"FROM POMPEY
TO PINDLING"

"Bahamians Who Made a Difference!"

By

The Rev. Dr. Joseph Emmette Augustus Weir, OM, JP, Bd, STM, PhD

Lyfe Publishing

Publishers Since 2012

Published by Lyfe Publishing LLC & Rich & Company Florida LLC

Lyfe Publishing, 10800 Nautica Place, White Plains MD 20695

Library of Congress Cataloging in Publications Data

The Rev. Dr. Joseph Emmette Augustus Weir, OM JP

Pompey to Pindling / The Rev. Dr. Joseph Emmette Augustus Weir, OM JP

ISBN: 978-1-957333-25-0

1.   Non-Fiction
2.   Bahamas–Nonfiction
3.   Pompey to Pindling–Nonfiction

Printed in the United States of America

1 2 3 4 5 6 7 8 9 10

Book design by Olivia Pro Designs and Aionios Designs

After eating his evening meal on April 30, 2021, his wife Ena Weir recounted that The Late Rev. Dr. Joseph Emmette Weir with The Holy Bible in his hand, leaned back in his chair, closed his eyes and quietly slipped away to "forever be with Our Lord and Saviour Jesus Christ."

A prolific writer, this his last and final book "From Pompey to Pindling – Bahamians Who Made a Difference!" was resting prominently on his desk with chapters all in order, awaiting one missing chapter which was the chapter allotted to Mary Ingraham, Leader of the Women's Suffrage Movement in the Bahamas. Information on her has been included as Dr. Weir desired.

Realizing that the time was at hand to see this epic Bahamian historical document completed, the decision was made by his wife to proceed.

This book is an excellent and insightful personal recounting by The Rev. Dr. Joseph Emmette Weir of the backgrounds and historical contributions of Bahamians who became key in the progress, values and development of the Bahama Islands.

January 15, 2022

Thanks to Roger Weir

Thanks to Dr. Roger Weir, MD (M, BS) brother of The Rev. Dr. J. Emmette Weir for making this publication possible.

Special Mention

The Rev. Dr. Emmette Weir was blessed to be wedded to his lovely spouse Ena who ensured that this historical book written and compiled by her husband over many years was finally brought to completion in his absence. She was a prayer warrior and armor bearer for her late husband who served in multiple ministerial posts in the Methodist Church which they loved dearly. Ena Weir née Johnson hailed from the beautiful island of Jamaica, West Indies and holds a Bachelor of Arts in Education awarded by St. Benedict University, Minnesota, USA. She has 45 years teaching experience and has served at schools operated by the Ministry of Education in both Jamaica and the Bahamas; Queen's College, Nassau; St. Paul's Methodist College and Bishop Eldon Primary School in Freeport, Grand Bahama Island. Ena Weir in her own right is a multi-talented woman who is also an author, artist, seamstress, interior designer, cook and gardener to name a few of her many attributes. She is the epitome of the Biblical "Virtuous Woman" of Proverbs 31. Along with her late husband she nurtured and cared for their children Erica, musician and educator; Ellsworth, Director of Parks, Bahamas National Trust, his wife Teneille and their children Jayden and Jordan. The writer recalls her faithful ministry to the women's prayer group of the Methodist Church while in Nassau. A kind, humble and compassionate woman, Ena Weir quietly and wisely extended her hand to the poor and needy. As the faithful and devoted wife of a humble yet powerful and influential member of the Christian faith found in her late husband, it can be said she served as his number one intercessor and jointly they interceded for many at breakfast daily. Ena Weir is truly a woman of distinction and honour.

Ava Forbes
Secretary to Ena Weir

From Pompey to Pindling
Bahamians Who Made a Difference!

Table of Contents

ABOUT THE BOOK   387

Part I
The Pioneers

Foreword

I t is indeed a privilege for me to contribute the Foreword to this book written by Reverend Dr. J. Emmette Weir, a former student of mine at the Government High School. Throughout his professional life as a minister and as a teacher, he has published a number of interesting books intended to inspire critical thinking and to enrich the lives of his readers.

Dr. Weir has experienced the dire and urgent need for Bahamians to become more knowledgeable about their past history and especially to be better informed about persons who have contributed positively to the development of the Commonwealth of The Bahamas. This need is especially evident among the young people of our Nation.

This book records significant facts about persons, who have had the opportunities to effect change and who have become significant contributors to our nation building process. Their influence has, indeed, made a difference.

Dr. Weir's great interest in historical events generally, has inspired him to disseminate knowledge about personalities, who have worked long and hard to accomplish worthwhile achievements for themselves and for their fellowmen. In doing so, they have left a legacy for subsequent generations to emulate.

There is no doubt that much research has been put into making this book informative, historic and meaningful. It covers a wide period of history and includes persons from varying strata of society and in many professions, some of whom are well known and others not so well known. I highly commend the sterling efforts of the author, who has compiled and disseminated much information in the pages of this book, which should enable Bahamians to know their past, appreciate the present and be inspired to help to shape the future of our Bahamaland.

I congratulate Dr. Weir and hopefully, this book "Bahamians Who Made a Difference," will arouse the interest of many and appeal especially to our young people to do their best to excel and to set high goals so that they too may make a difference and contribute positively to the present and future development of our country.

Marjorie Davis (Miss)

Former Director of Education

Introduction

O n Thursday, December 5, 2013 Rolihlahla Madiba Nelson Dalibunga Manson Mandela first Black President of South Africa, universally respected civil rights icon, passed away peacefully at his residence in his beloved homeland.[i] So great was his stature at both national and international levels, that political potentates and eminent religious leaders everywhere, including the Rt. Hon. Perry Gladstone Christie, Prime Minister of The Commonwealth of The Bahamas, the Hon. Hubert Alexander Minnis, Official Leader of Her Majesty's Loyal Opposition, the Rev. Dr. Rainford Patterson, President of The Bahamas Christian Council and the Hon. Hubert Alexander Ingraham, immediate Past Prime Minister, all joined in gracious and generous expressions of admiration and gratitude for his many achievements! President Barak Obama, First African-American President of the United States (himself a protégé of this "giant of a man") expressed, most appropriately the sentiments of many, drawn from "all walks of life" in proclaiming "He no longer belongs to us. He belongs to the ages!" Eulogized by one authority as a "master example of non-violence," his "death" made the headlines in the media (mass and social) "in every corner of the globe!"

What, evidently, most impressed the highly influential international anchor people and news commentators, was the fact that when the charismatic Nelson Mandela, emerged from twenty-six long years of imprisonment, being punished (believed by many, including this writer "unjustly") for his uncompromising condemnation of and strong principled popular resistance to the white dominated government's apartheid "racist"—policies, without the slightest sign of acrimony or seeking of revenge! Rather, he chose the path of reconciliation and reconstruction, and thus went on to become his nation's Prime Minister, uniting all its peoples, drawn from many races, tribes, classes and creeds, to work together for the socio-economic, political, moral and spiritual development of their mineral rich and exquisitely beautiful country.

What the news commentators "on the international scene" failed to mention, however, was the fact that one of the Third World Leaders who played a pivotal role in securing the release of Nelson Mandela from prison, was none other than the then Prime Minister of The Commonwealth of The Bahamas—The Rt. Hon. Sir Lynden Oscar Pindling, KCMG PC JP!

Sir Lynden Oscar Pindling, NH, KCMG, PC, JP

(22 March, 1930 – 26 August, 2000)

I. "Father of the Nation"

In an illustrious and most eventful political career stretching over five decades, Sir Lynden Oscar Pindling, "The Father of the Nation," exercised a tremendous amount of influence upon the socio-economic, political, educational and moral development of the people of the Commonwealth of the Bahamas.

Hailed by some authorities as the greatest Bahamian of the twentieth century,[ii] this diminutive "fella from over the hill" really proved to be a tremendous force for change, leading the Bahamas into Independence in 1973 and continuing to serve as its Prime Minister for a quarter of a century.

Despite the tremendously important part he played in the development of The Bahamas, there are many in the Bahamas today, especially of "the younger generation" who evidently know very little about him. For instance, the narrator was utterly appalled when he heard about the students of a graduating class of a prominent institution of secondary education in this country, who confessed that they knew virtually "next to nothing" about this great Bahamian.

Who, then, was Sir Lynden Oscar Pindling? What do we know about his family? What were the factors in his early life which motivated him in his meteoric rise to prominence in the Bahamas? What were the main contributions that he made to the advance of the land of his birth? What were his human weaknesses and failings? Most importantly, what lessons can we glean from his life which may prove useful to us in our own aspirations and earnest endeavours to be, by the Grace of God, "the best that we can be?" These are the weighty questions which shall comprise the focus of our attention in this contribution to our understanding and appreciation of the life and times of "The Father of the Nation!'

II. "Growing up on East Street"

Lynden Oscar Pindling was born on March 22, 1930, AD, being the only child of Arnold Pindling and his wife Viola! His father, who hailed from Jamaica, came to the Bahamas to serve as an officer of the Royal Bahamas Police Force.

Medium in height, dark in complexion, dignified, stately and always neatly attired, Arnold Pindling was ambitious and enterprising. Accordingly, after serving on the Police Force for about eight years, he embarked upon an entrepreneurial career in various enterprises including shop keeping, farming at Eleuthera and the breeding of race horses for competition at Hobby Horse Hall, commonly called "The Race Track!"

Little Lynden's mother, Viola Pindling née Bain, who could trace her roots to Acklins via Andros, came from an old Bahamian sea faring family. Her father Captain Bain was one of the most competent mail boat captains of the early twentieth century. Arnold and Viola were united in matrimony at Zion Baptist Church on May 15, 1929 by the Rev. R. P. Dyer, a Methodist Minister then Principal of Queen's College.

Being the enterprising person that he was, Arnold Pindling, with the assistance of his in-laws, purchased property on East Street. There he established the family homestead including the family residence and a shop. Lynden Pindling then spent the formative years of his life "growing up on East Street."

A disciplinarian "from the Old School," Arnold Pindling brought up his son in a methodical manner. He was expected to fulfil his chores and assist in the family businesses while, of course, keeping up with his studies. For, both his parents placed high priority upon education. Indeed, as Sir Lynden himself testified at the home-going services for his parents, they poured all their love upon him and dedicated what resources they had to his physical, mental, moral and spiritual development.

Young Pindling, then, was expected to work diligently and to attain high standards in academics, which he did. After attending several schools operated by the Ministry of Education, he was successful in the very highly competitive examination at the premier institution of education of that time – the "Old Government High (GHS)." While there he proved to be an able student graduating with enough passes in the Cambridge Senior Examination to enable him to study at a British University. However, he excelled in leadership being awarded the Dux Prize on two occasions, a feat matched by few other students in the history of "the high school" as its strict headmaster, Dr. Deans Peggs delighted to call the leading government institution of education. At "Government High" then, young Pindling demonstrated that he was endowed by The Almighty with the charismatic gift of leadership, which, indeed proved prophetic, indicating that here was a young man destined for leadership in the progress of the people of his homeland.

Not only did his time of study at GHS indicate that he was gifted as a leader; at that institution he met several students who would turn out to work along with him in the years ahead, including Paul Adderley, Arthur Hanna and Cecil Wallace Whitfield.

Upon Graduation from GHS, young Pindling worked for two years at the Post Office along with other graduates of that institution originally established to train persons to work as civil servants. Being quite ambitious, Sir Lynden encouraged by his father and a prominent black lawyer Thaddeus Augustus Toote, decided to enter the legal profession. Thus he embarked on the flight to London to study to become a lawyer. Throughout the formative years of his life, then, from early childhood through the years of study at primary schools operated by the Ministry of Education, Government High, and his stint in the civil service, Lynden Pindling resided at the homestead on East Street.

Now, it is recognized that one's childhood experiences, training and impressions are of pivotal importance in development throughout life. In this regard, Lynden Pindling is no exception. It is submitted, therefore, that a knowledge and appreciation of East Street in the early forties is essential for an understanding of the forces which motivated and inspired Lynden Pindling throughout his long, distinguished and eventful career.

What, then, was it like for young ambitious black men and women "growing up on East Street" in the forties and fifties?

Lynden Oscar Pindling was born in Mason's Addition (which may be described as "a tributary road running into the main street named East Street!) The Bahamas then a tiny colony of the Mighty British Empire was under the control of a white merchant Oligarchy known as "The Bay Street Boys" (so styled because their business enterprises were concentrated along Bay Street, the main thoroughfare running east to west along the north coast or bay of the island of New Providence). Indeed, this powerful socio-political, socio-economic minority comprising only fifteen percent of the total population, wielded tremendous political and economic authority in the Colony.

Through an antiquated electoral system which included plural voting, "The Company Vote," and a long out-dated constitutional structure which gave certain constituencies in

"The Out Islands" (now known as The Family Islands) more seats in the House of Assembly than their dwindling populations merited, they managed to dominate the political arena. Moreover, General Elections taking place only once in every seven years, tended to foster an attitude of complacency on the part of some of the twenty-nine members of the House of Assembly, becoming, as it were, "absentee representatives," residing in Nassau, seldom visiting their constituencies except "at election time!'

The dominance of "The Bay Street Boys" in the political realm was matched only by their stranglehold of the economy of the Colony. For, being "commission merchants" they had the "agency" (i.e. franchise or exclusive right of distribution of products which they imported from abroad, mainly from the United States of America and Canada and to a lesser extent from Europe) and the other parts of the Caribbean. They, in turn, sold these products, often at an exorbitant "mark up" to shopkeepers, who operated petty shops in "the over the hill "communities.

Now, if "Bay Street" was symbolic of the mighty political and economic clout of "The Bay Street Boys," then East Street was symbolic of the struggle of the Black majority to wrest political and economic hegemony from them! Here it is germane to point out that the choice properties on Bay Street, and the prime beachfront lots "out East" and "out West" were owned by "The Bay Street Boys" and wealthy expatriates such as Sir Harry Oakes and deep pocketed winter residents. The vast majority of the black Bahamians occupied the inland areas known as "over the hill."

Inevitably, there were those amongst the black population who were not satisfied with the *status quo* and summoned up the courage to challenge the control exercised by the white minority. Thus, by the time young Lynden Pindling was a school boy "in short pants," the Burma Road Riot of 1942 clearly indicated that they were prepared "to take a stand against social injustice," protesting against the low wages that kept them in poverty! And while much of this resistance against "the powers that be" came from those in the long established black communities such as Grant's and Bain Town, as so well documented by Dr. Cleveland Eneas; strong and growing opposition came from the residents at the eastern boundary—East Street! A walk along East Street "in those days" would certainly make one aware of the pivotal place it occupied in the advance of the "Black Majority," especially those who were making strides in the business and commercial field of human endeavour.

Thus perched "on top of the hill" was "Mortimer's Candy Kitchen," operated by the enterprising Mortimers who hailed from Inagua. Black Bahamians on their way to and from Bay Street were refreshed by stopping there to purchase peanuts, popcorn, the famous Mortimer candies, cool drinks and snow cones! It was a major black Bahamian enterprise. Continuing there were many other small businesses including those of craftsmen such as Thad Wilson (shoemakers) and many shops including that operated by The Pindlings. There were also dry goods and other products available along East Street—including liquor merchant Audley Kemp.

Secondly, East Street was a major centre for black entertainment. Just "down the road" from the Mortimer enterprise was "The Silver Slipper," a very popular night club. Bahamians "from all walks of life" as well as tourists flocked there for entertainment. It was the venue of the annual gala of the Old Scholars Association of Government High School. Gentlemen dressed in tuxedo formal wear danced through the night with the lovely ladies of their choice. "The Silver Slipper" was a leading place of entertainment "in those days."

Nearly opposite to "The Silver Slipper" was another very popular venue of entertainment for Bahamian blacks – "The Cinema!" (True it was "a cinema" but it was known as "The Cinema" just as the old GHS was known as "The High School!') People, young and old, went "to The Cinema" to watch the latest movies from Hollywood.

Boys and young men, in particular, enjoyed "Cowboys and Crooks," "Tarzan," "Superman," "Batman and Robin," and the ever popular "serials," highly sensational, action packed, suspense filled dramas, each episode leaving one eagerly awaiting...next week! Those of the older generation delighted to watch films about "The War" (World War II), the fights of Joe Louis; and they took pride in watching films featuring up and coming Bahamian actor, "Son of the Soil," Sidney Poitier. And the children were thrilled by Walt Disney, Mickey Mouse, and "The Wizard of Oz" and...Shirley Temple.

Denied access to "The Savoy" on Bay Street, the hard working Bahamian blacks found a place of entertainment and solace in "The Cinema" of East Street as they watched the latest movies, forgetting for a while the harsh realities of their oppressed socio-economic condition! Ironically, it did not matter to them that this popular rendezvous was owned by The Bethel Brothers...Bay Street Boys!

It is of interest to reveal here that Mr. McPherson Williams told the narrator that one of the victories of a group formed to assert the rights of "the people over the hill" was obtaining provision for the movie "No Way Out," featuring Sidney Poitier to be shown at "The Cinema!"[iii]

Thirdly, besides being a bastion of black Bahamian commercial entertainment, East Street was centre for the religious and spiritual nurture of the Black community. At its North, at the busy intersection of East Street and Shirley Street, was the ancient Zion Baptist Church, where the Pastor was The Rev. Talmadge Sands, a towering religious figure, highly respected by "Bahamians in all walks of life"! Then, just "down the road" from "The Silver Slipper" was the East Street Gospel Hall renowned not only for its evangelical services when the Gospel was proclaimed by fiery Evangelists but also as a citadel of religious and moral instruction. At its Sunday School, elders from the McCartney, Thompson, and Wallace families instructed hundreds of Bahamian children and young people in the moral and spiritual principles of The Christian faith.

Midway on "the other side of East Street" was the Lily of the Valley Church of God, where the Pastor was another leading and most influential clergyman of yesteryear—Bishop W. V. Eneas, father of Dr. Cleveland Eneas, dentist and Bahamian historian. At the Southern end of that famous street that "never sleeps" was the huge, newly constructed edifice of The Church of God of Prophecy. The Pastor was another Bahamian religious and theological giant, the urbane patriarchal Bishop Alvin Moss, General Overseer of his rapidly growing denomination in the Bahamas, Turks & Caicos Islands. While preaching from the pulpit of its large sanctuary on Sundays for the moral and spiritual nurture of his members, he presided over a church office "just across the street" during the week catering to their domestic and social welfare as well as their economic empowerment![iv]

East Street, then, was very lively even "in those day!' For, you see, in many communities in New Providence and The Family Islands, then, when electricity was not as widely available as it is today, many people "went to bed with the chickens" and so they were very quiet at night. But, not East Street! There was something going on all the time! So, any hour of the day or night you could find something to do...whether you were engaged in shopping, entertainment or Divine Worship, or were suffering from a bout of insomnia. Truly, it could be described then and most certainly known as..."The Street that Never Sleeps!"

Now, "Needless to say," "growing up on East Street" in the days of Pindling's youth, you had to be tough, bold, willing, if necessary, to enter into combat "to defend your rights!" For, "make no mistake about it" you had to develop "survival skills" based upon courage, tenacity and "guts!"

Yet, you could walk along East Street feeling "safe and sound" any hour of the day or night! That was precisely because there was little or no fear of crime. Why? Because right at "the top of the hill" was "The Police Barracks," headquarters of The Royal Bahamas Police Force. So, although you certainly were expected to be tough, if you were not, you still felt secure because the Police were never far away. Such then was life "growing up on East Street" during the formative years of the life of Lynden Oscar Pindling!

Now, "growing up on East Street" in that turbulent post-World War II era, Lynden Pindling, being an observant and sensitive young man, would have been painfully aware of the tremendous political and economic clout of the powerful Bay Street oligarchy! By the same token, he most certainly would have been acutely conscious of "the second class status," suffering and oppression of the black majority living "over the hill." Thus, it is submitted that it was precisely for this reason that he was able not only to identify with "the man on the street" but also to communicate, gracefully and most effectively, with the vast majority of the Bahamian electorate throughout his long and eventful career. Indeed, it was this rare ability *"to walk with kings and not lose the common touch,"* which was pivotal to his long dominance in the highly competitive arena of political leadership.

Moreover, Pindling, in those formative years of his life, would have come to realize the crucial significance of education as "the passport" to moving from a status of subservience and dependence to one of progress, prosperity and upward social mobility. This, no doubt, resulted in the very high priority he placed on education in his many years of service to the people of his native land.

Then, Lynden Oscar Pindling, as he grew older would have become more and more concerned about the status of the Bahamas as a Colony of Great Britain, firmly under the control of "The Mother Country," and therefore, without control of its national destiny under God. His studies, at primary and secondary level in the Bahamas, and later, at tertiary level, in England, would, understandably have led to dissatisfaction with Colonialism and a corresponding intense inner burning desire for the political independence of the land of his birth!

"The lust for liberty,

The desire to be free..."

It is submitted, therefore, that the key to understanding the incipient influences, motivational forces, achievements, and contributions of Sir Lynden Oscar Pindling over the many years of his illustrious career is an appreciation of the lasting effect upon him of the conditions under which he grew up on East Street during the post-World War II era. Concisely, the position maintained here is that you can't understand Sir Lynden without knowing something of his East Street background.

Accordingly, it is submitted that four major contributions to the socio-economic and political progress of the people of The Bahamas distinguished the long most eventful political tenure of Lynden Oscar Pindling. These include:

- Leading the people of The Bahamas from colonialism to independence in a democratic manner.

- The establishment of The College of The Bahamas.

- The implementation of the concept of National Insurance.

- The establishment of The Royal Bahamas Defence Force.

It is appropriate now, to proceed by discussing each of these major contributions of this Great "Bahamian Who Made a Difference!"

III. The Four Major Contributions of Sir Lynden Oscar Pindling

1. Leading the people of the Bahamas from colonialism to independence in a democratic, non-violent manner

When, on July 11, 1953, Patricia Cole-Cozzi and Sir Lynden Oscar Pindling were, simultaneously, "called to the Bar," the winds of inevitable political change were blowing, placidly, through the normally tranquil "Isles of June!"

For, it was during that very year that the Progressive Liberal Party ("The PLP) became the first political organization to be established in this country.

In this regard, it may be confidently asserted that these political zephyrs were coming from a direction that was not expected by "the powers that be!" For, "The Founding Fathers" of this rapidly escalating challenge to the political hegemony of "Bay Street" were not Black Protestant Politicians "from over the hill," but indeed, were "brown skinned men (mulattoes/ 'bright people'/Conchy Joes), most of whom either hailed from or could trace their roots to Long Island, being deeply influenced by the increasingly radical Christian Social Ethics of the Catholic Church!

They included Henry Milton (later Sir Henry Milton Taylor), Junior Member of the House of Assembly for the Long Island Constituency, Cyril St. John Stevenson, Editor of "The Herald," a fiery weekly tabloid, highly critical of the machinations of "The Bay Street Boys" and William Cartwright, Realtor, publisher of the magazine "Bahamian Review," who eventually became the historian of the moment.

Because it championed the cause of those who were oppressed, "the wretched of the earth" as a Caribbean sociologist described them, and since most of them were black or Afro-Bahamians (although there were some poor whites who also cowered under the dominating power of "The Bay Street Boys,") the PLP almost immediately was perceived as "The Black Man's or Coloured People's Party." By the same token, the United Bahamian Party (The UBP) which was established in 1956, came to be perceived as "The White People's Party."[v] However, in all fairness, to both entities, it has to be noted that in their respective "platforms," it was clearly stated that persons of all colours, classes and creeds were welcome to become members.

Now, as we have seen, the young Lynden Oscar Pindling, now a budding Attorney-at-Law, knew from bitter experience "growing up on East Street," the oppressive power of the Bay Street Boys. It was not surprising, therefore, that soon after being "called to the Bar," he plunged into the challenging political arena by joining the PLP. Also becoming a member of this growing young political organization was his colleague, Arthur Hanna. They then had much in common! Both attended the Government High School, both of them had studied law in the Mother Country and both had recently been called to the Bar. Later they were joined by another up and coming black attorney, Labour Leader Sir Randol Fawkes. These young attorneys were welcomed by "The Founding Fathers" into the PLP with open arms, for in so doing, they encouraged many other Bahamians to become members of the PLP which kept on growing!

Lynden Pindling demonstrated charismatic gifts of leadership. As an attorney he was appointed legal adviser to the Party. He proved to be very capable in guiding the leaders of the Party in dealing with the legal challenges they faced in their struggle to wrest political control of the Colony from the Bay Street Boys.

The PLP, then continued to grow very rapidly especially in the black belt communities "over the hill" and communities in the Family Islands with a predominantly black population. On the other hand, growth was comparatively slow in the predominantly white constituencies in Nassau and those in the Family Islands where the population was predominantly comprised of white Bahamians.

This demographic trend was reflected in the keenly contested election of 1956. For, although the PLP attracted more than a third of the votes cast, it was represented by only six members of Parliament. "The Magnificent Six" as they were known, included:

Milo B. Butler

Cyril St. John Stevenson

Clarence A. Bain

Lynden Oscar Pindling

Randol Fawkes

Samuel Isaacs

On the other hand, Henry Milton Taylor, one of the Founding Fathers of the PLP found himself in a very awkward position having been defeated by The UBP in his native Long Island. As he then did not have a seat in the House of Assembly, it became necessary to elect a sitting Member of Parliament as the Parliamentary Leader of the Party.

Sir Lynden Oscar Pindling, in his capacity as legal adviser was considered ideally suited to serve in this capacity. Accordingly, he was elected Parliamentary Leader of the PLP. It can be observed, retrospectively, that this marked a major turning point in his life, and never looking back, he moved decisively to maintain leadership in front line politics for many years to come!

During the years following the General Election held in 1956 the PLP grew most rapidly, with new persons swelling its ranks day by day! Meanwhile, "The Magnificent Six" kept "the feet of the Bay Street Boys to the fire" as they constantly challenged the members of the Government. Early in 1956 a delegation including the highly respected Chairman of the PLP, Henry Milton Taylor, The Hon. Milo Butler, and Sir Lynden Pindling, its legal adviser went to London seeking political reforms. Not to be outdone, representatives of the Bay Street Boys also sent a delegation to London. Upon their return, they established the United Bahamian Party. As the late Shirley Wright observed, the establishment of this party was merely a formality as the Bay Street Boys had been acting virtually as a political party for centuries!

"The winds of change" which had been blowing placidly through "The Isles of June" now began to blow with greater intensity. Thus in 1958, Randol Fawkes, President of the Bahamas Federation of Labour, leader, and member of the House representing the Southern District, led the General Strike which brought about major reforms. These included the abolition of the company vote and pluralism, and the addition of four seats representing the rapidly increasing population of New Providence.

These most welcome reforms, however, lacked one which was sorely desired by all progressive thinking Bahamians, the enfranchisement (granting of the right to vote) of Bahamian women. This most important objective did not come until 1962, largely through the untiring efforts of the leaders of the Suffrage Movement such as Mary Ingraham, Georgianna Symonette, mother of Sir Clement Maynard, Sylvia Johnson and Dame Doris Johnson.

Buoyed up by these reforms, especially the enfranchisement of women, who had always given their full support to the leaders, and increasingly large number of members The PLP, approached the General Election of 1962 with extreme confidence and boundless enthusiasm! For after years of serving in Opposition, many months of energetic campaigning throughout the length and breadth of the Bahamian archipelago from Abaco to Inagua, Andros to San Salvador) they confidently expected that at long last the PLP would wrest political control of the country from the Bay Street Boys, and so form the next government. Thus at political rallies, attracting thousands convening at the Southern Recreation Grounds and Windsor Field in New Providence and in all the major Family Islands, triumphant cries of "PLP all the way!" summoned the faithful of the party, to exercise their right to vote and to participate in the formation of the new (black) government. Many Bahamian

Blacks declared. "We are preparing to take over this country." But that was not to be!

For amazingly, to the great surprise and utter disappointment of the black majority, the powerful moneyed UBP, operating its powerful propaganda machine including broadcasts from Radio Stations in Miami...won! The results of the General Election, held on November 26, 1962 merit the most careful examination and reflection! Simply and acidly put, these results could be summed up, thus:[vi]

Although garnering the minority of the votes at the poll, the UBP, nevertheless, retained political control of the colony by gaining the majority of the seats in the House!

Two fundamentally contrasting emotions characterized the responses of "the people." On the one hand, there was great regret. It is reported that "big men wept like babies" when "the results" came in. The feeling of regret was so severe, that you could feel it in the atmosphere!

The other emotion was—unbridled rage--for, there were those "hotheads" who came to the conclusion that the only way to grasp political control from the white merchant oligarchy was by means of resorting to violence. Indeed, there were those who wanted to "March on Bay Street" and seize political and economic domination violently, even shedding blood if necessary!

But The Hon. Lynden Oscar Pindling, Leader of Her Majesty's Loyal Opposition, would have no part in such a violent course of action! As one well known and most influential Bahamian columnist has brilliantly chronicled, his wise decisive leadership at this crucial juncture in the historical development of the people of the Bahamas.

"Following the bitter loss of 1962, an election which many PLPs were convinced they would win, especially after women were newly enfranchised that year, a group of men approached Sir Lynden about the party's response to an election they felt the UBP had stolen by massively outspending the PLP and through outrageously undemocratic means.

"These men and others were not prepared to accept the defeat and continued rule by a racist and greedy oligarchy determined to retain economic and political power by manipulation of the instruments of state and government. One of the men who approached Sir Lynden was enraged by such a defeat and wanted, in the words of some 'to tear down the town!'"

Having considered democratic action ineffective and non-violent action insufficient, there were those who wanted to immediately, "March on Bay Street and wreak mayhem."

To his everlasting credit, Sir Lynden, supported by his close colleagues, quenched the rage and stopped what would have been a disaster for the country, the movement and the PLP. He was determined for his party to triumph by the ballot box.[vii]

Pindling's Wise Men... and Women

Why then, did Sir Lynden Pindling choose the path of democracy and peace rather than that of violence? To put it another way, "How did 'The Quiet Revolution' come about?"

Well, it may be stated, with confidence that there were at least five reasons why in leading "All the way," Pindling decided to act in this manner.

First, Lynden Oscar Pindling was not naturally a violent person. Like his father, Arnold Pindling, he was always neatly attired, dignified, reserved in demeanour. Accordingly, he was always polite and respectful to others whatever may have been their status in society, reflecting the values of one brought up in a disciplined Christian home.

Moreover, his educational background, including his days at The Government High School under the tutelage of Dr. Dean Peggs and his training as a lawyer in London, groomed him into a person with a fundamental respect for law and order. Thus, by nature and nurture, the young Lynden Oscar Pindling was inclined to choose the path of peace and democracy rather than that of violence in his leadership (the ballot box rather than bullets) from Colonialism to Independence!

Secondly, there was a very long tradition of democracy in the Bahamas. For in 1729 The Bahamas became a colony of Great Britain with a government structure modelled on that of "The Mother Country." The Bahamas then was never "A Crown Colony" governed directly by the Colonial Office, but one like, Bermuda and Barbados, with an advanced Parliamentary Constitution. In 1964, a new Constitution granting full internal self-government came into force. Pindling, then as a lawyer, realized that it would be more effective to continue along this path of constitutional reform rather than resorting to violence, which would, indeed, be a retrogressive step!

Closely related to the second was the third—the mild temperament of the Bahamian People. Brought up in a country with a mild temperate climate (other than in hurricane season) and one with a long tradition of democracy, they were not inclined to act violently. True, they would express themselves vociferously at times of national debate, but would generally refrain from inflicting bodily harm on anyone even in the most heated political controversy! Bahamians have demonstrated a gentle hospitable manner towards tourists over many years which have been attested to by many visitors. "True" Bahamians are appalled at any display to the contrary and identify such behaviour as "non-Bahamian."

Fourthly, there was the powerful, moderating influence of The Church. Generally speaking, Pindling and the hierarchy of the PLP accorded great respect to the message of The Church. During the formative years of the nation, clergy persons such as the Rev. Dr. W. H. Brown, the Rev. Dr. Reuben Cooper, the Rev. Edwin Taylor, the Rev. Joseph Perna, Canon William Thompson and Bishop Michael Eldon were very active and vocal.[viii]

Being deeply religious, the Bahamian people listened to their spiritual leaders.

Moreover, as we have seen, "The Founding Fathers" of the PLP came deeply under the influence of the radical social teaching of the

Catholic Church. Very significantly, according to the late Rev. Joseph Perna, Lynden Oscar Pindling read, with great intensity, the various Papal Encyclicals "as they came out." In all these universally recognized ecclesiastical documents there was the call to social reform without resorting to violence. It is certainly germane to note here that all this was in line with the teaching and practice of the late Martin Luther King, Jr. Indeed, the famed Civil Rights leader, who had already demonstrated the power of non-violent action, visited the Bahamas during this period. There can be no doubt that the nonviolent effective approach of Dr. Martin Luther King, Jr. deeply impacted Sir Lynden Oscar Pindling in his eventful political career.

We come now to the summit of the reasons why the leader of Her Majesty's Loyal Opposition rejected the way of violence, holding tenaciously to that of democracy and non-violence—the advice of those described as "his close colleagues!" A Biblical episode is helpful here!

When Moses had led the children of Israel out of Egypt, he took responsibility of the administration of justice for the entire people of God. He was visited by his father-in-law, Jethro Priest of Midian. Jethro, observing the great strain that this was placing upon Moses advised him to delegate some of his judicial authority. "Moses" he exhorted, "You are trying to accomplish too much on your own." Then he urged Moses to select wise men of integrity who could assist him. They dealt with all the minor cases and referred only the most difficult ones to Moses. Much more was accomplished with the officers with delegated authority being gratified and Moses himself being much more relaxed. (Exodus 18)

Here then, the ancient priest laid down a principle that has proved most useful in administration ever since: 'no one person is incompetent.' Each of us receives gifts endowed by The Creator which must be used for the benefit of the whole community. (Eph. 4:1-16).

The wise leader then, is not necessarily the person who is multi-talented or very capable but rather it is he/she who is most discerning in selecting persons with competent abilities to help him, one who inspires others to use their particular gifts for the benefit of the kingdom. Throughout the ages, leaders in all walks of life—kings, presidents, bishops and prime ministers—have selected wise, competent and talented men and women to assist them in their administration.

Who, then were "Pindling's wise men," those on whom he could depend for sound advice especially during the crucial early years of his service? Those who exercised a moderating influence upon him in contrast to "the hotheads" who advocated a violent "March on Bay Street?

Well, holding "pride of place" amongst them in those early days, were those who might be described as "The elder statesmen" of the movement. These included The Hon. Henry Milton Taylor, a "Founding Father" of the PLP, The Hon. Milo B. Butler, who as has been demonstrated, was a Lion on the campaign trail and a Lamb in administration. Thirdly, there was the Hon. Carlton Francis, a mentor of Sir Lynden, then there were those who at Government High School, had studied law in London and had returned home to make their contribution in the competitive arena of politics. Included in this group were The Hon. Arthur Hanna, who later served as Deputy

Leader Prime Minister; The Hon. Paul Adderley, brilliant attorney and Cecil Wallace Whitfield, who later left the PLP to help in the formation of the Free National Movement.

Then there was Sir Clement Maynard. Urbane and dignified, always neatly dressed, punctual, he was totally loyal to Sir Lynden throughout his own long most distinguished tenure of service to his native land.

Besides, these wise men, there were also several wise women who advised the young Bahamian politician. Taking a leading place amongst them was Dame Doris Johnson, first Bahamian woman to serve in the Cabinet. Like the Hon. Carlton Francis, she was already a veteran educator when she entered the arena of politics. She carefully chronicled the events leading up to Independence in her most useful book, "The Quiet Revolution!"

Finally, the other "wise woman" amongst Pindling's "wise men...and women" was none other than his wife, the elegant Lady Marguerite Pindling; the love of his life, his constant confidant and soul mate. Tall, graceful, impeccably and tastefully dressed at all times, this discreet lady certainly had the ear of her husband.

These, then were Sir Lynden's close colleagues, the wise men and women who guided, stood by, advised and encouraged him especially in the early years of his long and distinguished career. Truly profound truth is embedded in the contemporary declaration "None of us as heroes stands alone!"

"Black Tuesday"

Now, as we have seen, the Hon. Lynden Oscar Pindling (now Official Leader of Her Majesty's Opposition) and the hierarchy of The Progressive Liberal Party had decided against resorting to violence in their quest to achieve political control of the self-governing colony. In so doing, they came up against one intractable fact—the urgent need for constitutional reform. Concisely, it was imperative that there should be a redistribution of the seats in The House of Assembly to reflect the major demographic shift of its population since the turn of the century.

For over the years, many of the natives residing in the Family Islands (aka "The Out Islands") relocated to New Providence in "search of a better way of life." The search for employment and advanced educational opportunities were the main motivating factors in this internal migration. Indeed, this trend rapidly accelerated during the post-World War II era with the population of the Family Islands gradually decreasing (with the shining exception of Grand Bahama site of the "Magic City," Freeport), and that of New Providence, site of the capital city, Nassau, rapidly increasing. Thus by the middle of the twentieth century, there were more people resident in New Providence than all of the other islands of the Bahamian archipelago, combined!

Despite this major demographic shift in favour of New Providence, however, there were more seats in the House of Assembly representing the Family Islands than those located there.

Clearly this was not satisfactory! It was realized by all concerned that this situation had to be changed. A step in that direction had taken place as a direct result of the 1958 General Strike when four additional seats in Parliament had been allocated to New Providence. However, in the wake of the defeat of the PLP in The General Election, held in 1962, although it had garnered more votes "at the Poll" than the victorious UBP, it was clear that that did not go far enough, Concisely, a much more radical realignment of the seats in the House of Assembly, in line with the major demographic shift that had taken place since the turn of the century was urgently required. Absolutely!

It was agreed, therefore by all concerned that a redistribution of the seats in the House of Assembly was a matter of top priority. Indeed, provisions for such an important constitutional reform had been made in the New 1964 Constitution.

However, when it came to the details as to how this objective might be attained, a major difference in the respective positions of the ruling United Bahamian Party and the Opposition Progressive Liberal Party, emerged. Accordingly, from early in 1965 there was long and protracted debate and lively discussion on this matter carried out everywhere—in the halls of the House of Assembly, editorials and "Letters to the Editor" and commentaries in the media, in the petty shops and barber shops. These, of course, tended to be highly polarized. The battle lines were drawn! A showdown was inevitable.

This came about when the United Bahamian Party came out with its plan for the determination of the boundaries of the constituencies in New Providence and the Family Islands – the Draft Order providing for The New Constitutional Boundaries under Section 63 of the 1964 Constitution. This clearly did not meet the approval of the supporters of the PLP. For, they regarded it as nothing other than a subtle exercise in "gerrymandering" designed to keep the UBP in power. As the Hon. Sir Milo Boughton Butler, bluntly put it in a debate in the House on this "burning issue" "Mr. Chairman, this Constituency Commission has done a wicked thing in cutting up New Providence and the Out Islands in a damnable way in order to give themselves— the minority government—a distinct advantage in the next General Elections."[ix]

In response, therefore, the Council of the Progressive Liberal Party organized demonstrations against the proposed boundaries throughout New Providence. Leading these demonstrations were the diminutive Lynden Pindling and the giant Milo Butler carrying placards denouncing the activities of the Bay Street Boys. Thousands of the people also turned out for rallies held mainly on the Southern Recreation Grounds and Windsor Field when the leaders of the PLP soundly condemned the proposals for the redistribution of the seats as set forth by the Commission.

Thus, on Tuesday, April 27, 1965 when this matter came up for further debate (having been first raised in the House on April 16) a large crowd gathered outside the precincts of the ancient (1729) House of Assembly.

High tension prevailed as the moment for the discussion of this highly controversial matter approached. The crowds outside the House on Parliament Street and Bay Street were instructed, "Watch the Eastern Window." Meanwhile the members, including the Premier and Leader of the UBP, Sir Roland Symonette, The Hon. Lynden Pindling Leader of the Opposition and the Speaker Mr. Bobby Symonette and the other members of the House of Assembly took their places in that ancient Assembly. After prayer by the Chaplain, the Speaker called the House to order. Everyone present, no doubt, was deeply conscious that they were about to participate in an event of tremendous significance. When the Speaker called for the Reading of The Recommendation of the Constitutional Commission, a dramatic move was made by The Hon. Lynden Pindling.

Moving decisively, he approached the Table where the Speaker's Mace was in place. Gripping the Mace, he declared:

> "This Mace is the symbol of authority and the authority for the islands belong to the people, and the people are outside of this House and so this Mace belongs outside too."[x]

He then threw the Mace out of the open eastern window. Amongst loud shouts, this ancient symbol of parliamentary authority fell on the street and was broken into several pieces. Immediately afterwards The Hon. Milo Butler too seized the two hour glasses and also threw them out of the eastern window.

Persons "eyewitnesses" who were present when this historic event transpired, such as veteran broadcaster Calsey Johnson, The Rev. Dr. Moultrie and Mrs. Armbrister could testify when the 40th Anniversary of Independence was celebrated on July 10, 2013, "I was there when the Mace flew out of the eastern window!"

Sir Randol Fawkes, who was present in the House of Assembly on that fateful, historic evening vividly describes what, happened after the Mace was thrown out:

> "Then all of the PLPs stormed out of the House. When they made their grand entrance to Bay Street they were granted a

hero's welcome by a crowd who yearned to breathe." Pindling addressed the people from the top of a van and then at a rally on The Southern Recreation Grounds.

Meanwhile, greatly to his credit, the Hon. Bobby Symonette demonstrated remarkable constraint and composure throughout this dramatic episode. Indeed, he waited for more than an hour until after two policemen brought the broken mace into the House and put it back in its place. And the UBP did pass the controversial Constituency Order into law.

Thus ended the proceedings of a most historic day in the Bahamas, or as American ace anchor man the late Walter Cronkite would put it, "And that's the way it was Tuesday, "Black Tuesday," Tuesday, April 27, 1965, "Black Tuesday" in the islands of the Bahamas!

It has to be observed, however, that despite the fact that the Constituency Bill was passed by the UBP, "Black Tuesday" was recognized as an historic turning point in the history of the Bahamas. In time it was vested with new meaning. It was regarded as a major step in the struggle for liberation by the people of The Bahamas.

"The lust for liberty...the desire to be free."

"The Tenth Day"

Events moved rapidly in the years that followed with "the winds of political change" blowing so powerfully that they approached the velocity of the tropical storms which threatened the tranquillity of the islands "during hurricane season!"

43

Thus, on January 10, 1967 when the next General Election was held, based on the constitutional boundaries set in 1965, the UBP and PLP were tied each winning eighteen seats. The two members who did not belong to either of the main political parties were the Hon. Alvin Brennen (Independent Harbour Island,) and the Hon. Randol Fawkes, the sole member of the Labour Party). After the former accepted the offer to serve as Speaker, both major parties eagerly sought the support of the Hon. Randol Fawkes, after much activity, including most attractive offers by the UBP, Sir Randol threw his full support behind the PLP. This made it possible for Sir Lynden Pindling to form the new government in his capacity as Premier.

(Interestingly enough, January 10, was vested with both religious and political significance. Largely through the influence of clergymen such as the Rev, Dr. H. W. Brown, The Rev. Dr. Reuben Cooper, Fr. Joseph Perna and The Rev. Edwin Taylor of The Bahamas Christian Council, the *Tenth Day*, based on the Exodus, was highly regarded in events up until the attainment of Independence.[xi] Politically speaking, it became known as "Majority Rule Day," a major event in the struggle of black Bahamians for social justice and political liberation. Accordingly it was observed with special events for many years and on January 10, 2014 it was celebrated as a public holiday for the first time!)[xii]

The death of the PLP Member of Parliament, The Hon. Uriah McPhee (in whose honour a school is named) afforded the young Premier the opportunity to call another General Election in 1968 when the PLP won by a large majority in the House of Assembly.

Then, in 1969 further changes were made in the Constitution bringing about

1. The change of the name of the political leader of the country from "Premier" to "Prime Minister"

2. Reduction in the power of the Governor

3. The islands were to be known officially as "The Commonwealth of The Bahamas."

In the General Election of 1972, Sir Lynden Pindling again led the PLP to victory. The dominating issue was that of Independence as Sir Lynden, hierarchy and general membership of the PLP were crystal clear in their desire for Independence. The resounding victory of the PLP at the polls indicated that the majority of the people were in favour of the move towards Independence. Accordingly, a precise date was set for the attainment of Independence—July 10, 1973.

The preparation of the Colony for transition from colonialism to independence included the adoption of a new colourful "Coat of Arms" designed by the Rev. Dr. Hervis Bain, underlined by the new national motto "Forward Upward Onward Together." The new flag featured a black triangle at its base, gold middle strip and two enveloping aquamarine stripes. The inspiring National Anthem, was written and composed by eminent Bahamian educator Timothy Gibson with its patriotic clarion call to excellence, national unity and reverence for God. The National Pledge contributed by the Rev. Dr. Philip Rahming, another very patriotic Bahamian and several other National Symbols.

A White Paper on Independence, issued on October 18, 1972, proved to be the subject of lively discussions throughout the length and breadth of the Bahamian archipelago. This was precisely because it consists of the principles and democratic concepts which would inform the content of the Constitution of The Bahamas as an independent nation under God.

Meanwhile, the Prime Minister devoted much of his time and energy to promoting the need for national unity in moving towards independence. There were those, notably the proponents of the Abaco Independence Movement, who had reservations about Independence, his endeavour in this regard proved effective.

Opposition to the concept of Independence gradually evaporated. Moreover, the able leadership of the Rev. Dr. R. E. Cooper and Rev. Philip Rahming was very active, during this period, in promoting national unity, patriotism and reverence for God throughout the Bahamas. Thus Bahamians approached the celebration of this momentous event as a united, confident and God fearing people.

Therefore, on July 9th a huge crowd, estimated at 50,000 gathered at Clifford Park for this historic ceremony heralding "The Birth of a Nation." At midnight the "Union Jack" was lowered even as the impressive flag of the emerging nation was hoisted and was soon "blowing in the breeze" to the delights, "pride and joy" of all the people residing in "The Isles of June!" Prince Charles represented the Queen at these celebrations. (The narrator attended a similar ceremony in Governor's Harbour, Eleuthera where he was serving as a young minister of the Gospel).

And so "The Quiet Revolution" was completed. Sir Lynden Oscar Pindling had proudly and triumphantly led the people of the Bahamas from Colonialism to Independence without violence! A major achievement in every way! The lust for liberty, the desire to be free has motivated humankind throughout the ages.

2. The Establishment of the College of the Bahamas

Now, as we have seen, Sir Lynden placed very high priority upon education as the master key to opening up opportunities for the socio-economic, intellectual and moral progress of the oppressed and poor members of the Bahamian community. This conviction was certainly shared with all the officers of the Progressive Liberal Party. Accordingly, much was done in the field of education, especially during the early years of the Pindling administration.

Scholarships were generously provided to enable Bahamians to serve more effectively in the classroom. Many of the recipients of these scholarships studied abroad, at leading institutions of tertiary education, mainly in the United Kingdom, The United States of America, and Canada and at the University of the West Indies in Jamaica. Upon completion of their studies they returned home bursting with new ideas, enthusiastic about making their contribution to the education and advancement of their fellow Bahamians. It was during this period that The Bahamas became more closely affiliated to the University of the West Indies, with this well-established institution opening a campus in Nassau. An ambitious program for the building of new institutions of education was embarked upon both in New Providence and The Family Islands. Sir Cecil Wallace Whitfield, who was appointed Minister of Education when the PLP became the governing party in 1968, with his energy and organizational skills, spearheaded this project; and after he left the PLP, several others notably the Hon. Livingston Coakley, The Hon. Darrell Rolle, The Hon. Paul Adderley, The Hon. Arthur Hanna served in this capacity.

With regard to national examinations, the Bahamas elected not to join the other Anglophone Caribbean territories in adopting the Caribbean Common Examinations (CXC). Instead, largely through the initiative and influence of the Hon. Paul Adderley, it established two major national examinations, endorsed by Cambridge University—The Bahamas Junior Certificate (BJC) and The Bahamas General Certificate of Education (BGCSE). The latter replaced the GCE.

Very significant strides were also made in the area of tertiary education. Indeed, the Bahamas had, traditionally "lagged behind" other territories in the English speaking Caribbean in this aspect of education, with many Bahamians (including the narrator) having to travel abroad for advanced educational opportunities. With the coming of Independence, therefore, Bahamians "in all walks of life" realized that there was "a crying and urgent need" for a major institution of tertiary education in their small nation, struggling "to make its mark" in a most competitive world.

It was, therefore, an occasion for great "pride and joy" when The College of the Bahamas was established on July 14, 1977, just three years after the attainment of Independence. This important institution came about by the amalgamation of four institutions:

The Bahamas Teachers' College, Nassau

The San Salvador Teachers' College

C. R. Walker Technical College

The Sixth Form of the Government High School

Speaking at the Opening Ceremony, Sir Lynden Pindling very optimistically expressed confidence that it would become the University of the Bahamas within a decade.[xiii] In reality, however, the process of attaining university status proved to be too ambitious to take place in such a short time. Steady progress, however, was made toward this goal under the leadership of a series of outstanding Presidents including Professor Knowles, founding President, Dr. Bacchus, and Dr. Keva Bethel. In 1995 the College was granted full autonomy. The College of the Bahamas in 2013 at the celebration of the 40th year of Independence offered more than forty courses at Bachelors and Master Degree levels and had a student body of 5,000 at campuses in Nassau, Freeport and other Family Islands. It boasted a large cadre of Bahamian lecturers, most of them having earned degrees at Masters and Doctoral level. It was then confidently expected that this, the premier institution of tertiary education in the nation would soon become The University of The Bahamas in fulfilment of the vision of Sir Lynden Pindling expressed at its establishment.

3. Implementation of the Concept of National Insurance

The establishment and operation of a project to provide for the socio-economic welfare of its citizens is a concept which prevails in most modern states. Described as "The Welfare State" in the European nations and as "Social Security" in the USA, it is designed to provide assistance especially for the poor members of society, and on a broader scale to help those who may experience hardship on a temporary basis— e.g. persons laid off when a company downsizes. It is a concept at the heart of the teaching of Christ and which was demonstrated in his Ministry (see; Matt. 6:1-5; Mark 5; Luke 4:18-20; John 10:1-17). This is evident in the fact that one of the foundational documents of "The Welfare State" was written by Archbishop of Canterbury William Temple.[xiv]

Now as we have seen the youthful Lynden Pindling "growing up on East Street, was painfully aware of the plight of the poor.[xv] Then, the concept of a Christian nation was incorporated into the preamble to the Constitution of the Bahamas.[xvi] Moreover, as has been demonstrated, "The Founding Fathers of the PLP came heavily under the social teaching of the Catholic Church which was at one with Liberation Theology in challenging all Christians to make sacrificial contributions for the welfare of the poor and oppressed of society.[xvii] Concisely, Pindling and the Founding Fathers of the PLP regarded provision for the welfare of the underprivileged of society, like education a matter of top priority.

In keeping then with all these factors, every effort was made to implement the concept of National Insurance early in the tenure of Sir Lynden. Thus, in October 1974, just fifteen months after the attainment of Independence, the National

Insurance Programme was launched. That there was a crying need for such a plan for the welfare of the Bahamian people was attested to by the fact that it "took off like a rocket." A broad number of National Insurance services were introduced over the years including old age pensions for those who were unable to make the necessary number of contributions, pensions for all contributors, Unemployment Benefit, Disability Benefit and even a Death Benefit. While originally it was conceived of as designed to assist the poor, over the years, its scope has broadened and so Bahamians drawn from every facet of society benefit unashamedly greatly from this method of providing for their needs. Moreover, with the funds accumulated over the years, National Insurance has been able to provide funding for major projects, especially clinics for the welfare of Bahamians in Nassau, and the most remote communities in the Family Islands. Moreover, the National Insurance Board has provided well-paying and secure jobs for many Bahamians as it is staffed entirely by natives.

In 2014 at the celebration of its fortieth anniversary, the assets of National Insurance were estimated at 1.65 billion (i.e. one thousand six hundred and fifty million) dollars. With great insight, the rate of contributions has been adjusted to ensure that the NIB will remain viable and so beneficial to Bahamians in all walks of life for many years to come. It can be stated, therefore, without fear of contradiction that the implementation and operation of the concept of National Insurance in the Commonwealth of The Bahamas has proved to be "a smashing unqualified success!"

4. The Establishment of the Royal Bahamas Defence Force

The Bahamas as a colony of Great Britain from the establishment of democratic government in 1729 was in charge of its internal affairs, while the important matters of external affairs and defence remained the responsibility of "The Mother Country." However, with the coming of Independence on July 10, 1973, the Bahamas had to take responsibility for these areas.

Accordingly, very soon after Independence, Sir Lynden led the way in getting the Bahamas to take care of its own defence. Consequently, in consultation with the military authorities of England, he appointed Captain William Swingley a swash buckling, energetic and enthusiastic military officer to spearhead the launching of this project. This took place early in 1980.

Concerning this important event, a young officer wrote:

> "Which of us will deny the higher call to service, this great mark of self-reliance on this superior march to progress? This was the question posed with urgency by former Prime Minister Sir Lynden O. Pindling, as he determined to establish a defence force."[xviii]

The "Father of the Nation" naturally being deeply concerned for its defence, envisioned marine defence organized along the lines of the US Coast Guard, with the following mandates:

1. Generally to protect the sovereignty of the young nation

2. To tackle bravely the constant challenge of illegal immigration

3. To deal effectively with preventing trafficking in illegal drugs and "smuggling" (importation of goods without paying customs Duty!)

4. To prevent poaching in Bahamian waters by foreign fishermen.

Its mettle was soon to be severely tested. For on May 10, 1980 just forty days after its establishment, the Royal Bahamas Defence Force was made to realize how very challenging indeed, dangerous, was the fulfilment of its mandate to protect the precious marine resources of the Bahamian archipelago from the illegal fishing expeditions of poachers from neighbouring Caribbean territories.

From all reports, it was a beautiful sunny morning, typical of the finest climate of the Isles of June, when the HMBS "Flamingo" was escorting two Cuban ships which were engaged in illegal fishing in the tranquil southern waters of the Bahamian archipelago in the vicinity of the Ragged Islands. Suddenly two Russian built Cuban MIG jets attacked the Bahamian ship. In the battle that followed, the ship eventually sank when four of its crew lost their lives including Able Seamen David Tucker, Arnold Williams, Austin Smith and Frederick Sturrup.

These four brave Bahamian seamen were numbered amongst those (who fought in the World Wars of the twentieth century) to make the supreme sacrifice in the service of their homeland. Ever since that fateful day, Bahamians have mourned the passing of these gallant young men on the anniversary of "The Flamingo Incident."[xix]

Sir Lynden Pindling, who was away when this event occurred, demonstrated great diplomatic skill in dealing with this matter. He sought to preserve the dignity and sovereignty of the nation while realistically recognizing that there was no way the Bahamas could, at that time, enter into military combat with its Communist neighbour. The Cuban government was apologetic and made monetary compensations to the families of those who lost their lives. However, the loss of our Bahamian sons can never be replaced and will forever be engraved on our hearts. It is hoped that Cuba learnt a valuable lesson from this tragedy and this sacrifice may well have opened the door for mutual respect and understanding over the ensuing years; Bahamians having since benefitted from opportunities opened by Cuba for free medical care and educational advancement. It was indeed, "the finest hour" of the Royal Bahamas Defence Force.

During the years following "The Flamingo Incident," the Royal Bahamas Police Force grew very rapidly, providing not only defence and the prevention of drug running and illegal fishing, but also a promising new career path for many Bahamian young men and women. Competent Bahamians have succeeded Capt. Swingley and the Bahamas is justly honoured at the service of this marine branch of its military defence organization. While primarily concerned with activities at sea, there have been times when it officers have been called upon to assist the Royal Bahamas Police Force in "keeping the peace" on the land. The high ideals of the Royal Bahamas Defence Force are encapsulated in the verse of the National Cenotaph in memory of the Gallant four who made the supreme sacrifice on May 10, 1980:

IV. The Challenges of Sir Lynden Oscar Pindling

It has been stated that: "Success is not about what one accomplish by himself: but what he inspires others to do." Measured in terms of this anonymous saying, inscribed in the great hall of the Moore (College of the Bahamas) Library, the life of Sir Lynden Pindling was a great success. He certainly inspired many others to serve to the best of each one's ability in the process of making his contributions to the development of the people of the Commonwealth of the Bahamas. But, like any other great leader, he had his own human weaknesses and inadequacies "his ups and downs," his failures as well as his triumphs. Here it is essential to bear in mind that success depends, to a large extent, upon how we deal with our times of despair and disappointment. Let us, then, reflect upon the challenges encountered by Sir Lynden Pindling and how he sought to cope with them.

Failure to Establish a National Youth Service

Early in the eighties, it was realized that the Bahamas faced major challenges in the proper training of its young people. This was manifested in a growing lack of respect for the older generation by many of the young people, a higher rate of teenage pregnancy and drug addiction, a disturbingly high rate of crime and violence amongst youth...all posited upon a major breakdown in the quality of home and family life in the Bahamas. Church leaders such as the Rev. Kenneth Huggins of The Methodist Church, staunch advocate of Christian Home and Family Life, Archbishop Drexel Gomez, The Rev. Dr. Simeon Hall, and social worker Dr. Sandra Dean Patterson all expressed major concern about this situation. The narrator was amongst those who called for the establishment of a National Youth Service dedicated to the training of Bahamian youth.

When, therefore, the Government put forward proposals for the establishment of a National Youth Service it was a concept which was not unknown to the Bahamian community. A period of national debate, carried on in every facet of Bahamian society emerged. Bishop Lawrence Burke of the Roman Catholic Church was amongst the first persons to voice objections to the bill. He was followed by many others in the community drawn from all walks of life. The objections were two-fold:

1. The military, "boot camp like" nature of the proposed National Youth Service

2. The fact that it would be compulsory.

Eventually in the light of such strong public outrage and objection, Sir Lynden decided not to proceed with the proposal to establish a Bahamian National Youth Service. Over the years, various attempts were made to establish a Youth Service Programme but these proved quite inadequate to deal with the challenges facing our youth as outlined above. Notable amongst these efforts was Y.E.A.S.T program organized by Deacon Jeffrey Lloyd of the Roman Catholic Church.

During the ensuing years, the social problems of the nation, especially a high rate of crime amongst youth, have gradually increased. One is left to wonder whether these most disturbing trends would have developed to the extent that they have had a National Youth Service been implemented.

2. The Ongoing Effort to Implement a National Health Scheme

Now, as we have seen, the implementation of National Insurance proved to be a huge success. The same cannot be said of what may be considered its "twin sister"—National Health Insurance. For, in countries where the "Welfare State" is practiced, the provisions of National Insurance and National Health Insurance have developed together.

On the other hand, while National Insurance has been fully operational since the early years of Independence, the implementation of a National Health Insurance scheme has proved most challenging.

Proposals for the establishment of a National Health Insurance initiative were discussed during the latter years of the Pindling administration. Indeed, a discussion paper was widely circulated. But these did not get very far, and indeed, were left unattended to when the Progressive Liberal Party lost the election in 1992. It has been raised on several occasions since and in 2014 ad., the Hon. Perry Gomez, Minister of Health, announced that definite steps would be taken to implement a National Health Insurance programme by 2015 ad.

3. The Challenge of the Economic Empowerment of All Bahamians

With the coming of Majority Rule in 1967 and Independence in 1973, "The Quiet Revolution," the political liberation of the people of the Bahamas was accomplished, or at least fulfilled to a very large extent. This was one of the major goals of Sir Lynden Pindling.

It has to be pointed out, however, that the attainment of the economic empowerment of the masses has proved much more intransigent. Pindling himself realized how challenging but most necessary was this ideal.

In one of his well-known addresses, he put it thusly:

> "Political independence for the Bahamas is almost meaningless unless it holds forth the prospect of economic independence. Just as a target date was set for political independence so a target date should be

set for economic independence. And just as the path to political independence was taken through stages, similarly the path to economic independence should be taken through stages."[xx]

Detailed discussion of this very complex multi-faceted issue is beyond the scope of study here. It is sufficient to note that on July 10, 2013, forty years after the attainment of political independence, there remained a vast disparity between the rich and poor in the Bahamas with "The Great Recession" of 2008--2012 having diminished much of the wealth of the Bahamian middle class while there were many communities in the Family Islands lacking the basic infrastructure required for classification as "First World." Concisely, while great progress has been made in attaining political independence, the attainment of national economic independence remains "an unfinished task" demanding the best efforts of those who are called upon to exercise leadership—political, socio-economic, and ecclesiastical—in the Commonwealth of The Bahamas.

4. The Commission of Inquiry

There were other inadequacies which were evident in the administration of Sir Lynden Pindling. Amongst them were the matter of the proliferation of drug-running in the 1980s and questions raised about his finances resulting in the appointment of a Commission of Inquiry. Despite much probing amidst widespread publicity nothing was proved and no prosecutions ensued.

The Policy of "Bahamianization"

It is germane to emphasize here that Sir Lynden Pindling, and his colleagues in the early years of his administration, notably The Hon. Arthur Hanna, the Hon. Loftus Roker, the Hon. (later Sir) Arthur Foulkes, the Hon. (later Sir) Cecil Wallace Whitfield and the Hon. Paul Adderley, were all fierce nationalists, dedicated to advancing the rights and promoting the welfare of Bahamians. This was manifested in the exercise of the policy of Bahamianization. Very profoundly, it was at the heart of the famous "Bend or Break" speech delivered by Pindling at Freeport as far back as 1969. For, although that landmark address left some expatriates uncomfortable, it resulted in the advancement of many Bahamians in "The Second City."

What then can be said, summarily, about the general performance of Sir Lynden Oscar Pindling at the domestic level of his many outstanding endeavours?

Here it is submitted that the brilliant assessment by noted Bahamian historian, Professor Don Maples, is most useful:

> Under Pindling's leadership, all Bahamians were provided with an education. The middle class, whether black, coloured, or white expanded and became better off. Medical and social services were made available to all. Sir Lynden supported Bahamian culture, promoted pride in being Bahamian and being black. He achieved the emancipation of black Bahamians. At the same time he persuaded white

Bahamians that they too were important to the Bahamas' future.[xxi]

5. Sir Lynden Pindling, "International Elder Statesman"

Thus far, we have discussed the outstanding record of service that Sir Lynden Oscar Pindling accomplished at the local or national levels. It is appropriate then that we turn now to examine his achievements at the international level, beyond the geographical boundaries of "The Isles of June!'

Very early in his political career, Sir Lynden embarked upon regular visits to other parts of the Caribbean. Bearing in mind that his father hailed from Jamaica, it should not be surprising to learn that one of these trips was to Jamaica. The narrator, who at that time was a young Minister of The Gospel, serving in that island, vividly recalls the wife of a colleague in ministry expressing how impressed she was by the sincerity, humility, and fluency of the young Prime Minister of the Bahamas.

Very significantly, in stark contrast to the officers of the UBP who stood aloof from the other Islands of the English speaking Caribbean, Sir Lynden Pindling sought to forge closer links with them in many ways. Thus, in the area of tertiary education, as we have seen, closer links were established with the University of the West Indies, with many Bahamians being sent to study at its campuses in Jamaica, Trinidad and Tobago, and Barbados. Correspondingly, in due course, The Princess Margaret Hospital was recognized as a teaching hospital by the UWI, the Faculty of Tourism of the UWI was based in the Bahamas, and students from throughout the region came to study at the Eugene Dupuch Law School. Likewise in the area of sports, the Bahamas joined in the Carifta Games. Indeed, it was while the Hon. Kendal Nottage served as Minister of Sports that the Bahamas boasted of being "Numero Uno" in these highly competitive regional athletic and aquatic exercises.

Sir Lynden Pindling's foray into the field of international political affairs began very early in his career thus, in October, 1956 he was a member of the delegation, including also Mr. H. M. Taylor and the Hon. Milo B. Butler, which represented the PLP in discussions with the Colonial Office in the urgent need for political reforms in The Bahamas. Then in 1965 Sir Lynden Pindling was the brilliant spokesman of an eight person delegation of the PLP which met with the 24-member Special Committee on Decolonization of the United Nations. Soon after becoming Independent, the Bahamas became the 138th Member of the United Nations. Again, Sir Lynden made a brilliant speech before that august international body on September 18, 1973.

Craton comments:

"On that occasion, by all accounts, Pindling rose above the humble platitudes expected from a comparatively minor newcomer, to put in a memorable plea for the concept of interdependence: *'the need for all states to recognize that isolation enhances division, while unity promotes harmonization of action.'*[xxii]

In due course, the Bahamas joined other international organizations including the UNESCO (The United Educational Scientific and Cultural organization), the IMF (The International Monetary Fund) and OAS (The Organization of American States).

Turning to the region, as has been noted, Sir Lynden demonstrated deft diplomatic skill in dealing with the HMBS Flamingo incident.

Meanwhile in regional political circles, especially the English speaking Caribbean community, Sir Lynden gradually arose to a position of great influence and recognition. As the years passed and he remained in political leadership while many other Caribbean leaders appeared and then, after a short time, disappeared from the regional political arena, he was regarded, deferentially as an Elder Caribbean Statesman.

The influence of Sir Lynden eventually extended beyond the region. Sir Lynden made a favourable impression upon those in positions of leadership in the extensive Commonwealth of Nations.

The highlight of these endeavours was no doubt the holding of the Commonwealth Heads of Government Meeting (CHOGM) in Nassau in 1985. It was, indeed, "an honoured privilege" that the Bahamas, a little nation with just over a quarter million inhabitants, hosted the political leaders of the many nations of the British Commonwealth composed of many nations and territories, including huge democracies such as India and Canada, nations which recognized the

Queen as titular head (including the Bahamas, Jamaica, Barbados) and those which were republics such as Guyana; of large nations in Africa and small territories such as the Turks & Caicos Islands and the Cayman Islands, which were still colonies of "the mother country," the British Commonwealth, political remnant of the once mighty British Empire, was, indeed a very powerful, internationally recognized international socio-economic, loosely knit political body. With the Queen in attendance and political leaders of fifty-three nations, it was certainly an event which made all feel "proud to be Bahamian!"

While many important issues had to be dealt with at that most important international political gathering, there was one which stood "at the top of the agenda and dominated its deliberations—the challenge of dealing with South Africa where the policy of Apartheid was entrenched and the world famous hero and its major opponent Nelson Mandela was in prison.

The militant political potentates of the black nations of Africa and the Caribbean were bitterly opposed to this blatant form of racism in South Africa, a nation rich in natural resources but poor in human relationships! Moreover, there was a worldwide "Free Mandela Movement." Indeed, the narrator recalls that at that time there were many who called for the release of Mandela.

In this context, in the spotlight of the world, Sir Lynden Pindling rose to the challenge of that august occasion. He moderated the debate which led to signing of the Nassau

Declaration strongly condemning Apartheid, calling for the extension of the sanctions upon South Africa and calling for the release of Nelson Mandela. Then, on the day following the end of CHOGM, Pindling flew to New York where he addressed the General Assembly of The United Nations reinforcing the call for imposing sanctions upon South Africa. A major chain of events set into action, initiated by the bold speeches and actions of Sir Lynden Pindling. Under the weight of the international outcry, the government of South Africa freed Nelson Mandela. Hugely popular "at home and abroad," Mandela was elected to serve as the first African President of South Africa. Thus, as we have seen, Pindling was instrumental in initiating the political events which led to the release of Nelson Mandela.

Eminent Bahamian Historian Michael Craton sums up Pindling's achievements at the international level thus:

> "Prime Minister Pindling's widespread travels on Commonwealth business, especially in Africa and Asia, made him familiar to and with many fellow leaders. Besides showcasing the Bahamas and learning much from the problems encountered by other developing countries, he was able to offer encouragement and support. This was particularly true over the imposition of sanctions on Rhodesia and South Africa because of the racialist policies of their white minority rulers. The Rhodesian situation had (more or less) been resolved by the creation of Zimbabwe in 1980. But by fortunate chance, the South

African situation was the major issue dealt with at the 1985 CHOGM, leading to the landmark Nassau Declaration. The Bahamas and its leader were therefore indelibly associated with the events that led to the release of Nelson Mandela, the dismantling of apartheid, black majority rule and South Africa's readmission to the Commonwealth."[xxiii]

It was in terms of his achievements on the international level, Sir Lynden's "Finest Hour."

6. Pindling, Patriarch, "Father in the Home"

The Good Book warns that he who aspires to leadership in the Church should himself be a good leader in his own home. For, it is expected that the person who would lead others in the church should be able to manage his own household well! The same principle may be applied to the person who aspires to lead in the State. Accordingly, it is salutatory and most instructive to pause here to reflect profoundly upon the quality of the home and family life of "The Father of The Nation."

Bear in mind, therefore, that during the crucial years following his call to the Bar in 1953, the youthful Lynden Pindling made two decisions, which were destined to be of tremendous significance throughout the course of his life. The first of these (chronologically speaking) was his decision to join the fledgling Progressive Liberal Party, to throw his lot into the struggle for the political liberation of the people of his homeland. The second was the decision to get married.

As a young practising attorney, Lynden Pindling was attracted to a young pretty photography technician by the name of Marguerite McKenzie, who hailed from Andros. As their paths crossed often, it was not long before he entered into courtship with this brown skinned Bahamian beauty. It lasted several years and their relationship blossomed.

> "Lynden and Marguerite were married by the Anglican Father David Pugh, at six o'clock in the morning of Saturday, May 5, 1956. The place was St. Ann's Parish Church, way out of town, at the northern end of Fox Hill Road, overlooking New Providence's Eastern Bay. Including the priest and couple, there were just eight persons present. Lynden's fellow lawyer, Exumian Livingston B. Johnson, acted as best man and Marguerite's sisters: Doris and Julie were maid of honour and bridesmaid. A friend of Johnson's and Doris' fiancée, Lon Albury, made up the wedding party in its entirety.[xxiv]

Marguerite proved to be the ideal partner and soul mate for the young ambitious lawyer, determined "to make his mark" in the highly competitive arena of politics! For, it was only a "matter of weeks" after they were joined in matrimony that her spouse was "caught up" in the bid to win a seat as a representative of the PLP in the crucial 1956 General Election. She was very much his confidant who stood by his side in the "ups and downs" of his eventful political career. Thus, she continued to support and encourage him as he ascended the steep ladder of political leadership eventually becoming the first Prime Minister of the Bahamas.

Meanwhile, their relationship developed and deepened over the years. Accordingly this conjugal union produced four children including Obediah "Obi," Leslie, Michelle and Monique. Very importantly, much to her credit, Lady Pindling while very active in supporting her husband in his political career, even to the point of actively campaigning, managed to give herself diligently and uncompromisingly to the nurture of their children, all of whom eventually became law-abiding contributing citizens of their homeland.

Sir Lynden himself, despite his very busy schedule proved to be a devoted father who was loved and respected by his children. They always spoke very highly of him in conversations with the narrator. Sir Lynden made it clear that his family was very important to him. Large portraits of the members of his family adorned the impressive Office of the Prime Minister located at Rawson Square. At lunchtime, he usually went to the family residence "out West" instead of dining at one of the restaurants down town. He tried his best to be a father not only at home but to the nation as well, thus becoming a good "Father in the home" besides being recognized as "Father of the Nation."

7. Sir Lynden Pindling, "Father of the Nation!"

By the year 1997, Sir Lynden Oscar Pindling realized that "the time had come" for him to retire from front line politics. Burdened with the challenges, criticisms and conflicts which are part of the landscape of the cut and thrust of political leadership, and facing challenges in his health, he felt that it was time to pass the baton of leadership to a politician of "the younger generation." He had demitted the office of Prime Minister in 1992 when the Free National Movement won the General Election. Thus, by that time The Rt. Hon. Hubert Ingraham had served for five years "at the helm of the nation." (It is important to bear in mind that both the Rt. Hon. Hubert Ingraham and the Rt. Hon. Perry Christie who succeeded Sir Lynden in office, were selected by him as young politicians with great leadership potential. Events during the years since have indeed vindicated his ability to discern those who are gifted as leaders!)

On Monday, July 7, 1997, the Right Hon. Sir. Lynden Oscar Pindling delivered a highly emotionally charged speech confirming his resignation from front line politics. Expressing his appreciation to The Almighty for allowing him to serve his country for many years, and to his family and faithful followers for their unwavering support over these many years, he summed up his achievements with honour and dignity. At the same time, he was deeply conscious of his human failings and weaknesses expressing his regret for what he had failed to do. All in all, he was satisfied that he had done his best for his country. Indeed, this moving farewell oration of Sir Lynden reminded one of the immortal words of United States of America's President John Fitzgerald Kennedy:

> "Ask not what your country can do for you: but what you can do for your country."

And so the Old Warrior laid down the weapons of political warfare and retreated into the life of a private citizen. In the twilight years of his life, he courageously maintained a fairly rigid routine—carrying out his practise in his law office ("A man must make a living!" he declared), reading and spending quality time with his family, including Lady Pindling, their children and grandchildren. It was during this period of his life that he devoted more time to his spiritual development, spending much time in reading and reflection on the Bible. He became an active member of the church of his mother, The Seventh Day Adventist Church and Pastor Hugh Roach along with other pastors, notably Dr. Myles Munroe, Bahamas Faith Ministries International, rendered pastoral care especially as his health concerns were proving most challenging. During this time, he engaged in a long battle against cancer of the prostate gland, an ailment which afflicts many males in their senior years.[xxv] He bore his suffering with true Christian fortitude. Eventually, on August 16, 2000, surrounded by members of his family and pastor, Sir Lynden Oscar Pindling completed his earthly sojourn.

Thus this great Bahamian, this giant of a man, who rose from being "A little fella from East Street" to become the first Prime Minister of the Commonwealth of the Bahamas was laid to rest in an impressive and inspiring Memorial State Service at the imposing Church of God of Prophecy on East Street. Masses of Bahamians thronged the street from Wulff Road to top-of-the hill Baillou Hill Road to bid a mournful and loving farewell to a true son of Bahamian soil and one who left an indelible imprint in the annals of Bahamian history for all ages.

That he had achieved much for his nation there can be not the slightest doubt. He had led its people from colonialism to Independence without bloodshed in "The Quiet Revolution," and he had established or presided over the establishment of major Bahamian institutions including The College of the Bahamas, the National Insurance Board, The Bahamas Defence Force, and others. Despite his human weaknesses and failings, he had greatly inspired many Bahamians to strive to be and do their best. If the measure of one's success is the extent to which he/she inspires others to do their best, then his life was one of abundant success:

> "If I can help somebody, as I walk this way...then my living will not be in vain!"[xxvi]

Over the years which followed his passing, criticisms about Sir Lynden gradually subsided and there was a growing appreciation of his contributions to the development of the people of the Bahamas by Bahamians "in all walks of life." Thus, the Hon. Perry Christie, Prime Minister of the Commonwealth of the Bahamas took the initiative in renaming the Nassau International Airport, The Lynden Pindling International Airport. There was growing appreciation of what he had accomplished and this was by people of all racial groups and political and religious groups in the Bahamas. At least one authority claimed that he was the greatest Bahamian of the twentieth century. Thus, in due course, he came to be acknowledged by all Bahamians as "The Father of the Nation!"

What then should be our response as we reflect profoundly upon the life and contributions of this great Bahamian, who surely made a difference? Surely this is a clarion call, and existential challenge to each and every one of us to use our gifts and talents as we rededicate ourselves to Christian nation building. This is precisely what is implied in Archdeacon Ranfurly Brown's challenge to us to realize "The Divine Call in being Bahamian."

It was Nelson Mandela, that great champion of social justice, who asserted that we should strive to leave the world a better place when we leave it than what it was when we came here. This we can do by seeking to fulfil the Divine plan and purpose for our life as Dr. Myles Munroe ever delights to remind us!

Yes, as we read and reflect upon the life and contributions of Sir Lynden and other great Bahamians Who Made a Difference, we are led to do our part in making our family a better family; our community, a better community; our nation, a better nation; and our world, a better world. This call to engage in the transformation of our community is well expressed in the exhortation of St. Paul:

> "Be ye not conformed to this world, but be ye transformed by the renewing of your mind that ye may prove what is that good, and acceptable, and perfect will of God." (Roms. 12:3, AV)

This clarion call to participate authentically and enthusiastically in the transformation of the world around us, as expounded here by St. Paul and proclaimed by the prophets is at the heart of the life and teaching of Christ. Accordingly, there can be not a shadow of a doubt that it comes, with amazing relevance, pertinence and challenge, to each and every one of us who "lives and moves and have our being" in these beautiful Bahamian isles...and beyond.

It is submitted, however, that we can, indeed, attain this most noble and worthwhile objective by exercising that inherent freedom which is ours as dwellers in a nation established upon the principles of democracy, Christianity and the rule of law.

It was not, therefore, by chance that we began this study of "Bahamians Who Made a Difference" by examining the life and contribution of Pompey, that Bahamian champion of social justice, who was motivated by a burning desire for freedom.

The lust for liberty, the desire to be free.

It is therefore, most appropriate that we should complete it by meditating profoundly upon Sir Lynden Pindling's wise observation about freedom:

> Freedom does have a price, it is not free.
>
> Freedom means responsibility, a responsibility to properly look after our families and ourselves; and citizenship demands more than simply paying taxes and voting for one's leader. In addition each of us has a sacred duty to love and protect this blessed land God has given to us, to build it up and make it better

for future generations. All of us have a stake in being Bahamian.[xxvii]

Pompey
Courageous, Charismatic

First Bahamian Champion of Social Justice

"Nothing worthwhile is obtained easily."

President Barack Obama

"No man is really free, who does not dare to do the right."

"If you hold to my teaching, you are really my disciples. Then you will know the truth and the truth will make you free."

The Master

I.   **INTRODUCTION – "The Lust for Liberty!'**

"The lust for liberty,'

The burning desire to be free

From all the chains (metal or mental!),

Which restrain or restrict,

In any way

The freedom of humankind

Has, indeed, lifted the spirits,

Ignited the passions

And motivated the actions

Of people in all walks of life!'

Drawn from every race, religion, and culture

"Throughout the ages!'

Yet, "if truth be told,'

The achievement of this most noble goal,

To which so many aspired!

Has often proved...elusive

And always most expensive

Calling for relentless efforts,

Often leading to...tears...sweat...blood shed!

Major sacrifices by all those engaged

In the eternal pursuit of liberty!

Thus, Jacques Rousseau,

That famous philosopher of the French Revolution (1789)

Musing profoundly on this phenomenon,

Arrived at the conclusion

"Man is born free

But is everywhere in chains!'

II.   **"Stride toward freedom"**

Now, of all the chains that have impinged upon the freedom of humankind "throughout the ages,' none has proved more oppressive, repressive, abhorrent to the spirit of liberty, and downright de-humanizing than...slavery! And although it has been described in some quarters, as "the institution of slavery,' there can be no doubt that it has been the cause of tremendous store of suffering and cruelty most vile, inflicted upon the oppressed, the down-trodden, "the wretched of the earth,' from "time immemorial." Indeed, there has been no more poignant demonstration of "man's inhumanity to man."

Yet, there have been those, who thwarted in their endeavour to attain liberty, or discouraged in some way, have become complacent and even resigned to their miserable condition! However, in the mysterious working of Divine Providence, there have arisen in every generation, charismatic leaders (i.e., men and women endowed with the gift of leadership), who have sought to awaken their dozing oppressed and down-trodden companions from their complacent slumber, encouraging them to break the shackles restricting their freedom, inspiring them to rise up and fight for their liberation!

Thus, Moses, acting under divine inspiration when the children of Israel were slaves in Egypt their house of

77

bondage boldly approached Pharaoh demanding, "Let my people go!' (Exodus 5:1). Many centuries later, David, "A man after God's own heart,' was called upon to deliver them from the oppression of the Philistines! (II Samuel 1-7).

"The lust for liberty,' was at the heart of the rallying cry of that great American patriot Patrick Henry, during The American War of Independence (1776) "Give me liberty or give me death!' By the same token, "The burning desire to be free" informed this declaration of freedom of liberated African-Americans during the time of their emancipation:

"And before I be a slave

I'd be buried in my grave

And go home to my LORD

And be free!'

Coming to the Caribbean region, it is germane to note that there were several charismatic leaders who arose to protest against slavery, especially early in the Nineteenth Century after the abolition of the slave trade. Amongst them were "Black Harry" of Antigua, Sam Sharp of Barbados, and Paul Bogle and William Gordon of Jamaica.

The question that inevitably (if not immediately!) comes to mind here is, "was there a charismatic leader who emerged, or was "raised up" by God here in the Bahamas, to protest against the injustices of slavery?

The answer is at hand! "Yes! None other than Pompey, that legendary freedom fighter from Exuma!'

For, although there were others "who took up a cudgel" against slavery, there can be no doubt, that "historically speaking" when it comes to the early struggle for social justice in the Bahamas, "pride of place" must be attributed to...Pompey!

Now, despite his major contribution in this sphere resulting in the attainment of hero status during the post-emancipation era, amazingly little is known about Pompey in the Bahamas today! <u>Yet, it is submitted that, it is essential that all Bahamians—"especially those who belong to the younger generation!' – should get to know much more about this great liberator than his name!</u>

Who, then was Pompey? What motivated him in spearheading the struggle for liberation in the Bahamas? Why did the strongest and boldest protest against slavery in the Bahamas erupt in Exuma rather than New Providence, site of the Capital, Nassau? How could it be that Pompey's legacy which was well-recognized in the Bahamas during the post-emancipation period sank into oblivion in later years? What can be done (or is being done") to restore him to his rightful place in Bahamian history? Most of all, what lessons can we learn from Pompey to help us as we cope with the challenges of life in the Bahamas today? These are the questions for which we shall seek answers as we continue to read and meditate profoundly upon the exciting career of this early Bahamian champion of social justice?

Now, it is extremely important, in all thinking and discussion about slavery, to distinguish, clearly between "The Abolition of The Slave Trade" and "The Abolition of Slavery." For these two very significant historical events are often confused!

The slave trade, of which Elizabethan Adventurer, Sir John Hawkins, was a pioneer (soon followed by Spanish, Portuguese, Dutch and French traders) was designed to take full economic advantage of the vast mineral and agricultural resources of the then "New World!' Thus, their ships sailed from ports in Europe to West Africa where they purchased slaves, and transported them, to The Americas and The Caribbean. They made the long return voyage to Europe, laden with the products of their American colonies—precious metals, sugar, cotton, corn, tobacco, coffee, etc.

While lucrative for the traders and planters, the slave trade, especially "The Middle Passage" (the long dangerous trans-Atlantic voyage) was the cause of an incalculable amount of human suffering and anguish and even many deaths amongst the slaves. Accordingly, it was abolished by an Act passed by the British Parliament in 1807. This was, the direct result of the tireless efforts of Sir William Wilberforce and the other abolitionists, who strongly objected to the slave trade and slavery in general on the basis of their deeply held Christian convictions. Henceforth, all ships engaging in the illegal slave trade were intercepted by the Royal Navy and the slaves on board were freed, arriving in the ports of "The New World" as liberated men and women!

Meanwhile, those who worked on the plantations after the Abolition of The Slave Trade remained in slavery. Indeed, they were forced to endure their condition of bondage until slavery was abolished by The Act of Emancipation in 1834!

It was during this turbulent period—between the abolition of the slave trade and the abolition of slavery—that most of the protests against slavery took place in the Bahamas. Indeed, as Saunders has brilliantly documented, more than ten such slave "Revolts" in the Bahamas occurred during the period from 1829-1834. While there were revolts and protests against slavery in New Providence, Cat Island, Watlings Island (later San Salvador) and Eleuthera, the largest number, by far, took place in Exuma. Why that island?

Well, when the United Empire Loyalists left the United States after the American War of Independence, they sought to settle in the Bahamas. They brought with them their slaves and decided to establish cotton plantations along the lines of those they had operated in the Southern States whence they came, mainly the Carolinas and Georgia They found that the island of Exuma and their cultivation required the labour of many slaves.

The wealthiest and most influential landlord at Exuma early in the Nineteenth Century was and Englishman, Lord John Rolle of Stevenstone. He had inherited a plantation where 140 slaves laboured and lived from his father, Denys Rolle. A bold, ambitious developer, he greatly expanded the holdings inherited and eventually had operated five plantations in

Exuma, which were inhabited and cultivated by four hundred slaves.

It is interesting and significant to note that whereas in most of the other Caribbean territories notably Jamaica, Barbados, Antigua and Trinidad & Tobago, the main crop was sugar cane, in the Bahamas the main crop was cotton. Or, to put it another way, whereas in most Caribbean Islands, "Sugar was king!' In the Bahamas "Cotton was king!' Cotton was not as "labour intensive" as sugar. Accordingly, the slaves in Exuma, in addition to working on the plantation where cotton was the main crop were allowed to cultivate other products such as corn, peas, and sweet potatoes on small plots of land. Taking into consideration the large number of slaves required to cultivate the five plantations owned by Lord Rolle, it should not be surprising to learn that most of the "revolts" against the institution of slavery occurred amongst them.

Indeed, there were always ground of complaint on the part of the slaves as they boldly expressed their burning desire for freedom. No doubt the presence of "liberated slaves" amongst them or "the new negroes from Africa" who were liberated from slave ships by the British Navy, contributed to an atmosphere of growing dissatisfaction with their state of bondage! "Things came to a head'" then, "Early in 1830 when with only seven days' notice, a group of seventy-seven of Lord Rolle's slaves were told they would be sent to Cat Island." They strongly objected to being treated in this manner. The charismatic leader who emerged to lead them in their protest was 32-year-old slave "Pompey." Little is known about his background before he arose to lead this revolt.

Whatever else might be surmised about Pompey, evidently he was "a born leader." For the other slaves willingly looked to him for leadership and acted in accord with his instructions.

Led by this dynamic young man, the protesting slaves hid in the bushes of Exuma for five weeks. But they were not content to stay there for very long. Again, led by Pompey, forty-four of them took possession of Lord Rolle's salt ship (as salt was also produced on his vast holdings) and sailed to Nassau. They had heard that the Governor Carmichael Smyth (in whose honour Carmichael Road, Nassau, Bahamas is named!) was sympathetic towards the welfare of slaves and they hoped that he would assist them in their quest for freedom.

But such was not the case, at least not at the beginning. Treated initially as runaway slaves, they were captured, charged before local magistrates and sent to the dreaded workhouse. "Five of them were sentenced to be publicly flogged with 50 lashes each, and one boy and eight women were to receive 39 lashes each in the workhouse. The sentence was in fact carried out." Amongst those who were flogged was a female slave five months pregnant and nursing mothers. What cruelty!

When the Governor learned of the terrible manner in which the Exuma slaves were treated, he was furious. Accordingly, he immediately "fired" the magistrates and police involved and ordered that Pompey and his group of slaves be permitted to return to Exuma.

But that was not "the end of Pompey." By no means. Indeed, his undaunted spirit was not broken by the treatment received in Nassau and he continued to take a leading role in the revolts which continued in the Rolle plantations in Exuma. Concisely, he continued to be the ringleader of those who protested the conditions of their existence as slaves.

The supervisor at The Rolle plantations sent a report to the Governor in which he claimed that many of the slaves refused to work and that they were storing up ammunition in preparation for an armed insurrection!

In response to what appeared to be the brewing of a major slave rebellion, along the lines of those which had occurred in other British Caribbean colonies, Governor Carmichael Smyth, expeditiously, despatched a company of fifty soldiers, under the command of the Chief Constable of the Colony, to Exuma. Their landing at Georgetown late at night on June 30, 1830, must most certainly, be recognized as major event in the long, exciting history of the Bahamas!

The soldiers, however, met little resistance! A thorough search of the slave huts at Steventon resulted in the discovery of a few rusty muskets and a small quantity of ammunition required to sustain the major slave rebellion anticipated!

The Chief Constable, then, ordered the soldiers to proceed to Rolleville, another of Lord Rolle's five plantations in Exuma.

But, the ever vigilant Pompey, using "a short cut,' prevented them in getting there and warned the slaves of the imminent arrival of the armed brigade! Accordingly, they escaped into the bushes, and when the soldiers searched their abandoned huts, they found, as was the case in Steventon, a few virtually useless pieces of military equipment. Thus Pompey again surfaced as a strong leader, motivated by a burning desire for the liberation of his people!

The soldiers then returned to Steventon and ordered the slaves to go back to work. But they were reluctant to do so. In response, having captured Pompey, they severely punished the leader of their protest...with thirty-nine lashes! Thereupon, the slaves resumed their duties. The Chief Constable and the fifty soldiers, then, returned to Nassau, satisfied that their mission had been accomplished!

But the slaves they left behind in Exuma, while reluctantly complying with the order to return to work in the Rolle plantations, were, by no means, pacified!

For, the widespread conception that their liberation was indeed, very near combined with other pertinent factors to foster a volatile, restless condition amongst them. Not surprisingly, therefore, protests against slavery continued on the extensive Rolle holdings during the most turbulent period.

Indeed, peace and harmony did not come to the slaves toiling in the plantations in Exuma and the other islands of the Bahamas until the Proclamation of Emancipation in 1834.

III.   "Food or Freedom"

Now, it must be abundantly clear exactly why Pompey led that historic revolt of the slaves of Exuma! Here, it is extremely important to bear in mind that the vast majority of the slaves at Exuma, and the other islands of the Bahamas, were not totally oppressed minions, who led a wretched existence without any possessions of their own!

For, as Saunders pointed out:

It would seem, although the evidence is inconclusive, that the majority of the slaves brought to the Bahamas by The Loyalists were creole-born, lived in a society with an almost equal sex ratio, had a well-developed family life and had probably lived and worked on small farms in small holding-size units.

Moreover, as we have seen, the slaves working at Lord Rolle's estates, were allowed to engage in subsistence farming on their own plots of land. Indeed, their circumstances were more comfortable than that of many of their counterparts in other colonies of the West Indies.

Why then, were the slaves, led by Pompey, constantly in a state of unrest and protest? Why they were not satisfied with their condition? The answer is at hand:

The lust for liberty

The burning desire to be free

Once ignited in their hearts and minds

By Pompey

Could not be diminished.

You see, the revolt of the slaves at the extensive Rolle Estates in Exuma, began precisely when they realized that their freedom, their rights to participate in determining their destiny, were being violated! It was ignited when they commanded to leave Exuma for Cat Island with extremely short notice—just a few days to pack all their possessions, not being afforded the opportunity to harvest the crops they had planted for the benefit of their families. They objected then, to continue to being treated like "chattel,' as if they were objects to be used and abused rather than as persons who had emotions and rights, they protested because they had reached "the breaking point!" Their rights had been violated and they simply felt that "Enough is enough!" Concisely, they wanted to have "a say" with regard to their own destiny, and in keeping with their dignity as human beings created with rights by the Creator.

An illustration from ordinary domestic living is helpful here. A dog, a dog which is chained, may be well fed and cared for by its owner. But it is not free! For, as long as it is "in chains" it is not a free animal, able to roam where it may desire! Whenever freedom is restricted—whether in the case in the case of man or beast—there is bondage.

The Pompey revolt, then, confirmed in the Bahamas a profound truth "tried and tested" in the anvil of human experience "from time immemorial"; no matter how many material benefits you may supply to a people, no matter how comfortable you make their surroundings, no matter how big you make their pay check, if you deprive them of freedom, they will never be satisfied! For, as the Good Book advises, man cannot live "by bread alone,' that which satisfies the body, but must also have that which brings liberation.

IV.   **"Was Pompey a Christian?"**

Was Pompey a Christian? If so, to what extent did his religious faith play a part in the stand he took against slavery? The answers to these questions are pertinent to our discussion here as we seek to discern the reason why Pompey was so strong and consistent in his protest against slavery?

Here it is essential to bear in mind that there are in the Bible, two schools of thought when it comes to the relationship between the church and the state. On the one hand as demonstrated and discussed elsewhere, there is that approach which is in favour of the status quo calling for the support of the governing authorities. On the other hand, there is that strong "liberationist tradition, which is revolutionary in nature calling upon people to express their desire for freedom by taking action to bring about their liberation. Its chief paradigm is the Exodus and it is expounded in detail in the contributions of The Liberationist Theologians.

Coming now, specifically to the matter of the religious faith of Pompey, it is most significant that this matter is at the heart of a discussion which Sir Etienne Dupuch had with a group of Bahamian young people during the latter part of his long eventful life.

Here is what the famous Bahamian editor said to some of the young people of his generation:

> "The strength of the negro in history was that he understood better than anyone else the promise of Christ that even though His children might walk in the valley of the shadow of death, they should fear no evil for his rod and staff would comfort them and guard them safely on the road to "The Pearly Gates,' where he has a special place for them"

I will tell you just one of the stories ex-slaves would tell in Nassau when I was a boy:

> Pompey was a great Christian, but he did not want to keep his faith to himself. Every afternoon, just before sundown, he knelt down outside his small thatched hut and talked directly to his Lord.

> "Aww God, my one and only Jesus,

"Dis me now, your fateful servant, Pompey, talkin', an' I want you tea listen careful to my plea. I is jus' plain tired o' all de trials and tribylations on dis here sinful and "cruel" earth. I wants you ter take me o' de burden. I want you fer take me home ter yer bosom anytime, Lawd you sen' de Angel Gabriel, he will fine ya fateful servant anxious an' waitin.'"

One night the boys of the village decided to play a trick on Pompey. At midnight one of them rapped on his door.

"Who dat?" Pompey asked.

'Dis me now. De Angel Gabriel.

De Lord God sen' me ter bring his fateful servant home ter him."

"Go 'way Gabriel! Pompey said in a frightened voice, Pompey done move!"

I told this story to my friend, Rev. Harcourt Brown the other day, and he gave me a better version of it.

He said that Pompey was married and living with his wife "Samanta" (Samantha-Jane).

One night a boy climbed a tree outside Pompey's home and blew a horn.

"Pompey!' Samanta Jane whispered to him, "You hear dat?"

"What you tink 'oman, he whispered back, "You tink dat is Gabriel horn?"

"Cud be" she said, shakin' her head from side to side.

At that moment there was a rap on the door.

"If das Gabriel, tell him I gone out."

Once again there was a rap on the door, this time a little louder. "Who dat?" Samanta Jane asked.

"Dis me de angel Gabriel. De Lord sen' me fer his fateful servant Pompey."

"Sorry Gabriel" Samanta Jane said in her sweetest voice,

"Pompey don' jus' gone out!"

"Das alright" the voice outside the door said

"The Lord say if Pompey ain't dere, bring he wife!'

There followed a big commotion inside the house.

"No, Mr. Gabril! I was only jokin'" Samanta Jane said.

"Pompey ain' gone nowhere! He rite here.

"Pompey stop cuttin' de fool. Come out from under de bed.

"You all de time callin' on der Lord fe sen fer you."

"Now Gabriel come! Get outa 'dis house and go wit' him. Goodbye, Pompey!'

Now these stories about Pompey, which, according to two eminent Bahamian authorities, were being told amongst the ex-slaves during the late post-emancipation era are most interesting in every way. They certainly indicate that Pompey was very well respected in the African Bahamian community, and indeed, had become by then legendary. While somewhat amusing to us today they do certainly, at a profound level have a very powerful message about Pompey. Evidently, he was a deeply religious person and this aspect of his life must have been magnified as it was retold again and again in the communities of the ex-slaves and their children.

In the light of the above, it is submitted that Pompey was, indeed, a Christian. Moreover, it is submitted that he was a Christian who interpreted the scriptures in terms of the liberationist exodus tradition, and therefore, his faith was at the heart of his courageous struggle for the liberation of his people.

"Yes he was a deep committed Christian whose faith motivated his stand against injustice as has been the case with liberationist champions from Moses to Mandela!

V.   **Lessons from Pompey!**

Having carried out a study of the life and times of Pompey, as well as the forces which motivated him in his struggle for social justice for his people, we are now in a position to evaluate their significance for us. What lesson, then, can we learn from the life and times of Pompey to assist us as we seek to cope with the challenges of life in the Bahamas today? It is submitted that they are, indeed, two-fold – the priority of courage in the lives of all who would aspire "To Make a Difference,' and the paramount importance of passing down from one generation to the next, encouraging and inspiring stories of those who have achieved greatness.

Pompey, Man of Courage

With regard to courage, it is salutatory to pause here to reflect profoundly upon this most important virtue.

For you see, those who have become leaders, who have, indeed, "Made a Difference" have come from backgrounds "many and varied." They have emerged from and continue to arise from all the varied national and cultural entities, socio-economic classes, creeds, colours and genders, which comprise the human family in "the global village." Yet, it can be unequivocally asserted that, despite their peculiar characteristics, backgrounds and idiosyncrasies, they all have demonstrated one essential trait...courage!

Variously defined as "dogged determination,' "thinking out of the box,' "bravery,' "boldness,' "guts,' or as the late Dr. Cleveland Eneas, another Bahamian who made a difference,' relished to describe it "s-t-i-c-k-a-b-i-l-i-t-y" certainly the primary qualifications required of those who would "make a difference!'

For, it took courage for Father Abraham, in response to the Divine Call to leave his comfortable home in Ur of the Chaldees with his family, his entourage of workers and their employees and many animals (bear in mind that in today's terms, he was a multi-millionaire!) and to go to a land to which he was divinely directed (Gen. 12). It took courage, tremendous moral indignation for John the Baptist to condemn King Herod for his blatantly immoral lifestyle at a time when monarchs exercised unfettered executive authority (Mark 6:14-29). It took courage on the part of Christopher Columbus to defy those who feared that the world was flat, and to embark upon that historic voyage of discovery proving it to be a globe, making landfall on our Bahamian island of San Salvador on October 12, 1492. Martin Luther, "Father of the Reformation,' demonstrated great courage when asked to renounce his past theological statement at the Diet of Worms, October 31, 1517, declaring "Here I stand!' It took courage for "Mother Theresa" to leave her well-to-do family in Europe to serve amongst "the poorest of the poor" in the slums of India. And it took courage for Martin Luther King, Jr. to stand before a huge crowd on a "March to Washington" to declare "I have a dream that a time will come when men will not be judged by the colour of their skin but by the content of their character!'

Most of all it took courage beyond comprehension for the Galilean carpenter, Jesus the Christ, to leave the Galilean countryside to go to Jerusalem, place of his crucifixion for the salvation of humankind! (Mark 8:31, 9:31, 10:33)

What of Pompey? Surely, he was a man of tremendous courage. When he was called upon to lead the slaves in their protest against being treated like chattel, with no rights, the odds against him were formidable. After all the white slave masters were entrenched in their socio-economic and political control of the colony. Throughout his career, as has been demonstrated, he exercised a tremendous amount of courage. His was an indomitable spirit which was not easily intimidated or silenced. This is why he continued to demonstrate courage even after attempts were made to placate or coerce him into submission. He remained, even in submission, a man of undaunted determination and relentless courage. Truly a role model for all Bahamians who aspire "to make a difference."

The great importance of passing down stories of heroes to the younger generation!

Now, as we have seen, the memories of the exploits of Pompey were fresh in the minds of those ex-slaves who survived until the "turn of the century" when Sir Etienne Dupuch was a boy "growing up in Nassau." Indeed, according to the famous Bahamian editor, he had reached almost legendary status in the 'afro-Bahamian community of that era.

Yet, by the time of the boyhood of the narrator, more than a generation later, these memories of the great Bahamian liberator had virtually evaporated. For, in all the years of his boyhood, including his years of study at primary and secondary levels of education, he cannot recall a single person speaking about Pompey. Indeed, in long sessions when his grandmother, an amateur historian in her own right, he learned much about the exploits of William the

Conqueror and the many wives of King Henry, VIII and little or nothing about that great Bahamian hero, Pompey! Indeed, he graduated from institutions of education in the Bahamas and Jamaica, knowing much British history, some American history, a little history of the Caribbean and virtually nothing about the history of his homeland.

The reasons for this lack of information about the Bahamas in our educational system in those days need not detain us here. For, it has happened. What is necessary, however, is for us to ensure that this does not happen again. We must not allow the exciting history of our beloved Bahamaland to be neglected by the people of our nation, rather, it is our sacred responsibility to teach the younger generation about the great deeds of Pompey and the many other Bahamians "who made a difference." The children and young people of other Caribbean nations know much about the history of their respective nations. By the same token, it behoves us to educate our young people about "Bahamians who made a difference!' In this regard we must start with the children.

When the Israelites gathered for the celebration of the Feast of the Passover, the profound story of their liberation from Egypt, their house of bondage by divine intervention, the youngest of them inquired as to why they were assembled!

Then the eldest amongst them repeats the wonderful story of the miraculous redemption of their forefathers from the hands of Pharaoh by the mighty "Right Hand of

God" (Exodus 12-15). Thus, this story is passed down from one generation to another, and so it is an event which is never ever forgotten! Indeed, the memory of this epochal event appears as fresh as if it happened yesterday when rehearsed in the celebration of the Feast of the Passover today! Indeed, no child grows up in the sacral community of Israel without knowing about the liberation of its ancestors from bondage in Egypt under the leadership of Moses, Man of God!

Now, there can be not a shadow of a doubt that there is a lesson here most relevant to us in the Bahamas today! For as painfully demonstrated in the case of Pompey's memory fading away within a generation, we are prone to forget the great men and women who built our nation. For, it reminds us of the tremendous importance of the instruction of our children, "the younger generation" about the history of our beloved Bahamaland! It is something that they need to be taught, from very young, with due diligence, knowledge and dedication. This, indeed, is the favourite message of veteran educator, Mr Urban Gibbs.

This Christian gentleman, who hails from Barbados, has spent most of his teaching career in the Bahamas, serving many islands, but notably Andros and Grand Bahama. Highly respected by all who have come under his influence in the classroom, he is both a preacher and a teacher. His favourite theme, demonstrated in the classroom and proclaimed in the pulpit, is the supreme importance of the early instruction of children in Christian virtues.

Most appropriately, in such matters he took his didactic cue from that great text in which Moses, under divine inspiration conveys to the Israelites, the absolute priority of the instruction of their children in the lofty ethical principle at the heart of their "salvation history!'

> "And thou shalt teach them _diligently_ unto thy children, and shalt talk about them when thou sittest in thine house, and who walkest by the way, and when thou liest down and when thou risest up." (Deut. 6:7, AV)

Concisely, diligent instruction of children, constant meditation and reflection upon the divine instructions must be carried on "24/7!'

The relevance of all this to us in the Bahamas today is abundantly clear! It behoves us, then to rededicate ourselves to the diligent instruction of our children in the history of our homeland! Never again must we allow the memory of the exciting exploits of "Pompey the Courageous" to fade into the background. Rather, we must ensure that our children, the vital "younger generation,' "read, mark, learn and inwardly digest" the history of the lives of Pompey and "other Bahamians who made a difference" that they too may be encouraged and inspired, by the grace of God, "to be the best that they can be!'

Dr. Robert Love

(1839-1914)

Priest, Physician, Civil Rights Activist, Journalist, Prophet

"A prophet is not without honour save in his own country."

(Jesus the Christ)

Introduction – Growing up in Grant's Town

Did you know that "Jamaica's leading black politician at the turn of the (Twentieth) Century" was, in fact...A Bahamian?[xxviii] Probably not.

For, in the long, exciting history of the Bahamas, there have emerged those, who, while making comparatively little impact upon the course of events at home, managed to accomplish much more abroad. Such person was the illustrious Rev. Dr. Joseph Robert Love! Beginning life in humble circumstances "Over the Hill," this remarkable "Son of Bahamian Soil" travelled abroad making very significant contributions in varied fields of human endeavour in the United States, Haiti, and most significantly, Jamaica. Despite his many achievements abroad, however, Dr. Robert Love remains a figure about whom the vast majority of Bahamians know "little or nothing!" Indeed, Bahamians who are well informed about the history of this nation have confessed that they are ignorant about the many achievements of this most remarkable gentleman!

Who then was Dr. Love? What do we know about his formative years "growing up" in the Bahamas? What were his accomplishments abroad? How has it transpired that one who is comparatively well remembered in at least two Caribbean territories has been virtually forgotten in the land of his birth? What can be done to turn around this situation? Most of all, what can Bahamians, learn about young Bahamians learn from the life and contributions of Dr. Love to assist them as they tackle challenges "at home and abroad?" These are the intriguing questions which will be the focus of our attention throughout this contribution.

Joseph Robert Love was born into a talented old Bahamian family in 1839. He grew up in Grant's Town where he received his education at primary level, evidently, he was "a bright student," who demonstrated great potential. For according to Thompson, The Rev. Father Hartman Fisher, The Rector of St. Agnes for fifty years supervised his "advance in education'" tutoring him in the theological languages of Latin and Greek.[xxix]

"Reading between the lines'" it would appear that this Anglican Priest, himself a fascinating personality, "saw something" in the budding young Bahamian and provided education for him with a view to preparing him for the Priesthood. Evidently, the young Bahamian was deeply influenced by this remarkable Anglican priest, a native of Jamaica, taking full advantage of what he imparted to him in academic pursuits.

Moreover, as will become patently clear, he received from this clergyman, a white priest who served virtually the whole of his Ministry in a black community, an attribute, non-academic in nature, but which was to prove most significant in his distinguished career—a passion for social justice!

Priest, Brilliant Scholar, Career in the USA

Joseph Robert Love did not remain in the Bahamas very long upon completing his studies under Father Fisher. He migrated to the United States of America. One need not be surprised because it was a period when many Bahamians were migrating to the USA in search of a better way of life. His studies in the Biblical languages proved significant because in 1877 he was ordained to the Priesthood. Though later in life, this multi-talented individual would engage in varied professional endeavours, he would always be recognized as a "Man of Cloth". It is precisely for this reason that he was listed by the Anglican Diocese of Nassau, The Turks & Caicos Islands amongst "Bahamian Priests Abroad"![xxx] He established several churches in the USA which are still places of worship.

As has been noted already, Robert Love was a brilliant student, endowed with great academic ability. Thus, having completed his theological studies, he embarked upon studies in the field of medicine. Accordingly, in 1879 at the age of forty he became the first black medical graduate of the University of Buffalo, New York. The significance of the young Bahamian's academic achievement here can hardly be overrated. He graduated from the Medical School of a well- recognized American institute of education at a time when very few black students made advances in tertiary education. There can be no doubt that his outstanding success proved to inspire many

African-American students to pursue studies at tertiary level, earning advanced degrees in many disciplines!

Missionary in Haiti

At that time, Haiti, being the first Republic resulting from the revolt of its citizens against their European Colonial masters, was attracting people from throughout the Caribbean and the Americas. It was a time of relative prosperity, and so in contrast to today when so many leave that Republic "for greener pastures" in other nations, including the Bahamas and the USA, Haiti was a magnet to which many foreign radicals and social activists were attracted!

When therefore, the opportunity came to serve in Haiti, young Dr. Robert Love, with his adventurous spirit, took full advantage of it. Thus, he left the "comfort zone" of the USA and served as a missionary physician in Haiti. Interestingly enough, however, he did not confine himself to his parochial and medical duties, but ventured into the highly polarized field of politics in the young black Republic. He did not remain in Haiti for very long, however, and after serving there headed for another island in the Caribbean, where he would make full use of his qualifications and his foray into the political arena—Jamaica.

Dr. Love, Social Activist and Politician—Service in Jamaica

Dr. Robert Love arrived in Jamaica late in the nineteenth century; a time of major social change, conflict and political turmoil in that Caribbean isle! For in this post Emancipation era, there continued to persist protracted tension between the liberated masses and the white owners of the plantations as sugar was "king" in the island's economy. Indeed, there were major differences between the poor and oppressed masses and the more wealthy groups who controlled the economy. Dr. Love participated in this conflict, siding with the poor against the wealthy land owners and merchants. His influence in this area proved to be immense.

During this period, this versatile journalist and gentleman excelled both as journalist and orator. In his articles published in the Jamaica Advocate, he boldly defended the rights of the poor. As an eloquent speaker he continued to champion the rights of the oppressed, and in this regard he foreshadowed the contribution of the Liberationist theologians of the mid-twentieth century.[xxxi] It should not be surprising, therefore, to learn that he rapidly "climbed the ladder" of political success and influence in Jamaica, so much so that he was regarded as a leading politician early in the Twentieth Century.

Thus, in 1906 he was elected a Member of the Legislative Council. And for the rest of his life he continued to play a most active part in the political development of Jamaica. What proved very significant, historically speaking, was the influence of Dr. Love on the great social activist and universally recognized icon of racial social justice, Marcus Mosiah Garvey (1888-1940 AD.)

In this regard, Sewell in his seminal Garvey's Children—The Legacy of Marcus Garvey, reveals that Dr. Love himself, an excellent orator, greatly assisted Garvey in the early years of his struggle as an advocate of the rights of the oppressed in Jamaica, by giving him "his lessons in elocution"![xxxii]

At a much more profound level, however, the Bahamian priest/politician, exerted a major stimulating, positive impact upon the budding Jamaican social activist by imparting and reinforcing in his consciousness an attribute, at once intriguing and most potent, which proved to be of key significance in the development of his flamboyant, most eventful career—a deep abiding, tenacious sense of pride in being black, a son/daughter of Mother Africa!

Thus, in responding to those in later years, who opposed him when he arose to champion the cause of the black economically deprived masses of Jamaica, Garvey testified:

"Much of my early education in race consciousness is from Dr. Robert Love." One cannot read his *Jamaica Advocate* without getting race consciousness. "...if Dr. Love was alive and in robust health, you would not be attacking me; you would be attacking him."[xxxiii]

Now, the ultimate historical significance and the profound implications of this confession by Garvey, for a just evaluation and appreciation of the contribution of Dr. Love in this area of human endeavour can hardly be over-estimated! For, since by his own admission, Dr. Love so deeply influenced Marcus Garvey, the significance of his endeavours proved to be much greater than is immediately realized!

For, bear in mind that Garvey's divinely endowed oratorical skills, fully developed under the mentoring of Dr. Love, was a key factor in his renowned ability to grasp the attention and maintain the allegiance of many throughout the Caribbean and The Americas. Like Dr. Love, Garvey travelled far and wide, from the land of his birth, in pursuit of his mission—awakening the consciousness of black people struggling for racial justice throughout the region. While in the United States, for instance, he established the United Negro Improvement Agency, which rapidly spread to every territory in the Caribbean, to some in South America, America, West Africa and indeed, every corner of the globe. Very significantly, his stature, over the years, has grown to legendary heights. For, as Nettleford observes:

> Marcus Mosiah Garvey deserves to be the icon he has become to millions of people of African ancestry throughout the world because of his seminal contribution he made to the liberation struggles of blacks both on the African Continent and in the Diaspora."[xxxiv] Duly recognized in the land of his birth, Marcus Mosiah Garvey is undoubtedly the greatest of Jamaica's National Heroes!

Now, despite the fact that he spent most of his life, and his major contributions abroad, it is germane to bear in mind that Dr. Love had roots deeply entrenched in the land of his birth! For instance, Miss Cynthia Love, a close relative, was a very competent veteran Bahamian educator, and many prominent Bahamians known to and including the chronicler, "got their start" in education under her disciplined compassionate tutoring! Another relative, Mr. Kenneth Love, leading Bahamian photographer, has accumulated a vast store house of valuable information about the amazing Dr. Love!

Born and nurtured in the Bahamas, ordained a priest and trained as a physician in the United States, revered as a Missionary Doctor in Haiti, distinguished as a politician and journalist in Jamaica, this versatile Bahamian, remains somewhat of an obscure figure in the land of his birth, "a prophet without honour in his own country".

Or, to put it another way, "Whereas Marcus Garvey, who was not well received in his homeland while alive and died in exile abroad, was eventually, highly recognized as a National Hero at home; Dr.

Love, a Bahamian, who gained wide recognition abroad, has yet to be duly recognized in the land of his birth! But, "All is not lost!" Indeed there is hope! For as more and more Bahamians learned about this great Bahamian, they will get to "love Dr. Love", and so attribute to him the long overdue recognition he merits in his homeland!

The Rev. Dr. Joseph Love

- Priest
- Physician
- Brilliant Scholar
- Medical Missionary
- Politician
- Eloquent Orator
- Journalist
- Staunch advocate of racial social justice
- Mentor of Marcus Mosiah Garvey

Truly "A Bahamian Who Made a Difference", at home and abroad!

Doctor Claudius Roland Walker

(May 6, 1892–November 15, 1971)

Physician, Politician, Educator, Builder and Patriot

There can be no doubt that one of the most versatile and charismatic figures ever to emerge in the Bahamas was none other than Dr. Claudius Roland Walker, aptly described as "a roly-poly, bald-headed, googly-eyed, flat nosed, thin lipped Afro Bahamian." He indeed was a pioneer in all the endeavours of his eventful life.[xxxv]

PIONEER IN MEDICINE

Born on May 6, 1892, he was the only off-spring of the union of Mr. & Mrs. Claudius F. Walker. Demonstrating great ability, he travelled to the United States of America, after receiving early education at home, to pursue his education at advanced levels. Accordingly, he earned his Bachelor of Science Degree, (BSc) at Howard University in Washington, DC, lectured for a short stint at Florida Memorial College in Florida and obtained his degree in Medicine (MD) at the prestigious Meharry Medical College in Nashville, Tennessee. His education at Historically Black Colleges and Universities (HBCUs) certainly was indicative of a person dedicated to the advance and upliftment of black people.

Now with such impeccable academic qualifications, there could be no doubt that he could have remained to serve in the USA, most likely at a large teaching hospital or as a professor at an important institution of tertiary education! Instead, as a patriotic Bahamian he elected to return to the Bahamas to serve his people.[xxxvi]

Thus in October, 1930 he returned home to embark upon an eventful life of service to the citizens of the land of his birth. In accord, then with his academic qualifications he began by serving among the pioneers in medicine in the Bahamas! He served with diligence at all times. A stickler for cleanliness, he insisted that all workers in the health industry should wear plastic gloves. He worked for long hours, often going beyond the call of duty in seeking to improve the health of his patients. As a General Practitioner, he treated people suffering from many diseases. Moreover, in those days when drugs and medical products were not readily available, he ventured in the area of pharmacology so that he could serve his people better. For "Doc" did not do anything in a slipshod or half-hearted manner, but fully committed himself, working with determination and zeal to pursue any goal with vigour and great attention to detail!

In the field of medicine, the "Doc" was truly a pioneer, and as such, it behoves every young Bahamian who aspires to become a doctor/physician to know something about this outstanding physician. "Doc" was truly a pioneer in medicine.

PIONEER IN POLITICS

When Dr. Walker returned to the Bahamas in 1930, it was an outpost of the then vast British Empire, existing under a colonial constitution, which had remained virtually the same for over two centuries![xxxvii] Accordingly, executive authority was vested in a colonial governor, the representative of the monarch of the "mother country," who was advised by an executive council and a legislative council, both appointed by the powers that be.

There was a House of Assembly, but elections to it were held every seven years, the concept of universal adult suffrage was not known as only males could vote and those who had property or were in control of companies could vote more than once. The elections were held over a period of three weeks providing ample opportunities for those with the property or companies to move from one constituency to another during election time. Indeed, both the political and economic life of the Colony was controlled by the wealthy white minority known as the "Bay Street Boys".[xxxviii] Dr. Walker, as a progressive black Bahamian dedicated his life to bringing about political and socio-economic change in the Bahamas.

It was not surprising, therefore, that very soon after returning home, he entered the arena of politics. He was successful in winning a seat, representing the Southern District; where he lived and served with pride all of his life. He served Parliament until 1956 during which time he lost his seat only to regain it in a bye-election.

Dr. Walker was like the Biblical Zacchaeus and the French General Napoleon was short in stature,[xxxix] but like David and the British Admiral Nelson, he was big in courage. As such, he courageously fought for the rights of the black people who lived "over the hill." He knew nothing of fear.

HIS FINEST HOUR CAME

When as a brilliant orator and one committed to the cause of the small man, he was chosen by the workers to represent them in speaking to the Governor, the Duke of Windsor in the wake of the Burma Road Riots in June, 1942.[xl] Dr. Walker certainly arose to the occasion, speaking with eloquence, energy and authority on behalf of those whom he described as "the wretched of the earth."[xli] With his knowledge of Bahamian history, he was able to trace the past and, indeed, greatly impressed the Duke of Windsor as he called for an end to social injustice and more opportunities for the poor. His appeals did not fall on deaf ears as the plight of the workers was improved and major reforms were promised by the powers that be![xlii]

In the struggle for social justice for "the people," Dr. Walker realized that it was essential to have a publication dedicated to this cause. Accordingly, along with a group of concerned citizens, he established a tabloid known as "The Voice". That he found the time and energy to edit a tabloid along with his other responsibilities certainly demonstrated his literary ability and dedication to the cause of the black man. Interestingly enough, its motto was the Latin Proverb *"Vox Populi Vox Dei"* which may be translated: The voice of the people is the voice of God.[xliii]

Like other political tabloids of that era, it was published on weekends after a huge amount of effort on rotary equipment which today seems primitive.[xliv]

While much of its content was political, seeking to represent the concerns of the people "over the hill", there was also the reports about the people of the community – births, marriages, education. Moreover, the narrator recalls that there was a religious section which he read with great interest. For, there were meditations and sermons by outstanding international religious contributors such as Norman Vincent Peale, Dr. Oswald Smith of The People's Church, Toronto and then young up and coming evangelist "Billy Graham!"

Yes, Dr. Walker was a pioneer politician, who paved the way for others to follow as the country moved toward majority rule and eventually independence. He helped to steer the winds of political change, blowing in other parts of the region, in the direction of the Bahamas.

As has been demonstrated, the knowledge of Dr. Walker was encyclopaedic. For, when he returned to the Bahamas with several academic degrees from distinguished American universities, there were very few Bahamians who had advanced to tertiary education, for there were no such institutions at the colony![xlv]

But the wonderful and positive thing was that Dr. Walker did not accumulate knowledge for himself! Rather, he was always willing to help others and was very interested in education. As such he was one of the moving spirits behind the establishment of Woodcock Primary School, located nearly opposite the Walker homestead on Hospital Lane. He also was instrumental in providing education for adults, who did not have the opportunity for education while in their childhood or youthful years. As such, he was an educator in the true sense of the word, one who sought to draw out the best from others and to train them in developing their God-given talents to the best of their ability.[xlvi]

In his deep concern for the education of the Bahamian people, he was fully supported by his wife Mabel. According to reports, Dr. Walker met her while they were studying German at university. She was an American who truly identified with the people of the Bahamas. Whereas, Dr. Walker was an educator by nature, she was an educator by profession. Very significantly, they have the distinction of being the only couple to have two educational institutions named in their honour.[xlvii]

The Walkers were the proud parents of six children, including Juliette, Rinehart, Roland, the twins and David. As might be expected, they did their best to provide their children with the best in education both at home and abroad.[xlviii]

Now, Dr. Walker was very competent in languages. For not only was he very eloquent in the English Language, with a vast vocabulary, but he was also fluent in German, French, Italian and Spanish. Yet his competence in the classic European languages did not, in any way cause him to despise the vernacular of the Bahamas. The narrator recalls Doctor Walker explains with pride, the etymology of a certain word as used only by Bahamians.[xlix]

Yes, Dr. Walker was Bahamian to the core!

PIONEER BUILDER

Now, Dr. Walker, despite his great knowledge, was by no means a bookworm, excelling in book knowledge without practical and technical knowledge. In fact, he was very practical and was good at using his hands as well as his braces!

Very ambitious, he was always willing to embark upon many building projects, indeed at a time when most Bahamians thought about one-storey cottages he was engaged in building two or three storey structures!

Because of racial discrimination, black tourists were not welcome in the main hotels in downtown Nassau back in the thirties and forties. Accordingly, Dr. Walker constructed a three-storey building known as The Rinehart Hotel for the accommodation of black American Tourists. The Walker homestead was a large impressive building as was the Woodcock Primary School. The narrator recalls conversations with his younger brother Dr. Roger Weir about the large building constructed by Dr. Walker.

In a sense most profound, Dr. C. R. Walker was a builder in every respect! Physically, he was a small man who courageously constructed big buildings. Morally, he was a builder of character. Politically, he was indeed a nation builder.

As such, he was greatly respected by Bahamians in all walks of life. No one dared address him by a Christian name or a "nickname". All inhabitants of the Bahamas, whether black or white, rich or poor, native or foreign born, educated or barely literate, referred to him, with great deference as Dr. Walker or more specifically Dr. C. R. Walker.

A pioneer in medicine, politics, education and building, Dr. C. R. Walker was indeed a small Bahamian who made a big difference in ways more than one!

Kate Moss
"Little Katie"
Also known as "Poor Black Kate"

"He hath showed strength with His arm: He hath

Scattered the proud in the imagination of their hearts.

He hath put down the mighty from their seat: and hath exalted the humble and meek."

Luke 1:51

I t is an axiom of universal human conduct, "tried and tested," in war and peace "throughout the ages," that "the female of the species," should be treated in a manner more gentle and compassionate than the male.

Thus, in their fierce battles, all the "super powers" of antiquity— including the Egyptians, the Babylonians, the Persians, the Greeks, the Romans and even the Assyrians, the most cruel of conquerors, sought to kill the males, jealously regarded as potential rebellious rivals, while preserving their female counterparts. Indeed, the latter were regarded as the most valued "spoils" of war, prized as potential maid servants, concubines or even spouses of the warriors of the victorious nation.[1] It should not be surprising to note, then, that the

Pharaoh, fearful of the growing number of Hebrew slaves in ancient Egypt, ordered their midwives to kill all baby boys at birth, while sparing all baby girls. (Exodus 1:16)

Indeed, in virtually all civilizations it has been the practise to show a special concern for the welfare of females, for deep within the psyche of humankind, created "in the image and likeness of The Divine One," is the instructive propensity to apply justice in the treatment of males, while protectively extending mercy toward females!

Now, "generally speaking," in keeping with this long established custom, the female slaves on the plantations of the countries of "The New World," were dealt with, in a manner, significantly different from that meted out to their male counterparts. For, while the men were recruited to engage in the hard, demanding "sweaty labour required for the cultivation of crops in the field, the women, for the most part, were employed in domestic chores in their master's household. Moreover, when it came to the punishment of their slaves, whether for minor infractions or deliberate acts of defiance, the proprietors were, usually, much more severe in dealing with their male than their female slaves. Indeed, nothing incited the anger and sense of righteous indignation of those opposed to slavery than the oppression of female slaves! While, then, in the harsh treatment of a slave "of the gentler sex" such a person was "Little Katie".

Also known as "Kate" or "Poor Black Kate," the story of this early Bahamian female suffering servant, is at once intriguing, tragic, infuriating; yet...most instructive! As such, it merits our most careful attention!

The Hon. Henry Moss, and Helen, his loyal wife were prominent members of the Bahamian aristocracy during the early years of the Nineteenth Century. For, he was a member of the House of Assembly and a Justice of the Peace. Amongst the United Empire Loyalists who fled from the United States to the Bahamas after the American War of Independence, the Mosses were wealthy landowners with a pioneering spirit, having established large plantations in Crooked Island, a remote island of the Bahamas.[li]

While comparatively little is known about the Moss properties, there can be no doubt that they were used, mainly for the cultivation of cotton. For, just as "Sugar was king!" in the plantations of the other islands of the British Caribbean, so "Cotton was king" in the Bahamas at the turn of the nineteenth century.[lii]

Now, amongst the domestic slaves on the Moss Plantation was a young lady named "Kate". Evidently, she was not as docile and servile as her master and mistress expected a slave girl to be! It was not long, therefore, before she was summoned by them to face "trumped up" charges of "theft and insubordination". Consequently, she was punished by them with such severity and cruelty that reaction was very strong with repercussions which were felt not only throughout the Colony but also throughout the entire British Empire!

Dr. Gail Saunders, distinguished Bahamian historian, has vividly encapsulated the most severe, and indeed, cruel and unjust treatment inflicted upon this young Bahamian slave girl:

> "On the 22nd July, 1826, she was confined to the stocks and was not released until 8th August – that is seventeen days later. The stocks were so built that she could neither sit nor lie

down "at pleasure" and she remained in them night and day. During this period, she was beaten repeatedly, perhaps six times and pepper was rubbed in her eyes to prevent her from sleeping."[liii]

Indeed, as the noted historian goes on to explain, her punishment by the proprietors of the Moss Estate was threefold!

First, she was subjected to confinement to the stocks, a most cruel form of punishment, deliberately designed, like crucifixion of antiquity to inflict maximum torture upon the victim.

Secondly, while confined to the stocks, she was subjected to constant beating, was deprived of much needed sleep, and at the end of this ordeal, was severely flogged.

But that was not all! As if confinement to the stocks and beating were not enough punishment, "to add insult to injury" this brave domestic slave, upon release, was relegated to the harsh labour of the field, a task which as we have seen was usually assigned to males!

Kate, indomitable in character, strong in spirit, was nevertheless, "from all reports," physically frail. This is why she was also known as "Little Katie". Finally, already weakened by harsh persistent punishment, unsuited for the rigorous conditions and lacking the robust physical stature required for work in the field, this long suffering Bahamian female slave, perished. She succumbed to a fever prevalent in those days of comparatively primitive medical treatment!

What utterly cruel and barbaric treatment! Entirely lacking in the compassion expected in dealing with the committal of infractions by a female! But that was not the end of the story of "little Katie" by no means, for, news of the harsh, cruel manner which the Mosses dealt with their slave girl, "spread like wildfire" throughout the Bahamian community. Indeed there was public outcry when the facts were revealed! And, in what was, done retrospectively, may aptly be described as the exercise of "swift justice," Henry Moss, Honourable Member of the House of Assembly, wealthy planter, Justice of the Peace, and Helen his wife, were summoned to appear before the Chief Magistrate charged with inflicting cruelty upon a slave, convicted and sentenced to spend six months in jail! Requiring the courage to act impartially in the trial of two of the most powerful figures of the Bahamian community. It certainly proved to be one of the most celebrated and significant cases in the history of the administration of justice in the Bahamas.

"What is the status of slaves in relation to their masters/mistresses?" "Are they their property, mere chattels, like their material possessions and domestic animals, which they may use (or abuse) at will, or are they also fellow human beings, created in the Divine image and likeness, and therefore, entitled to rights and privileges?" "Moreover, are slaves bound to remain in their servile and subordinate positions for life or can they rise to take on positions of responsibility?" Questions such as these have been discussed and keenly debated, often with great emotion, "from time immemorial"?

Now, with regard to the third, it is most interesting and somewhat intriguing to note that in antiquity (dating to centuries before Christ), it was recognized that slaves could, indeed, rise to occupy positions of responsibility, influence and wealth. "I have seen" observed the preacher, "slaves riding on horses and princes walking on foot like slaves!" (Ecclesiastes 10:7, NRSV).

When, however, the slave trade was initiated in the sixteenth century, slaves were, indeed, regarded as property, commodities in The Triangular Trade, whereby slaves were transported from West Africa to be sold to the proprietors of cotton, tobacco and sugar in North and South America and the Caribbean. As Maples points out:

> "Slavery is usually economic—the slave is used by the master to make money for himself. Slaves work for their masters for no wages. In return, their master usually provides them with basic food, shelter and clothing but nothing else. The slave has no choice about what to do or what to become; they can be bought or sold as if they were a commodity."[liv]

Such was the condition of the slaves on the plantations of the Americas and the Caribbean up until the Eighteenth Century.

In the same vein, both Dr. Gail Saunders and Bahamian Church historian Bishop Gilbert Thompson confirm that slaves, in the early centuries of the slave trade and slavery were regarded as "chattel."[lv]

Gradually, however, the attitude of masters and mistresses to their slaves was changing, due to the major socio-economic, political, moral and spiritual factors which fostered a more humane concept of the status of slaves.

Thus, the Loyalists who came to the Bahamas late in the eighteenth century "considered their slaves the most valuable property they brought" to the Colony. Or to put it another way, the Loyalists did not regard their slaves as merely chattel. Indeed, as persons who were fleeing from oppressive treatment in North America, they were not inclined to be oppressive in dealing with their own slaves! The Loyalists, for the most part, then, treated their slaves humanely, granting them a certain degree of independence being allowed to farm on their own small plots of land in close proximity to the large plantations.

Not all the Loyalists, however, shared in their enlightened attitude to their slaves. There were those who persisted "in the old ways," stubbornly clinging to the concept of slaves as chattels, their property which they could treat as they liked. Amongst them were Henry and Helen Moss. For, how else is it possible to understand why they treated their female slave "Little Katie" in the cruel manner that they did! Evidently, they laboured under the impression that they could "get away" with such cruel, unjust acts precisely because of their exalted status in contemporary Bahamian society. In so doing, however, they demonstrated not only gross arrogance but also a woefully inadequate ability to discern "the signs of the times!" For, the winds of most rapid socio-economic, political, moral and religious change were blowing furiously throughout the region.

In the first place, nearly two decades had transpired since the Abolition of the Slave Trade. As we have seen, this was a very turbulent period when resistance to slavery was rapidly growing.

Secondly, and logically, then, there was a strong spirit of liberation amongst the slaves on many plantations. The presence of a rapidly growing number of "liberated Africans" amongst them (slaves liberated by the British Navy which intercepted ships carrying slaves) fostered this attitude. Indeed, there were some slaves who were motivated by "The lust for liberty, the desire to be free."

Moreover, this desire for emancipation was reinforced and undergirded by the preaching of missionaries, notably Baptists and Methodists, who proclaimed the liberating aspect of the Gospel.

Thirdly, the Abolition of Slavery Movement was vibrant and robust, growing rapidly in scope and influence throughout the extensive British Empire. Thus in England, "The Mother Country," these abolitionists, following in the footsteps of William Wilberforce and others, whose strong objection to slavery on the grounds of their Christian principles and conscience, succeeded in attaining the Abolition of the Slave Trade in 1807. Likewise the Abolitionists sought to bring about the Abolition of slavery by means of an Act of Parliament. Not surprisingly, some of the Governors and civil servants who came to the Bahamas during this period were either themselves Abolitionists (e.g. Governor Grant and Governor Carmichael Smythe) or were very sympathetic to their cause.

It is submitted, therefore, that the action of the Mosses—inflicting severe, inhumane punishment upon a young female slave, which resulted in her death—was at once unwarranted, unwise, most of all...untimely!

Now, it is indeed easy to underestimate the ultimate significance and effects of the momentous events leading up to and emanating from the severe punishment meted out on July 22, 1826 to "Little Katie". For, they proved to be far-reaching, intensive and extensive with historical, ethical, judicial, philosophical and moral ramifications far more profound than may be appreciated in initial cursory consideration. It is germane, therefore, to examine them carefully with a view to attaining an accurate evaluation of their significance and challenge to us in the Bahamas today.

Two principles of fundamental importance were at stake in this landmark judicial inquiry, the one being humanitarian in nature and the other having to do with the universal validity of "The Law of the Land"!

With regard to the humanitarian/civil rights aspect, it is illuminating to bear in mind that this case took place against the backdrop of the demand for liberation by the slaves and the strong Abolitionist Movement in England. The case against the Mosses turned upon the morality of the authority of Proprietors to inflict punishment upon their slaves.

As intimated, at its core it dealt with the question, "Is the slave the property of his/her master without rights or is he/she a person created in the Divine image and, therefore, entitled to rights and to be treated with respect and consideration?"

As has been demonstrated, the long held concept of slaves as chattel had been challenged by the time the Mosses treated their slave girl Kate in such a cruel, disgraceful manner.

Concisely, they made the grave error of treating her as a thing rather than as a person. (It is relevant to bear in mind that the famous philosopher/theologian Martin Buber conclusively demonstrated that we relate to people in a fundamentally different manner than we relate to things. The first is known as an I–thou relationship, the latter as an I–it relationship. In dealing with things, we regard same as objects to be used and discarded when no more useful. On the other hand, we are bound to treat them as things). At a time when public opinion was moving in the direction of treating all persons in a humane manner, the Mosses greatly erred in treating little Katie not as a person without rights but as a thing, chattel without rights.

It is extremely important to bear in mind that the action of the Mosses was illegal. For, both in the British Parliament and the House of Assembly, legislation had been passed which strictly prohibited cruelty to slaves, especially female slaves! Here the main piece of legislation was The Consolidation Slave Act passed in the House of Assembly in 1524 under strong persuasion from the British Parliament which urged that the legislation be passed which would provide for the recognition of the rights of slaves, that there should be adequate provision for their instruction in the Christian Religion and "that the flogging of female slaves be stopped." While the Amelioration Laws of the Bahamas did not go that far, it was patently clear that cruelty to slaves in general, and to female slaves in particular should not be tolerated. Or, to put it in language which has since been used by the officers of the Royal Bahamas Police Force, the legislation of the day decreed "zero tolerance" for the cruel treatment of slaves!

This leads us directly to the second principle at stake in the case "The Crown vs. Henry and Helen Moss"—the universal validity of the law of the land. You see, had the Mosses acted the way they did a decade earlier (i.e., before the passing of the Consolidated Slave Act of 1824), they just might have been able "to get away with it" taking into consideration their status in society. But, once legislation had been passed prohibiting the mistreatment of slaves, there was no way that they could have acted in the way they did without being themselves punished! For, their action was not only in clear violation of the law but also out of sync with the long established convention that "the female of the species" should be treated in a manner more gentle and compassionate than the male."

The case, then certainly was very significant in the history of the judiciary in the Bahamas. For it established once and for all that people who break the law, regardless of their status in society, whatever may be their financial resources, class, colour or creed, must be punished. Or, to put it another way, it is established that no one is above the law! It also highlighted and consolidated the independence of the Judiciary, and decreed that the Bahamas was a colony in which the Rule of Law should always be respected. Indeed, as the late Hon. Paul Adderley, first Attorney General of the Bahamas under Majority Rule, delighted to emphasize the Bahamas is a nation in which the Rule of Law is respected.

In a sense most profound, the Moss case may be described "as the Magna Carta of The Bahamas," the moment when the rights of the individual were established, and the time when it was made clear that no one is above the law.

Henceforth, no one dared to inflict such cruel punishment upon their slaves. It was the death knell of slavery in the Bahamas!

It is submitted, therefore, that in the long eventful and exciting history of the Bahamas, "the moment of truth," the decisive hour when the universal validity of the Rule of Law, was established "once and for all," came when William Moss, Member of the House of Assembly, Justice of the Peace, wealthy planter, and his wife, Helen, were sentenced to spend six months in H.M. Prison for the most cruel punishment of their female slave, "Little Katie".

Once to every man and nation,

Comes the moment to decide,

In the strife of truth and falsehood,

For the good or evil side.

Some great name, the new Messiah,

Offering each the bloom or blight—

And the choice goes on forever

'Twixt that darkness and that light.

-James Russell Lowell, 1819—1991

Now this historic judicial decision, coming precisely at the time when the Abolitionist Movement was gathering increasing momentum throughout the British Empire, inevitably attracted worldwide attention! It came as no surprise, then, when in 1829, the principals of the African Institute, a London based organization, dedicated to the abolition of slavery published the pamphlet "Poor Black Kate"! Widely circulated, it brought to the attention of people in every corner of the globe the utterly cruel manner in which this Bahamian female slave suffered and eventually died. Indeed, has been pointed out by leading authorities, the case of Kate. "Poor Black Kate" featured prominently in the endeavours of those who diligently sought to bring about the abolition of slavery. By exposing the oppression of females, as epitomized in the fate of "Poor Black Kate," as the most abhorrent aspect of slavery, they certainly garnered tremendous public support for its abolition. For, nothing could more strongly arouse the righteous indignation of Abolitionists, and by the same token, invoke the

THE REV. DR. JOSEPH EMMETTE AUGUSTUS WEIR, OM JP

sympathy of feminists, than instances of the harsh treatment of slaves "of the weaker sex"!

Concisely, then the vindication of the rights of this young Bahamian female slave (albeit posthumously) "who suffered the ultimate sacrifice exerted positive effects upon the movement to bring about the elimination of "the institute of slavery"; which extended far beyond the shores of these islands. Truly, the excruciating suffering and tragic death of "Poor Black Kate" were then by no means...in vain!

What then is the challenge of the amazing legacy of this early female Bahamian champion of social justice? It is submitted that it is threefold:

First, it is incumbent upon us to learn more about her and, consequently to take definite steps to ensure that her legacy is preserved in a manner commensurate with her tremendously important contribution to the abolition of slavery. As Prime Minister, The Hon. Perry Gladstone Christie, emphasized at the ceremony of the recognition of forty-two Bahamians "Who Made a Difference" in our cultural development, we need to engage in more research and devote more of our resources to this particular project. It must be, therefore, a matter of priority to identify the exact location of the Moss property at Crooked Island where "Little Katie" worked as a slave. The effort should be made to restore it and make it an historical site (like Clifton Pier) to which "people from all walks of life," throughout the length and breadth of the Bahamas, Turks and Caicos Islands and abroad, may travel and draw knowledge and inspiration from the historic events which transpired there. The development of this site, attracting visitors "from all over the world," would certainly prove to provide a much needed economic boost to the once flourishing communities of Crooked Island!

Closely related to this call for the restoration of The Moss properties in Crooked Island is the sacred obligation "to tell the story of Little Katie" to the younger generation. Having learned as much as we can about her, it is incumbent upon us to impart this most significant information to them. For, just as we have noted in discussing the study of Pompey that Mr. Urban Gibbs, veteran Bahamian educator emphasized that we should "diligently" teach the young people, so we must do the same with regard to "Little Katie".

It is certainly worth observing here that the appeal of the story of Kate is universal, there can be no doubt that it is vested, potentially with a very special appeal to Bahamian women. For Bahamian women, who are in any way disadvantaged, or "stressed out" battered wives, those who take refuge in the crisis centres designed especially for females, single mothers struggling "to make ends meet" with a lot of hungry mouths to feed with very limited financial resources, victims of rape or incest, desperate women, homeless women, all can find consolation, and draw encouragement and inspiration from the heart-warming story of "Little Katie".

Indeed, "pride of place" as the pioneer epitome of courageous Bahamian womanhood must be attributed to this most impressive diminutive early Bahamian champion of social justice, amongst that august company of Bahamian heroines—including Mary Moseley, Mary Ingraham, Patricia Cozzi, Keva Bethel, Ruby Ann Cooper-Darling, Eileen Dupuch-Carron, Janet Bostwick, Cynthia "Mother Pratt," Ivy Dumont, Rubie Bethel-Nottage, Angela Palacious,

Marguerite Pindling and a host of "unsung heroines" – who have contributed richly, each in her own unique way, to the socio-economic, political, educational, cultural, moral and spiritual advancement of our beloved Bahamaland!

Though the cause of evil prosper,

Yes 'tis truth alone is strong,

And upon the throne be wrong—

Yet that scaffold sways the future,

And behind the dim unknown,

Standeth God within the shadow,

Keeping watch above His own...

"Little Katie," truly a great "Bahamian Who Made a Difference" at home and abroad!

Sir Etienne Dupuch, OBE

(16 February 1899 – 23 August 1991)

Journalist, Churchman, Social Activist, Politician

"The pen is mightier than the sword!"

Introduction

1. **Nature or Nurture?**

   What is more important in the development of the career and contribution of an individual—heredity or environment? What takes priority, that which he/she has inherited from their parents or the atmosphere in which they are brought up? Or, as some would put it, "What is more important in the mental, moral and spiritual growth of us all—our nature or our nurture? Questions such as these have proved to be the subject of much discussion from time immemorial. There is no consensus on this matter. This is not surprising because given the complex nature of the human personality; it is never easy to determine the relationship between these two essential factors in human development.

Be that as it may, there can be no doubt that there are individuals in whom heredity and environment combine very effectively and complimentarily to make them into highly motivated and influential citizens of their homeland. Such a person was Sir Etienne Dupuch. for, he was brought up in such an environment which enhanced his God-given flair for writing to prepare him for a most illustrious, eventful and outstanding career in journalism!

2. Sir Etienne Dupuch, Journalist/Editor par excellence!

Etienne Dupuch was born on February 16, 1899, into a family which had a rich cultural background coming from France in the early nineteenth century. His father was Leon Dupuch, who with great determination had established "The Tribune" in 1903. It has to be appreciated that the establishment of a newspaper in that time was no mean feat. For, during the early and middle years of that century, a number of newspapers were started, only to disappear after only a few years in circulation. Only "The Nassau Guardian," established in 1844 (and like "Johnny Walker," still going strong!) had survived. There can be no doubt that the existence of only one "daily" in the capital city of the Bahamas, was not satisfactory. There was, indeed, need and space for another newspaper.

This lacuna was filled by Mr. Leon Dupuch, who in 1903 established "The Tribune!" The operation of a newspaper was quite demanding. Working on what now seems a most primitive press. Mr. Dupuch managed to produce a four-page journal which was circulated throughout the community by newspaper boys riding bicycles. There can be no doubt that the hard work and anxiety coming from the production of a newspaper with limited financial resources took a heavy toll upon the elder Dupuch and he passed at the early age of thirty-one, leaving his son to continue the operation of the newspaper which he had established. 'Twas Shakespeare who said:

"Some are born great,

Some achieve greatness,

And some have greatness thrust upon them."

Now Etienne Dupuch certainly was not born great and whether in being called upon to serve as Editor of a major newspaper he had "greatness thrust upon him" can prove to be quite debatable. What is irrefutable is the fact that he achieved greatness!

For, he certainly "rose to the occasion" when he took on the challenge to edit "The Tribune". Over a period of more than 53 years from 1919 to 1972, he served at the helm of "The Tribune" as Editor, and as Contributing Editor for 19 years from 1972 to 1991 leaving a record of service worthy of mention in the Guinness Book of World Records. Thus it is now well-established and universally recognized that Etienne Dupuch was one of the greatest journalists ever to emerge in the region. Under his stewardship "The Tribune" grew rapidly in circulation.

As intimated above, he grew up in an environment which fostered his development as a journalist. During his youth, he saw action as a soldier "on the front lines" in the First World War. Moreover, he came under the influence of the Catholic Church. All these experiences factored in his life and prepared him for a life dedicated to journalism. As it has been truly said, "When preparation meets action then success is bound to come."

There can be no doubt, then that Etienne Dupuch was first and foremost a journalist. Writing in a crisp, clear, attractive style which could be readily understood by a child with a good basic education, Dupuch managed to grasp the attention of Bahamians "in all walks of life," especially the men of the various communities of the capital.

A bold and courageous person, Sir Etienne tackled a wide variety of subjects ranging from politics, economics, social justice, race relations and international affairs. No subject was too big or important for him to challenge, none judged too small or trivial for his all-engaging pen.

"The Dupuch Editorial," then was an essential feature of daily living for many Bahamians. In the early nineteenth and up until the mid-twentieth century, "The Tribune" was distributed in the evening. The narrator, then a school-boy, vividly remembers the men of his community waiting to purchase their copy of "The Tribune". These men often stayed up late in the night reading The Tribune. The next morning, what Dupuch wrote in The Tribune last evening became the subject of lively discussion amongst the patriarchs as well as the

FROM POMPEY TO PINDLING"

young Turks of that community. The "Dupuch Editorials," then were most informative, stimulating, never ever dull, and to borrow an expression made popular by dynamic talk show host Darold Miller... "Provocative!"

While concentrating on the local scene (especially at "election time"), Sir Etienne often commented on events on the international scene. The boldness and clarity which characterized his literary endeavors at the local level, also featured prominently in his comments on events abroad. During the Suez Canal Crisis (1955-'56), he wrote a series of articles in which he took a strong stand in support of The British Government. He was highly commended by Lord Beaverbrook, then a major stakeholder in the British newspaper and media industry. Yes, Sir Etienne Dupuch was a great Bahamian journalist, and many others, who excelled in this area of human endeavors, got their start under his leadership and many others, including this writer, were deeply influenced and inspired by his outstanding journalistic ability.

3. Sir Etienne Dupuch, Champion of Social Justice

Now Sir Etienne Dupuch was always a champion of social justice. At a time of racial discrimination, he stood for the rights of the poor and oppressed. Racial discrimination was evident in that there were certain hotels and restaurants where black Bahamians were not welcome. Clearly this situation could not continue for long especially as in other parts of the Caribbean, rapid strides were being made by the black majority and all signs of racism had been obliterated.

The division between the races was accentuated by the establishment of the PLP, which was conceived of as the party of the blacks, just as the UBP and the chamber of commerce were considered the power bases of the "Bay Street Boys". In this atmosphere of increasing polarization, Sir Etienne Dupuch sought to bring about unity between the major racial groups of the nation. Thus he had already entered the political arena having been elected an MP for the East. _The Bahamas Democratic League,_ then was conceived of as a political party of reconciliation and unity—the voice of moderation in an increasingly polarized society. Its purpose was to unite all Bahamians, regardless of race, color or creed to bring about prosperity in the Bahamas. As leader of this new party, Sir Etienne Dupuch sought to establish viable mediation between the black racism of the PLP on the one hand, and the white racism of the UBP. As such, the party strongly protested against racial discrimination. In this regard, it was at one with the fledgling PLP.

Black, white or brown, Catholic or Protestant, rich or poor, highly educated or illiterate—were invited and indeed, expected to join the Bahamas Democratic League. It was highly idealistic and certainly had an appeal to all who were fair minded and yearned for unity. The Party, then, was more closely at one with the PLP than the UBP when it came to the fight for social justice for those oppressed on account of their racial background.

Now as we have seen, racial tension was growing during World War II as indicated by the Burma Road Riot and the formation of the PLP. More and more the rising black Middle Class protested against this injustice. Very significantly, it was the maltreatment of prominent Caribbean personnel while visiting or *en route* through the Bahamas and the plight of the Bahamian blacks which brought these matters to a head.

Thus, attempts by black members of the House of Assembly such as Dr. C. R. Walker and Bert Cambridge, musician, proved futile. Sir Etienne Dupuch, however, had always demonstrated a concern for the welfare of people who were in any way mistreated on account of race. Thus, when in December, 1953, Sir Hugh Springer, the well-respected Registrar of the University of The West Indies was denied accommodation at a prominent hotel, it was Sir Etienne Dupuch who took him in as a house guest. Moreover, he highlighted this incident in "The Tribune" calling for an end to racial discrimination in the Bahamas.

Two years later, a similar incident occurred. Dr. Lenworth Jacobs, prominent Jamaican physician of St. Ann's Bay, and his wife Beth, were denied accommodation at the Fort Montague Hotel as stopover passengers on a BOAC (British Overseas Airways Corporation) flight from London to Kingston via Nassau. Mrs. Jacobs, in a highly publicized report, vividly described how she and her husband was taken by taxi through a community she compared to "Trench Town" (a ghetto of Kingston, Jamaica) to be accommodated in a second rate guest house "over the hill," while all the white passengers were guests at the luxurious beachfront resort."

THE REV. DR. JOSEPH EMMETTE AUGUSTUS WEIR, OM JP

Upon arrival "back home" the Jacobs did not hesitate to complain "loud and clear" about the manner in which they had been treated in the Bahamian capital. The reaction, in strong condemnation of this blatant act of racial discrimination was, likewise, "loud and clear"!

Indeed, in Jamaica there was widespread discussion of this incident, led by the media, including "The Gleaner" and Mr. Eyrell (known as Evon) Blake, outspoken Editor of the magazine "Spotlight". The narrator, then a student in Jamaica vividly recalls the response of the Jamaican people which was very severe. The Prime Minister of Jamaica, the highly influential The Hon. Norman Washington Manley went so far as to call for a boycott of BOAC flights from Nassau to Kingston and called upon the Governor, Sir Hugh Foot, to lodge an official complain to the Colonial Office in London.

In the Bahamas, again, "The pen proved mightier than the sword". For, Sir Etienne, as a writer, strongly protested against the shabby manner in which the Jacobs were treated in the columns of "The Tribune," as indeed, he had done, two years earlier in the case of Sir Hugh Springer of Barbados. But, as a politician, he went a step further. As leader of The Bahamas Democratic Party, he sprang into action!

Thus, on January 17 he brought to the House of Assembly a two-fold resolution calling for the end of racial discrimination and the appointment of a Commission of Inquiry into racial discrimination in the Bahamas. There was much debate on the matter. Then on January 23rd, the motion, seconded by Bert Cambridge, was debated in The House of Assembly. As might be expected the galley was packed with the supporters of both the BDL and the PLP. The House Speaker's decision to send the motion to a Select Committee, dominated by Bay Street Boys (the minority being Sir Etienne and Gerald Cash) was like placing a red flag before an angry bull. Sir Etienne protested and when called upon to sit down by Asa Pritchard he responded:

> "You may call the whole Police Force, you may call the whole British Army...I will go to gaol tonight, but sit down, and am ready to resign and go back to the people."

The House was adjourned and the crowd in full support of Sir Etienne carried him triumphant on their shoulders. It was, indeed, his finest hour!

The response of the business community was immediate and decisive. All the major hotels, including the Royal Victoria Hotel, the British Colonial Hotel, and the Fort Montague Beach Hotel as well as those at Cable Beach, placed notices in the local newspapers to the effect that they were open for business to all regardless of race, colour and creed. During the weeks and months that followed, Bahamians of colour, visited the hotels and enjoyed the privilege of being served as guests. Moreover, when they had visiting black friends from the USA or the Caribbean they proudly visited these hotels and restaurants, often pointing out that "We were not welcome here not long ago" or words to that effect.

In retrospect, there can be no doubt that the greatest achievement of Sir Etienne Dupuch was his firm stand against racism and his sterling contribution to the inevitable demise of racial discrimination in The Commonwealth of the Bahamas. It was to have a profound effect upon the direction of social equality in the Bahamas, and indeed, earned him the admiration of Bahamians for generations to come. It is, indeed, most instructive to heed and ponder carefully the voice of a Bahamian of "the younger generation".

4. Sir Etienne Dupuch, Devout Churchman

Evidently Etienne Dupuch was gifted as a journalist. However, no matter how gifted a person may be, so endowed by The Almighty who in His wisdom has bestowed gifts many and varied upon humankind (Matt. 25:14-30; II Cor. 2; Ephesians 4:1-15), it is one's duty to enhance them by diligent study and education.

In the case of Sir Etienne, his gift as a journalist was developed by the training he received from Roman Catholic Priests. Thus, in his editorials, he often paid tribute to those who helped to provide education and guidance for him, notably Father Bonaventure Dean. He made it crystal clear that he was a member of the Catholic Church. Thus, it is not without significance, that he selected as the cover of his autobiography a picture of himself in the regalia of the Knights of Columbus. There can be no doubt, therefore, that his Catholic faith had a profound effect upon his thinking and actions. Let us explore this matter in more depth.

The relationship between the religious convictions and the actions of Sir Etienne in the political and social justice arenas is at once complex and intriguing. Yet, it is submitted that a clear understanding of this relationship is of crucial importance in evaluating his actions and assessing his legacy. Here it is essential to take into consideration the social teaching of the Catholic Church.

As we reflect profoundly upon the political and social activism of Sir Etienne, several questions come to mind. What motivated him to take such a strong, principled stand against racial discrimination in the Bahamas? How could it be that in bringing a resolution to The House of Assembly calling for its dissolution, he received such strong support from not only his own BDL but also the PLP? What gave him the courage to stand up, when ordered to sit down by The Speaker, declaring that he was prepared to face the British Army or to go to prison rather than backing down...or sitting down"? The answer is at hand—his Christian faith and influence of The Catholic Church.

Here it is extremely important to bear in mind that early in his life, he converted to Catholicism. Moreover, in his education he came heavily under the influence of the Benedictine monks who were diligent in propagating Catholicism in the formative years of his life. Having once become a Catholic, he never looked back. In his editorials he often wrote about the Catholic Missionaries, confessing how much he benefitted from them.

Because of his lifelong commitment, he was made a Papal Knight. That he was a devout member of his church was demonstrated by his choosing for the arresting cover of his autobiography he elected to have a portrait of himself proudly regaled in the colorful vestments—Black helmet, red cape of The Knights of Columbus. There can be no doubt, it is reasonable to surmise that his thinking, actions and *Weltanschauung* were informed by the Theology and Social Teaching of The Roman Catholic Church.

Now, for many centuries, going back to the Middle Ages, the theology, and social teaching of the Church placed high priority upon harmony. Theologians, on the basis of the teaching of the Philosopher Plato, conceived of society as static, rigidly divided into the rich, middle class and the poor. This concept is to be expressed in the nineteenth century hymn:

The rich man in his castle

The poor man at his gate,

God made them all

And each in his state.

Gradually, however, the position of the Church was undergoing radical change. Thus, late in the nineteenth and in the twentieth century, the social teaching was marked by a paradigm shift from this static view of society into a more dynamic one of allowing for the upward mobility of the poor and oppressed, and justice for the downtrodden of humankind.

This radical shift in the social teaching of the Catholic Church called for the abolition of all distinctions between people based on colour, class or nationality. As such it placed very high priority upon human rights and the right of the individual to express his or her opinion. It also led to the rejection of abortion and as well as the rejection of capital punishment.

Now, Etienne Dupuch, and indeed, other devout Catholic laymen were certainly aware of the shift in the social teaching of the Catholic Church. While not going as far as the most radical of the Catholic theologians he nevertheless placed very high priority upon the concept of human dignity, the equality of all persons being created in the image and likeness of GOD. This, indeed, was what motivated him when he boldly called for the elimination of racial discrimination from the social life of the people of his beloved Bahamaland! In this regard, Sir Etienne took a position which was very close to that of other outstanding Catholic laymen, including some of the Founding Fathers of the Progressive Liberal Party. This is why when he took a stand against racism in Parliament; he was strongly supported not only by the members of his BDL but also by the members of the PLP.

You see, after many centuries of siding with the rich and powerful, during the late nineteenth and early twentieth century, the social teaching of the Church was marked by a new paradigm with emphasis upon the principles of liberty, justice and brotherhood. This trend continued with the social teaching of the Church during the twentieth century taking a position on the side of the poor and oppressed. Indeed, so radical was one of them that upon publication in 1967 it was branded by Conservatives as Marxist. Indeed the Liberationist theologians in Latin America and young Catholic Priests such as Prosper Burrows, took a radical stance on behalf of the poor and oppressed in society. As one authority sums up this "growing radicalism of this period, The Roman Catholic Church has long been criticized for helping to maintain an anachronistic social system and economic underdevelopment. ...Yet today no organization in Latin America is changing more rapidly than the Catholic Church."

At the heart of this paradigm shift was the concept, of the infinite value of each person being created in the image and likeness of The Divine. There could then be no racism or any other way of thinking or action which made a distinction between people on the basis of race, nationality or even gender.

Now Dupuch, as a devout Catholic was certainly deeply aware of this development in the social teaching of the Catholic Church. This then was the reason for his action not only in the establishment of the Bahamas Democratic League but also his strong stand against racial discrimination in The House of Assembly on January 23rd, 1956.

It is germane to observe here that most politicians and the attitude of politicians to religion are quite varied.

In the Bahamas, being a deeply religious nation, with the concept of Christian nation, enshrined in its Constitution, those who are involved in politics or aspire to become politicians do certainly demonstrate an abiding respect for religion. Many make it a point to attend memorial services for their constituents which certainly makes a good impression upon grieving relatives. Religion then may be very significant or it may be peripheral, demonstrating a concern for this spirituality in public while not very strong in their religious convictions.

But not Sir Etienne Dupuch, His religious convictions were by no means demonstrative or ostentatious. Rather it stood at the core of his being, and proved to be the driving force behind the informed opinions expressed in his editorials, animated the way in which he regarded others and motivated his actions in the political arena. Yes, Sir Etienne Dupuch, Papal Knight, or recognized as a Knight of both Church and State, took very seriously the Theology and Social Teaching of the Catholic Church.

Concisely, it is impossible to fully appreciate the content of his editorial columns, political and social activism patriotism and patriarchal demeanor of Etienne Dupuch without taking into consideration his deep-seated, tenaciously held and unashamedly expressed religious conviction. (Rom. 1:16-17) Religion, than was not the embellishment of his politics; on the contrary it was the well-spring of his political activity.

5. Sir Etienne Dupuch – Fundamental Differences

Now, as we have seen, Sir Etienne Dupuch was hailed as a national hero on the night when his historic resolution, calling for the end of racial discrimination in the Bahamas and the appointment of a Royal Commission to investigate all socio-economic disparities in the Colony was debated in the House of Assembly. Indeed, he received the enthusiastic support not only of his associates of the Bahamas Democratic League but also of the Progressive Liberal Party, evidenced by the fact that members of both these political bodies packed the gallery and joined in escorting him on their shoulders at that historical juncture in our development as a people.

Such being the case, one would have expected that after that moment of triumph and demonstration of unity, both these political organizations would work closely together in a common desire to improve the lot of the masses. But, such was not the case. Indeed, hardly had the euphoria of that triumphant action evaporated that signs of a rift between them emerged. For, when the Bahamian business community responded positively to the first part of the resolution, Sir Etienne did not pursue the second – the appointment of a Royal Commission.

The genesis of this differentiation was a fundamental difference of approach to the social challenges between Dupuch and the PLP.

Concisely, Sir Etienne Dupuch with his emphasis on moderation always manifested a divergent approach to that

144

of the politicians of the PLP, whom he felt were either too extremist in their views, whether conceived of as "too anti-white" or "too pro-black". Thus he was not entirely comfortable with the manner in which Cyril Stevenson in the columns of The Herald, and Sir Lynden Pindling, Milo Butler and Clarence Bain, in their oratory, strongly condemned and attacked the Bay Street Boys. This was, of course, out of sync with his emphasis on moderation in forming the Bahamas Democratic League.

Thus, in the months and years following the triumph of Dupuch in bringing about the sudden dissolution of racial discrimination, the cleavage of the gap between Dupuch and the BDL, on the one hand, and Sir Lynden Pindling and the PLP, on the other, gradually widened. Indeed, Dupuch in his well-read, highly influential editorials became increasingly critical of the PLP, even as its membership was rapidly increasing and the Bahamas Democratic League was as rapidly declining, eventually sinking into oblivion. Meanwhile Dupuch made it very clear that he was opposed to the tactics of the PLP and the polarization reached the point of antipathy.

What was the reason for this? Why did such a wide rift develop between Dupuch and the advocates of the PLP? The answer is at hand - the fundamental difference between politicians and journalists. It has been observed by a contemporary sage that there are three kinds of people "in the world today":

Those who make things happen

Those who watch things happen

Those who don't know what happened

Now, broadly speaking, it may be observed that politicians are amongst "those who make things happen" or profess to make things happen; they campaign at election time promising to bring about change and to make things better for those whom they seek to represent in the echelons of political power. Thus, politicians tend to place high priority on loyalty to their political party or organization. Journalists, on the other hand are those who "watch things happen". As such their approach is much more sanguine than that of the politicians and they feel that it is their responsibility "to hold the feet of the politicians to the fire"; calling upon them to fulfill the promises they made in election time when elected to serve in positions of authority. In this regard, the journalist is closer to the prophet than he/she is to the politician!

Almost inevitably, therefore, there develops a tension between politicians and journalists. For, whereas politicians tend to be bound by loyalty to their particular party, journalists are wary of allegiance to any group (political or otherwise) jealously guarding their right to express their opinions on issues as they see them without being limited to the dictates of any political organization. It is for this reason that, generally speaking, journalists do not make good politicians and vice versa. Indeed, the motto of the Tribune, which must have guided Mr. Dupuch over all his years as a journalist: "Being bound to the dogmas of no master" may indeed be applied to all effective journalists! When this fact is taken into consideration, it is possible to understand why Sir Etienne and the leaders of the PLP became so polarized in the years following his triumphal stand against racism in 1956.

While, then he did make forays into the political arena, Etienne Dupuch of the Bahamas (like Woodward of the USA and the late Theodore Sealy of Jamaica) was first and foremost, a journalist! As such, he was motivated by a deep inner conviction, "a call" from a religious perspective, to comment, fearlessly on the turn of events in the community – whether political socio-economic, cultural, domestic or religious – as he saw them, without in any way whatsoever, being bound by the dictates of any individual or corporate entity. He believed that, "Being bound to swear by the dogmas of no master," he reserved the right to evaluate, assess, and judge and "speak out" on any burning issue" of his time. More profoundly, he tenaciously and courageously held that, as a journalist, it was incumbent upon him to commend, or even to call into account any individual in society, regardless of his/her political clout, wealth, influence or religious persuasion.

Specifically, he believed that he had the editorial responsibility to side with the PLP or UBP when they "got it right," on the one hand, or to criticize, even condemn, them when he believed that they were heading in the wrong direction. Writing in this candid manner, then, Sir Etienne Dupuch managed to exert a tremendous amount of influence upon the minds of those who dutifully read his columns daily, whether, they totally agreed or strongly disagreed with him!

Concisely, Sir Etienne Dupuch throughout his distinguished six decade long literary career, convincingly demonstrated that "The pen is mightier than the sword."

6. Sir Etienne Dupuch, Patriarch in Every Way

In the realm of home and family life, , the religious faith of Sir Etienne Dupuch, as in the case of his journalism and political contribution, played an important part. As such, his was exemplary in keeping with his religious conviction Early in life he married and their marriage lasted until "death did them part" in accord with the tried and tested marriage vows of The Church. As a devout Catholic, he was faithful to his wife and no "sip sip" or gossipy innuendoes tarnished his reputation as a good husband and father to the children of this union

Very significantly, most of his children "followed in the footsteps of their father" in making their respective contributions in some area of the vast publishing industry. Thus, his son, Bernard and Pierre, operate a large printing company. His daughter, Mrs. Eileen Dupuch-Carron succeeded her father as Editor of "The Tribune"; another of his sons, Etienne, Jr. has for many years produced the most informative and useful "Bahamas Business Annual".

The interest of the family in the field of communications continues in the third generation with his grandson serving as Manager of a leading local radio station. There can be no doubt that it has been through the influence and the high esteem in which his children held him that they have continued the major contribution in the field of publishing that he established as the world's longest serving editor.

Moreover, as we have seen, many other Bahamians, who are not members of the Dupuch family, got their start in the field of journalism from this great literary giant. Thus he has proved to be the father not only of those related to him by blood but also all those who benefited from his literary genius. Indeed, it is hard to estimate the extent of his influence upon the development of journalism in the Bahamas...and beyond. For, not only in his native land but in many nations of the world, he was highly respected as a first class and courageous writer.

Indeed, Sir Etienne Dupuch, by demonstrating that "The pen is mightier than the sword" proved to be without a shadow of a doubt, "A Bahamian Who Made a Difference".

REFERENCES

Thomas G. Sanders, "The Church in Latin America, Foreign Affairs" 48 No. 2 (January, 1970).

Cited by Gustavo Gutierrez, ET "A Theology of Liberation" London: Student Christian Movement Press, 1974, p. 215.

See Vincent P. Mainelli, "Official Catholic Teaching on Social Justice," Wilmington, North Carolina, 1978

The writer has discussed this matter in detail in *Exodus and Sinai in The Theology of Liberation: A Discussion of The Relationship Between Biblical and Marxist Concepts in Liberation Theology with Special Reference to the Works of Jose Porfirio Miranda and Gustavo Gutierrez," The Dissertation in Fulfillment of the Requirements for the Degree Doctor of Philosophy,* University of Aberdeen, 1984.

The Most Excellent Sir Roland Theodore Symonette, ONH

(December 16, 1898–1980)

First Premier of the Bahamas,

"Father of the House," Industrialist, Philanthropist, Elder Statesman

"Early to bed and early to rise, make a man healthy, wealthy and wise."

Traditional British Proverb

Introduction

That Sir Roland Theodore Symonette, first Premier of the Bahamas, must be ranked amongst those great "Bahamians Who Made a Difference" there can be not a shadow of a doubt! For by grit, mother's wit, an uncanny business acumen, and a robust faith in divine providence, he managed to rise from comparative poverty and obscurity in a small out island community, to attain fame and fortune in our nation's capital.

Now, the Europeans in the medieval era were in the habit of using a single word or phrase to encapsulate the character and achievements of their political rulers. Thus, an early monarch of outstanding ability and magnanimity was affectionately known as "King Alfred the Great". The one who distinguished himself by his prowess in battle earned the title "William the Conqueror". Another who developed the unenviable reputation for consistent tardiness and lack of preparation was dubbed "The Unready". And the urbane devout German prince who was the patron and protector of Martin Luther "Father of the Reformation," was most appropriately, nicknamed Simon the Wise!

Now if one were to suggest one word which accurately sums up the character and illustrious career of Sir Roland Symonette, it would be none other than one which is peculiar to the Bahamas – "Stickability". Literally meaning "the ability to stick to a particular project until it is completed," it combines the cardinal virtues of determination, courage, "guts" and persistence. Perhaps the expression in "The Queen's English which best expresses this "Bahamianism" is "dogged determination". Interestingly enough, it was a favourite word of another Bahamian Who Made a Difference – Dr. Cleveland Eneas. It is submitted that in every aspect of his long distinguished career, Sir Roland Symonette demonstrated "stickability" and this is the reason why he achieved so very much.

"THE FATHER OF THE HOUSE," "STICKABAILITY IN POLITICS"

Sir Roland Symonette was born on December 16, 1898, being the youngest of the nine children of Edwin Lofthouse Symonette and his wife Lavina Alstyne. They were hard working, decent, well respected citizens of The Current, a settlement in North Eleuthera. He received his early education at the public school there and as an outstanding student he served for a short time as an assistant teacher or "monitor". In his capacity as a teacher he accompanied an elder brother to Inagua and remained there until the beginning of the First World War (1914) when he returned to The Current.

An enterprising young man, he often made the trip to Nassau to sell the produce of the farm operated by his father. Eventually, after a short stint in Florida where he engaged in fishing, he settled down in Nassau. Indeed, like many other "Island Boys," realizing that there were limited opportunities for progress in the "Out Islands" (later called The Family Islands), young ambitious Symonette relocated to the Capital.

Taking into consideration his adventurous character and background, along with his popularity amongst the people of his community, it was not surprising that he entered into the arena of politics. The sudden death of Captain Vespa Munroe, one of the three representatives of his home contituency, Harbour Island, afforded him the opportunity to gain a foothold in politics. Encouraged by colleagues and natives of Eleuthera he offered himself as a candidate and was elected to the House of Assembly thereupon he embarked upon a long and distinguished career in active politics unmatched by any other politician in the long history of democracy in the Bahamas.

Eminent Bahamian Attorney Ms. Jeanne Thompson, in an article in recognition of his fiftieth anniversary as a Member of Parliament, has documented it thus:

March 3, 1925   First elected to the House of
                       Assembly as one of the three

representatives of the Harbour Island Constituency

June 13, 1925	Re-elected for the Harbour Island Constituency
June 20, 1928	Re-elected for Harbour Island
May 31, 1935	First elected for the Eastern District, New Providence
June 17, 1942	Re-elected for the Eastern District
June 22, 1949	Re-elected for the Eastern District
June 8, 1956–	Re-elected for the Eastern District
November 26, 1962	Re-elected for the East Central District
January 10, 1967	Re-elected for the Centreville Constituency
April 10, 1968	Re-elected for the Shirlea Constituency
September 10, 1972	Re-elected for the Shirlea Constituency

The record certainly speaks volumes about the character and political savvy of Sir Roland. The record speaks for itself! Judged by any standard and in comparison with the political careers of people in any nation, Sir Roland's fifty-two years of service in the House of Assembly is most remarkable. Indeed, in the two hundred and eighty-nine years of existence of the House of Assembly, no other politician has served so long. He weathered the storm of tremendous change over this long period, holding the positions of Leader of the United Bahamian Party and becoming the first Premier of the Bahamas when a new Constitution granting internal self-government took effect in 1963.

How then, did he manage to win all the elections he participated in over the span of half a century (longer than the lifetime of many people!)? Well, bear in mind that when Sir Roland was elected as one of the representatives of the Harbour Island Constituency, elections to the House of Assembly took place only once every seven years. This very long period between elections was certainly open to abuse and lack of diligence on the part of politicians. Thus, there were those politicians who campaigned for a seat in the House just months before the election being highly visible in the community seeking to entice people to vote for them. Then when elected to the House, like Johnny Roker they could not be found in town, some becoming aloof and even inaccessible to their constituents, only to reappear to ask for their vote years later, months before the next election.

But not Roland Theodore Symonette! He kept in constant contact with those whom he represented, knowing many of them by their first name. Long before parliamentarians were provided with a stipend to fund their constituency office, the constituents of Sir

Roland knew that they could see him at his office on East Bay Street. All "budding Bahamian politicians, whatever may be their political affiliation, race or creed, would be well advised to study and emulate the shining example of Sir Roland who managed to serve in the House of Assembly for so long that he earned the title "Father of the House". Certainly, they can benefit from the lesson of his life when it comes to victory in the political arena—constant and effective contact with one's constituents is the key to victory at election time!

SIR ROLAND SYMONETTE DISCIPLINED PATRIARCH

As may be implied on the basis of our discussion thus far, Roland Theodore Symonette was a highly disciplined individual. The father of this writer, who in his capacity as a leading land surveyor worked for him, spoke very highly of his work ethic. He revealed that Sir Roland always arose early in the morning. In many respects he practised the virtues extolled by the wise writer of the Book of Proverbs in the Holy Bible: industry, honesty, thrift, prudence, diligence and justice.

In all his varied responsibilities and public appearances, Sir Roland Symonette was ably complimented by his wife, the gracious Lady Symonette, whom he greatly loved. He was very devoted to his family, and despite his activities, he found time to guide and provide fatherly direction to their sons Craig and Brent as in the case of his other children: Basil, eminent Bahamian yachtsman and business executive, "Bobby," and his charming daughters, Zelda and Margaret Ann. Thus, throughout his most productive, long and distinguished career, he ably and admirably succeeded in efficiently managing his many and varied administrative, civic, corporate-based responsibilities, while demonstrating tender care, affection and concern for the welfare of his family...immediate as well as extended!

All this has been very touchingly encapsulated by a biographer writing about Sir Roland at the peak of his most eventful life; in charge of the administration of his nation, as well as his extensive corporate enterprises.

In the peace and quiet of the pre-dawn, while the city and the majority of its people still sleep, a light burns brightly in the study of a waterfront home on East Bay Street. Behind a desk, still clad in his pyjamas, is a greying man of 61. He shuffles though a sheaf of government documents as quietly as possible lest he should awake his wife and two young sons. The light goes on at 4:30 a.m. and Sir Roland is at his desk until 6:30 a.m. Then he dresses, eats a light breakfast and goes to his office by 7 a.m. So starts the daily routine of one of the Bahamas' leading political and businessmen. Explaining why he rigidly adheres to this routine which would prove most challenging to many men more than half his age, the eminent Bahamian declared, "If I don't do my clerical and government work in the early morning, I won't be able to do it at all!

What a routine! Only a person who is disciplined, who has "Stickability" could manage to make it a habit practiced over many years.

SIR ROLAND SYMONETTE SUCCESSFUL BAHAMIAN BUSINESSMAN,

INDUSTRIALIST

As we have seen, Edwin Symonette, Sir Roland's father, supported his large family by farming in The Current, North Eleuthera, one of the major agricultural regions of the Bahamas. Very significantly, while the elder Symonette employed his elder sons to assist in the cultivation of the crops, he sent his youngest son, Roland to Nassau to market them. What motivated him to delegate this responsibility to the youngest of his many children is not clear. Perhaps, however, he detected in his youngest son a natural aptitude to carry out financial transactions. Whatever may have been his reasons, the actions of Mr. Edwin Symonette in reposing such entrepreneurial responsibilities in his youngest son proved to be wise, and indeed "prophetic". For starting in this manner, Sir Roland went on to become one of the most prominent entrepreneurs in Bahamian history.

The young Roland Symonette, as already indicated, resided in Florida where he was successful in the fishing industry. After returning to the capital, he acquired a boat which engaged in the lucrative trade of transporting food, vehicles and building materials between Miami and Nassau. Being very enterprising and innovative, the young Roland Symonette engaged in a number of business enterprises which greatly increased his wealth. These included the purchase and the development of huge tracts of land in Nassau and the Family Islands and a foray into the liquor business (euphemistically described as "wines and spirits") in partnership with a foreign capitalist.

There can be no doubt, however, that the major enterprise which Sir Roland Symonette initiated and operated for many years was a shipyard. While still comparatively young, this bold Bahamian acquired large tracts of land at Hog Island (now Paradise Island) where he established Symonette Shipyard. After a few years of operation there, he moved it to a new location on East Bay Street, Nassau. There he employed as many as a hundred and fifty men, who carried out major repairs on large ships from all over the hemisphere as well as "mail boats" and small vessels which engaged in trade between Nassau and the Family Islands. Symonette Shipyards, later named Nassau Shipyards, then, was the largest industrial enterprise owned and operated by Bahamians. As pointed out above, Sir Roland was disciplined and hard-working always arriving on the job early and expecting the same high standard of performance from his workers. In addition to the building and repair of ships, the enterprising Bahamian businessman engaged in other activities including major public works, road building and bridge building in Nassau and throughout the family Islands. Thus, Sir Roland Symonette became one of the very few Bahamians who could be accurately described as "Industrialist". Very significantly, the sons of Sir Roland (and now grandsons) have followed in his footsteps being engaged in business enterprises as diverse as shipping, construction and land development, agriculture, and most importantly of all, banking.

SIR ROLAND SYMONETTE LAND DEVELOPER, PHILANTHROPIST

Sir Roland Symonette, then, by making wise and lucrative investments, certainly acquired great wealth. What has to be stated, much to his credit, is the fact that in so doing he greatly assisted others. Concisely, he did not just accumulate wealth for himself and his family, but also in order to provide a generous measure of financial assistance to his fellow Bahamians regardless (or to use another "Bahamianism" (*irregardless*) to their race, financial standing or religion.

Nowhere was this altruistic concern for the welfare of others more evident than Sir Roland's well known development of property. During his youthful years, he served as much as he could, using the funds so earned to purchase huge tracts of land in New Providence and the Family Islands, notably Eleuthera and to a lesser extent other islands in the extensive Bahamian archipelago. In the course of time as the population of New Providence increased, due largely to migration from the Family Islands, Sir Roland had these properties surveyed and sub-divided into lots which were sold at very reasonable terms to those who required property for the building of their homes. These lots were sold for as little as fifty pounds with the purchasers making a small down payment and given time to pay the balance without interest! Shirley Heights in the north, Englerston in the south, and Blair in the east were the main subdivisions which he developed in this manner, enabling many Bahamians to acquire property in "subdivisions" or "developments" to acquire property with all the necessary infrastructure – well paved roads, water and electricity – necessary for the building of their own homes in well planned communities which earned Sir Roland the respect and gratitude of Bahamians "in all walks of life."

Explaining his reason for acting in this way Sir Roland revealed, "I was always for raising the standard of living of the poor man and I still feel that way. I entered into politics to help develop the Bahamas, particularly Out Islands and I try to help people throughout the country!" There are still many in the Bahamas who are grateful to Sir Roland for his generosity.

Here, it is germane to point out that Sir Roland was especially generous to the churches. He readily assisted them whenever they called upon him.

In this regard, this writer vividly recalls taking up his appointment as Pastor of Rhodes Memorial Methodist Church in September 1973 (the year of our Independence) and as Chaplain at Queens College, a Methodist foundation. At that time there was an urgent need for a church hall. The congregation had raised a considerable amount of money to begin construction but not nearly enough to complete. Further fundraising efforts would have proved challenging for the congregation. "Rev," the members requested: "Write to Sir Roland requesting his assistance in the construction of our church hall". After consultation with the authorities of the Methodist Church, the letter to Sir Roland was written. The reply of Sir Roland is permanently etched in my mind "I'll help you and I'll do so cheerfully!" he replied. True to his word, Sir Roland provided the funds to complete the building which was dedicated by the late Rev. Eric St. C. Clarke, Chairman and General Superintendent of the Bahamas, Turks and Caicos Islands District of the Methodist Church on Easter Sunday (Feast of the Resurrection), 1975.

SIR ROLAND SYMONETTE, UNIVERSALLY RESPECTED ELDER STATESMAN

There can be no doubt that the summit of the long, eventful and most distinguished career of Sir Roland Symonette was his appointment by Her Majesty Queen Elizabeth II as the first Premier of The Bahamas in 1963. It was an event of tremendous significance not only for Sir Roland but also for the people of the Bahamas.

This was precisely because it was the direct result of the granting of internal self-government under the new Constitution of the Bahamas. Indeed, it was a watershed in the historical and constitutional development of the Bahamas. For, in a sense most profound, it heralded the "beginning of the end of Colonialism" in the Bahamas, an essential step on the march to Independence.

You see, for more than two hundred and thirty-four years, since the establishment of the House of Assembly in 1729, the Bahamas had been a colony of Great Britain, governed by "The Mother Country" in every respect. The Bahamas was not a Crown Colony totally controlled by the Colonial Office, but one with a representative form of Government, and a replica of that of "The Mother Country" thus there was the Governor, appointed by the Colonial Office, representing the Queen, and the Executive Council, and Legislative Council and House of Assembly parallel to the House of Lords and the House of Commons, composed of politicians elected by the people. This pattern continued almost without change from the days of Captain Woodes Rodgers, 1729.

The winds of change, however, were blowing and the Old British Empire was rapidly undergoing major change as many nations in Asia,

Africa, and the Caribbean became Independent. In keeping with this trend, then the Bahamas was granted full internal self-government.

The Bahamas then had a Constitution in which Bahamians were in full control of the internal affairs of their country with "The Mother Country" still holding responsibility for external affairs and defence.

The implementation of the terms of the New Constitution called for the appointment of a Premier and a Cabinet.

Sir Roland Symonette as Leader of the United Bahamian Party, which then held the majority of seats in the House of Assembly became the first Premier of the Bahamas. He carried out his official duties with the confidence, grace and diligence fitting of the highest political post in the nation. With his wife, the elegant Lady Symonette constantly accompanying him, he served with dignity and decorum, demonstrating willingness and ability to adjust to changes in the political landscape of those turbulent times! Thus, when on January 10, 1967 the victory of the Progressive Liberal Party at the Polls and the coming of Majority Rule, and the subsequent defeat of the United Bahamian Party, he graciously resigned from his post. Unlike his colleague, Sir Stafford Sands, who fled the country never to return, Sir Roland continued to serve as a Member of Parliament. Indeed, as we have noted, he continued to serve for several more years; for while many of his colleagues lost their seat he proved to be the choice of the people he represented so well in Parliament until his tenure expired in 1977.

What, then, motivated Sir Roland Symonette to continue to serve in the political arena for a decade after the coming of Majority Rule when many of his colleagues either left the country or faded into oblivion as far as political action was concerned? What kept him going in his senior years at a time of great turbulence when the PLP suffered a major split with the departure of "The Dissident Eight," and his own party, the United Bahamian Party, gradually disintegrating; its remnants combining with former PLPs to form the Free National Movement (FNM)? The answer is at hand...patriotism! Yes, Roland Theodore Symonette, the island boy from The Current who rose to become the first Premier of the Bahamas was, at heart, a patriot who greatly loved his native land and dearly loved his fellow Bahamians. This patriotism informed the content of a speech he delivered during this period of his life:

> *"We have profound faith in the people of the Bahamas and we do not distrust your capacity of meeting the new responsibilities as you have met the old. If you do not fail us, we shall not fear your verdict."*

Concisely, as far as Sir Roland was concerned, loyalty to his native land took absolute priority over political expediency! It is submitted, therefore, that during those senior mature years when he served as Premier of all the people of the Bahamas, and as a Member of Parliament in Opposition after the attainment of Majority Rule, Roland Theodore Symonette graduated from being a politician to becoming recognized as a respected "Elder Statesman".

Here, it is germane to bear in mind that the difference between a politician and a statesman are profound. For, it has been rightly observed that whereas politicians think about the next elections, statesmen think about the next generation. "Moreover, whereas politicians tend to be divisive, eliciting the admiration and affection of members of their party with a corresponding antipathy on the part of those who belong to another party, statesmen tend to be unifying, earning the respect and affection of people in all walks of life. The great American President John Fitzgerald Kennedy captured the essence of statesmanlike thinking in his immortal exhortation:

"Ask not what your country can do for you,

But what you can do for your country!"

As one who in his mature years in Parliament was greatly respected by all Bahamians, especially his Constituents, one who placed loyalty to his country above party affiliation, and who was truly and unifying and conciliatory, Sir Roland was truly an Elder Statesman. Thus, it was not surprising that on the occasion of the celebration of his fifty years as a Member of Parliament, members of the House of all political parties joined in accolades to him. And so he continued as the respected Elder Statesman known affectionately as "RT," and 'Pop!" Indeed, there were those who repeated the slogan, ("Pop's Tops!" or "Pop's on Top!") in the highly polarized atmosphere of contemporary politics in most nations. "There are, indeed few who rise above the "trench warfare" of political struggle to become recognized as statesmen; such a person was Sir Roland Theodore Symonette.

SIR ROLAND SYMONETTE CHURCHMAN

The extent to which his religious faith played a part in the development of Sir Roland Symonette as a beloved "Elder Statesman" in his senior years does merit careful consideration.

Sir Roland Symonette was a lifelong Methodist. For, he hailed from The Current in North Eleuthera the island of the Bahamas where the Methodist Church is very strong both numerically and in influence upon the community. Evidently, however, his religious faith became more important in his life in the senior years as is often the case.

Thus, every Sunday morning (except when ill or abroad), Sir Roland and his gracious Lady attended Ebenezer Methodist Church. And Mrs. Maud Lowe ("Aunt Maud") saw to it that their sons—Craig the elder and young Brent)—attended Ebenezer Methodist Sunday School.

That Sir Roland took his Methodist heritage very seriously was evidenced by the fact that on the occasion of the celebration of the Fiftieth Anniversary as a Member of Parliament, he elected to attend a Service of Thanksgiving at Ebenezer Methodist Church rather than at the traditional venue of such state recognized services—Christ Church Cathedral.

More profoundly (and perhaps baffling to some), was the position he took in the debate on gambling which emerged when Sir Stafford Sands, in a bid to boost Tourism, advocated the introduction of casino gambling in the Bahamas. In the national debate that ensued (very much like the national debate on "numbers" now taking place in the Bahamian community), The Methodist Church came out strongly against gambling. Prominent Methodist pastors such as Rev. R. P. Dyer, The Rev. William Makepeace and the Rev. Edwin Taylor (all of blessed memory) courageously and uncompromisingly condemned the move to bring casinos to the Bahamas. Sir Roland, then, as a Methodist took a stand against gambling. It is extremely important to bear in mind that Sir Stafford Sands, in deference to the opposition of The Church, especially the Methodist Church, did not pursue the course of seeking to legalize gambling, but that of seeking to grant the hotels "a Certificate of Exemption" enabling them to bring in casino gambling. Sir Roland was resolute. Thus, he attended a rally organized by the Christian Council at Clifford Park against gambling. And when the matter came up for debate in the House of Assembly, he voted against it! What a Chairman!

As Craton stated, an ever stauncher member of the Methodist Church, Symonette even took a stand on principle against the widespread introduction of casinos despite the advocacy of the rest of the UBP. (Craton, Pindling p.110)

The senior years then, of Sir Roland Symonette were very delightful in every way in his capacity as Elder Statesman, serving at a level above the "cut and thrust" of party politics, he was greatly respected and held in high esteem by his fellow Bahamians "in all walks of life". He devoted much of his time to his ceremonial and social responsibilities inviting various groups to dine at the palatial Symonette mansion at East Bay Street. He was always accompanied by the gracious and petite Lady Symonette who complemented him on such occasions of conviviality. When he became ill and had to receive medical treatment abroad, he maintained the "stickability" for which he was known throughout life, bearing his suffering with true Christian fortitude. And so it was that this great Bahamian, who rose from obscurity in a Family Island community to become the first Premier of his beloved Bahamaland came gracefully to the end of his sojourn through life in 1980.

Distinguished Bahamian journalist Fred Sturrup appropriately sums up the eventful life and many contributions of this giant of a Bahamian with this observation:

> Sir Roland Symonette, the leader of the United Bahamian
> Party and the country's first Premier was perhaps the second

most popular individual in the nation's history. With the exception of his successor, Sir Lynden Pindling, the man adoringly called "Pop" by thousands of Bahamians, was generally regarded as being more beloved throughout the land than any other.

He had the special common touch that enabled him to connect with Bahamians of all ethnic backgrounds. Many stories have been told throughout the years of his assistance financially and otherwise to Bahamian families in New Providence and the outlying inhabited areas of the Bahamas.

Appropriately, on Monday, October 8th he was officially designated as a National Hero. The Most Excellent Sir Roland Symonette, ONH.

THEODORE ROLAND SYMONETTE

Family Man

Politician *par excellence*

Patriot

Industrialist

Land Developer

Philanthropist

Elder Statesman

Truly a Bahamian Who Made a Difference "in ways more than one."

Well-known by few outside his tightly-knit family circle;

Well loved by many Bahamians, especially those of the constituencies he served in his legendary parliamentary career!

Well respected by all inhabitants (Bahamians and tourists alike!) of his beloved Bahamaland!

QUESTIONS/EXERCISES FOR GROUP DISCUSSION AND ACTION

1. Why was Sir Roland Symonette described as "The Father of the House?"

2. "Early to bed and early to rise, make a man healthy, wealthy and wise." Do you agree that the truth of this old British proverb was demonstrated in the life and contributions of Sir Roland Symonette?

3. "Sir Roland was an able politician who became a respected Elder Statesman." Discuss.

4. Why and how did Sir Roland Symonette manage "to connect with Bahamians of all ethnic backgrounds?

5. What were the main provisions of the granting of full internal self-government to the Bahamas in 1963?

FOR FURTHER READING

1. Paul Albury, *The Story of The Bahamas*

2. Fred Sturrup, *A Modern Perspective of the UBP*, Nassau: The Nassau Guardian, 2008 ad.

3. Randol Fawkes, *The Faith that Moved the Mountain*, (Memorial Edition), edited by Rosalie Fawkes, Nassau, Bahamas: Estate of Sir Randol Fawkes, 2003 ad.

4. Craton, Michael, *Pindling*, Nassau, Bahamas: MacMillan/Caribbean, The Pindling Family Estate.

5. Jeanne Thompson

6. Wendell Jones, *The One Hundred Greatest Bahamians of the Twentieth Century.*

Part 2

The Pacesetters

Sir Milo Broughton Butler, G.C.M.G, G.C.V.O.

(August 11th, 1906--January 22nd, 1979)

FIRST BAHAMIAN GOVERNOR GENERAL

"...Can walk with kings...and not lose the common touch."

August 1st, 1973 was, indeed, a very special day in the history of the Bahamas; for, on that very day, for the first time in the two hundred and forty-four years since it was established as one of the oldest democracies in "The New World," a Bahamian took the oath of office as Governor General, the official representative of the reigning British Monarch...in this case Her Majesty Queen Elizabeth II.[lvi] Who was he? None other than His Excellency Sir Milo Broughton Butler, G.C.M.G., G.C.V.O., highly respected elder statesman, most distinguished "Son of the Soil".

Indeed, Sir Milo was held in high esteem by Bahamians "in all walks of life" having proved himself to be a successful businessman, veteran politician, devout churchman, and role model for many. What was it that motivated this great Bahamian to accomplish so much in his eventful lifetime? Why was he so concerned for the welfare of his fellow Bahamians? What lessons can we learn from his life to help us as citizens of the Commonwealth of the Bahamas today? The answers to these questions will come readily to the fore as we study the life and contributions of this noble Bahamian.

Sir Milo Butler, son of an old Bahamian family, was born on August 11th, 1906. Very significantly, Sir Milo was amongst the few Bahamians who could trace his ancestry back to emancipation. The Butlers were active, for many decades, as pineapple farmers and merchants, "making a living" in Eleuthera and Rum Cay, beginning with Glasgow Butler.

According to Sir Milo's biographer, Glasgow Butler, Sir Milo's great-great grandfather was an African slave owned by an Eleutheran planter named George Butler, an Englishman.[lvii] When the slaves in the British Empire were freed in 1834, "Glasgow assumed the surname of his former owner as was the general custom."[lviii]

There is something most relevant to us as Bahamians, especially when we celebrate National Heroes Day, Independence and other events of national significance. Many Bahamians are descendants of African slaves, who Like Glasgow Butler were freed at Emancipation and took the surnames of their white slave masters.[lix] Yet comparatively few of them can trace their ancestry to their African forefathers.[lx] At this time when so many people are anxious "to discover their roots," the success of The Butler family in tracing their ancestry back to their African patriarch comes as a source of tremendous encouragement![lxi]

Now Milo grew up in an environment in which he soon learned of hard work and the dignity of labour. His father, George Butler, died at a comparatively young age, leaving behind his widow and five children. As Milo was the only male" he was called upon, while still a

174

young man to help support his family. It was then that he developed the entrepreneurial spirit which enabled him to become a very successful businessman.

The young Milo Butler was deeply conscious of the suffering of many of the black people at the time when political and economic power were wielded by the powerful white oligarchy known as "The Bay Street Boys".[lxii]

It was no surprise, therefore, that very soon after he established himself in business that he ventured into the "Field of Politics". His opportunity came in 1938 when the Hon. A.F. Adderley was elevated to the Legislative Council. The youthful Milo Butler contested the seat in the Western District against Sir Harry Oakes, wealthy Canadian investor. He was defeated by the Canadian who was supported by the "Bay Street Boys".

Now after such an initial crushing defeat at the polls, any person lacking in stamina and *"stickability,"* would have "thrown in the towel" beating a hasty retreat from the highly competitive arena of "Front Line" political activity. But not the courageous Milo Broughton Butler! Instead, with the strong support of other black Bahamian leaders, notably eminent businessman Edgar Bain and his brother-in-law, the eloquent Mortician/Politician Marcus Bethel, he diligently pursed electoral reform. As a result of their relentless efforts, the secret ballot was introduced into the Bahamian electoral process. This marked a major advance in the Bahamian march to Democracy as people could vote for the candidate of their choice[lxiii] without being intimidated by "the powers that be".

In 1939, another by-election was required upon the elevation of Sir Harry Oakes[lxiv] to the Legislative Council. Again Sir Milo Butler contested the seat of the Western District. This time he won! Thereupon, he embarked upon a most outstanding political career. He soon gained a reputation as a fiery orator, who courageously championed the cause of the poor at political rallies on the campaign trail. Thus, soon after its inception in 1953, he joined the PLP. In 1956 he was amongst "The Magnificent Six" elected To Parliament. Then with the coming of Majority Rule in 1967, he served as a member of the first PLP Cabinet. As Minister of Health he adopted a hands-on approach which resulted in the efficient operation of the Princess Margaret Hospital and as we have seen, he was sworn in as the first Bahamian Governor General on August 1, 1973.

Sir Milo was a great family man. "He told his wife Caroline that he wanted seven sons and as many daughters as God would bless them with. They had seven sons and three daughters in the following order: Edna, Emaline, Raleigh, Joseph, Juanita, Milo, Franklyn, Asa, Basil and Matthew. There was no question of who was the head of the household."[lxv]

Sir Milo was greatly loved and respected by each and every one of his children and grandchildren. Moreover, he was blessed to have the full support, in all his many and varied activities, of his wife, the gracious Lady Caroline, and his highly respected mother, affectionately known by many as "Mother Butler." Concisely, he was an illustrious Bahamian Patriarch!

Now, there can be no doubt that the reason why Sir Milo Butler was successful as an entrepreneur was his practice of involving all his children in his various business enterprises. "There was no job too important and no job too demeaning for the Butler children." As a result they were well prepared to take on responsibility for the running of the family enterprises. Thus when Sir Milo became deeply involved in politics, his son Franklyn took over management of the main family business, Milo B. Butler and Sons, Ltd. It is now managed by his son Mr. Franklyn Butler, Jr. Today the business enterprises of the Butler Family are many and varied extending throughout the length and breadth of The Commonwealth of The Bahamas.

Despite his reputation as a fiery, orator on the campaign trail, Sir Milo Butler was at heart a kind, polite and compassionate person. Throughout his long career, he visited the patients at the Princess Margaret Hospital every Sunday, often accompanied by members of his family and friends. Moreover, he was instrumental in breaking down barriers leading to the employment of black Bahamians in banks and commercial enterprises. With typical boldness, he would enter the premises of any corporate body, suspected of practicing racial discrimination in the hiring of staff; demand to see the "boss" with a view to securing employment "for my people"! Thus, he played a major part in ensuring that opportunities for employment in all sectors of the booming Bahamian economy was, indeed, available to all qualified Bahamians regardless of race, colour or creed!

Sir Milo was a deeply religious man who worshipped regularly at St. Matthews Church and often attended, as a Lay Delegate, the Anglican Synod, held annually in Nassau. When called upon to deal with any matter, he appeared promptly with his Bible in his right hand. The Rt. Rev. Michael Eldon, Bishop of the Anglican Bahamas Diocese, eulogized him thus "Sir Milo was a deeply religious man throughout his life and he left us no doubt that this was the motivating force of his life.[lxvi] This is why the bust of Sir Milo at Rawson Square portrays him holding his Bible in his right hand.

Sir Milo Butler served his nation faithfully as a fiery politician, fine, caring, family man, and progressive businessman, humanitarian and respected Elder Statesman. Sir Lynden Pindling, our first Prime Minister described our first Governor General as "A friend of the poor, champion of the weak, national hero, chief warrior of the Bahamas."

In his own inimitable manner, Sir Milo Butler combined, in an amazing way, the respective, ostensibly incompatible characteristics of the wolf and the lamb. For, in the highly competitive and polarized arena of public activity, whether delivering a fiery speech "on the campaign trail' or advocating, with Bible in hand, for the rights of the disadvantaged, he was a wolf--fierce, fearless, confrontational, aggressive! On the other hand, in the tranquil atmosphere of private and domestic life, whether in an interview, giving fatherly advice to any member of his large family, or visiting institutions to distribute gifts to the needy, he was, indeed, a lamb--soft spoken, sensitive, gentle, and compassionate! Indeed, in a sense most profound, his life and contributions were in line with the prophecy of Isaiah:

> "The wolf shall live with the lamb, the leopard shall lie down with the kid, the calf and the lion and the fatling together, and a little child shall lead them. (Isaiah 1:6, NRSV)

Sir Milo Broughton Butler, successful businessman, fiery politician, patriot, elder statesman, devout churchman, patriarch, first Bahamian Governor General was truly indeed "A Bahamian Who Made a Difference!"

THE BUTLER FAMILY TREE

Glasgow Butler (Liberated African Slave),

Milo Butler I

Israel Butler

George Butler + "Mother Butler"

Sir Milo Butler + Lady Caroline Butler

Edna Emaline, Raleigh Joseph, Juanita Milo Jr., Franklyn Asa, Basil Matthew

QUESTIONS FOR GROUP DISCUSSION

1. Why is Sir Milo Butler acknowledged to be A Bahamian National Hero?

2. Sir Milo Butler was able to trace his roots to the founding patriarch of the Butler family, an African slave who was freed at Emancipation, 1834. How far back can you trace "the roots of your family?" Design a "Family Tree" to illustrate your answer.

3. Sir Milo Butler was the first Bahamian Governor General of The Commonwealth of The Bahamas. Who, then, was its first Governor General? List the names and dates of service, of four more Bahamian Governor Generals.

4. Why is Sir Milo Butler described as one who managed "to walk with kings and not lose the common touch?"

5. Politics and religion don't mix! Discuss with special reference to the life and contributions of Sir Milo Broughton Butler.

SUGGESTIONS FOR FURTHER READING

1. Patricia Patterson, *Milo Broughton Butler, GGMG, CVO Bahamian 1906 –1979, A Call To Service* (Kingston, Jamaica: New Way Educational Service) 2011 AD. This is the official biography of Sir Milo Butler, commissioned by and available from Milo Butler & Sons Ltd., Peet Street, Nassau, Bahamas.

2. Michael Craton, *Pindling* (Oxford: Macmillan Education), 2004 AD.

3. Randol Fawkes, *The Faith that Moved the Mountain* (Nassau: Estate of Sir Randol Fawkes), 2003 AD.

4. Don Maples, *The Making of the Bahamas,* (Essex. The Pearson Education, Ltd., and Kingston, Jamaica: Carlong Publishers Caribbean, Ltd., 2004 AD.

5. Gail Saunders *Slavery in the Bahamas,* Nassau: 6. Philip Galanis, The Freeport News, *Cecil, Lynden, and Milo,* "The Freeport News," Friday, January 3, 2014 AD.

6. Unpublished work, Emily Demeritte née Bain, "Sir Milo Butler" Dissertation in partial fulfillment of the requirements for a Bachelor of Arts Degree in Education, submitted to the University of the West Indies.

Excerpts from

Let us Build a Christian Nation

By J. Emmette Weir

Timothy Gibson, A Great "Son of the Soil"
(1903 – 1978)

The Bahamian national anthem was written by one who is nationally recognized as amongst the greatest of the sons of the Bahamian soil—Timothy Gibson.

Born on April 12, 1903, in the picturesque settlement of Savannah Sound on the beautiful isle of Eleuthera, he grew up in an old Bahamian family which had long distinguished itself in that vitally important area of human endeavour called education.

Nurtured in such an atmosphere, it was not surprising that this talented young man, following in the footsteps of his ancestors, decided upon a career dedicated to the physical, mental and moral development of his fellow human beings.

An educator, Mr. Gibson moved rapidly through the ranks, and was promoted to the post of headmaster of Western Junior School.

It was during this period that the writer, then an enthusiastic schoolboy, came into contact with Timothy Gibson!

The professional, serious and dedicated manner in which this great educator carried out his varied responsibilities made an indelible impression upon this individual in those formative years of his youth.

Among the many sterling qualities of Timothy Gibson, three in particular stood out as demonstrative of the kind of person that he was and as indicative of the reason why he achieved so much during his sojourn through this transitory life.

First and foremost, Timothy Gibson was a disciplinarian!

During school hours, Mr. Gibson often walked around the campus with cane in hand. And, in those days corporal punishment was an essential feature of the educative process, he did not hesitate to use the cane in the discipline of students who dared to violate the strict moral code of conduct he advocated every day!

In all fairness to this outstanding educator, it has to be pointed out; however, that Mr. Gibson administered discipline in such a manner that the students realized in the long run that it was for their benefit! For as a neat, well-groomed gentleman from the old school who doffed his hat in greeting ladies, he demonstrated disciplined behaviour in every way. As such, he was able to exercise discipline in all endeavours, thus gaining the respect, admiration and affection not only of his staff and students, but also of their parents and that of the entire community.

This leads us directly to his second great virtue demonstrated—encouragement. Yes, he was an encourager. Indeed, everyone who ever came under his influence can testify even now, that Timothy Gibson encouraged them to do their best.

As a perfectionist in his own right, he was utterly intolerant of mediocrity in any way, shape or form!

In a word, he exhorted his students to strive diligently for excellence. Yes, "excellence, excellence, excellence!" was his watchword. He never missed an opportunity to encourage his students to strive for high standards in all pursuits—physical, mental, moral and spiritual.

Thus, in morning assemblies, in the classroom, and at special school events Timothy Gibson persistently urged his students to be positive, to hold their heads high and to strive with all their energy to be the best that they could be.

The emphasis on excellence, manifested in the disciplinary aspects of education was evident also in the third area in which Mr. Gibson made an outstanding contribution – music.

Indeed, those who taught along with, as well as those who learned from Timothy Gibson, soon realized that he was a very talented and versatile musician. And, being at heart a teacher, he had a burning desire to impart to them something of his own great love for this international language.

Thus, all who attended educational institutions under the supervision of Mr. Gibson graduated with knowledge of the rudiments of music. In fact, a number of Bahamians who have excelled in music got their start under the tutelage of this talented Bahamian.

When not teaching music, Mr. Gibson devoted much of his time and energy to composing it. But not only was he a musician, he was also a poet, who greatly loved his homeland. Thus combining his musical literary gifts, with his strong patriotic desire to extol its unique marine beauty, he coined the expression "Bahamaland".

Early in 1955, the then extremely popular and highly acclaimed, Princess Margaret made a tour of the Caribbean. She concluded it with a visit to The Bahamas. In celebration of this great event, Timothy Gibson penned one of his greatest works, "Hail, Princess Britannia!" Thousands of Bahamian schoolchildren, waving their Union Jacks, warmly welcomed the charming young princess to "the Isles of June" as they sang the song that ended with the touching words, "we love you, we do!"

In retrospect, it can be asserted without a shadow of a doubt that this musical composition contributed in no small measure to the success of the visit of the princess to our beautiful Bahamaland!

In the eventful years following the visit of the princess, Mr. Gibson continued to make his contribution to education, administration and cultural affairs. As a result of these endeavours, he was honoured as a Commander of the British Empire by Her Majesty Queen Elizabeth II. But times were changing!

As a keen observer of events at the national and international levels, Timothy Gibson was sensitive to the changes taking place and his awareness of this was reflected in his literary and musical works.

He wrote against the backdrop of major developments in the political arena. As nationalism increased in every corner of the globe, the old

British Empire was gradually disintegrating, being replaced by a commonwealth of independent nations.

The Bahamas, like many other British colonies, was caught up in this movement towards self-determination and the control of its own national destiny!

Timothy Gibson, being very sensitive to this phenomenon, incorporated the concept of nationalism into his poetry and music. Thus, in 1969, he came out with his greatest work, "March on Bahamaland!"

This inspired song, which in a unique way captured the essence of Bahamian patriotism, proved to be very inspiring to all Bahamians. Thus, it was not surprising that when the Bahamas became an independent nation in 1973, it was adopted as its national anthem.

Today, thirty years later, it is still sung with pride by Bahamians in all walks of life.

Mr Gibson continued to write poetry and music, and to promote the culture of The Bahamas after his retirement. Then in 1978 this giant of a man, this truly great Bahamian educator, musician, poet, patriot, "family man," one who must be recognized as a founding father of our young nation, passed from time to eternity.,

It is most fitting that one who contributed so richly to the cultural development of The Bahamas should leave as his greatest legacy its national Anthem!

Let Us Build a Christian Nation,

By J. Emmette Weir,

THE REV. DR. JOSEPH EMMETTE AUGUSTUS WEIR, OM JP

Freeport, Grand Bahama Island,

2004

Our National Anthem is Not a Solo!

There can be not a shadow of a doubt that our proximity to the United States of America is a major cultural hazard!

For, too often, it is the case that we adopt customs of the people of our "great neighbour to the north" in an uncritical manner, mimicking them without reflecting upon whether they are relevant to our culture.

Take for instance, one very important expression of our sovereignty—the singing of our national anthem.

Whereas, traditionally, it has been our custom as a people to sing the national anthem together, the practice has developed in the United States for just one person to sing it while the others silently stand until him/her "has done it!"

How often have we watched major games on American TV when just one person sang their national anthem, while thousands of athletes and "fans" stood silently, in some cases, bursting out in applause when the soloist has done his/her part

Well, much to my concern, I have noticed that more and more, step-by-step, we as a people are adopting the American practice rather than continuing our tradition of singing together our national anthem.

So, just as is the case in the United States, most of our sporting events begin with just one person singing our national anthem while others silently listed to him/her! Likewise, at the huge crowded political rallies leading up to the recent general election, one person sang the National Anthem. How much more effective would it have been if the multitudes present united in singing OUR NATIONAL ANTHEM whether it be at Government House or in church or in a hotel or...on the playing field!

Concisely, our National Anthem is not a solo to be appreciated but a song in which we should participate in rendering the superb corporate expression of our national consciousness...our "Bahamianess!"

Let us, then, reject this practice of allowing one person to sing our national anthem and "go back" to our tradition of singing together our national anthem!

Extract from: Let Us Build a Christian Nation,

By J. Emmette Weir,

Freeport, Grand Bahama Island,

2004

Dame Dr. Doris Louise Sands Johnson, DBE

(June 19, 1921 – June 21, 1983)

Brilliant Bahamian Educator

BACKGROUND

Doris Louise Sands was born on 19 June, 1921 in St. Agnes, New Providence, Bahamas to Sarah Elizabeth (née Fyne) and John Albert Sands. A diligent student, who took a very serious approach to her studies, she demonstrated, early in life, a special interest in and aptitude for education. Thus at the comparatively tender age of fifteen she was appointed to the staff of Eastern Senior School, where renowned Bahamian educator Donald Davis was Headmaster. There she remained, faithfully and competently carrying out her responsibilities as a teacher for seventeen years. Very ambitious, this young Bahamian teacher took full advantage of all opportunities afforded her to improve her educational qualifications.

On 3 January, 1943, at Zion Baptist Church in Nassau, Sands married Ratal Allen Johnson. They subsequently had one son.

Polite, petite, always smartly attired, articulate, demonstrating an excellent command of "The Queen's English", Dr. Doris Johnson at the height of her educational career, could be truly described as "the consummate educator." Throughout her long career of service to the Bahamian public, she remained at heart an educator. Indeed, in a way most profound and providential, her impeccable qualifications in education, placed her in a unique position to make the contributions she did – her amazing achievements in the political arena, her reputation as a trusted adviser to people in all "walks of life" and her great ability as a writer!

DORIS JOHNSON – PIONEER FEMALE POLITICIAN

When the youthful, energetic and ambitious Doris Johnson returned home on completing her studies at the University of Virginia, the winds of political change were blowing furiously throughout the length and breadth of the Bahamas. The Progressive Liberal Party was engaged in a struggle to wrest political power from the United Bahamian Party under the control of Sir Stafford Sands. The highly respected teacher threw her full support behind the PLP. Given her background in education and reputation as a woman of wisdom, she soon gained the confidence of the PLP executives. Thus, the advance of this ambitious Bahamian lady "through the ranks" in the highly competitive arena of "frontline politics" was extremely rapid and truly historic. Indeed, she was a pioneer, achieving several "firsts" As she courageously participated in political activity. As one authority put it: "She had the habit of being first." History was made, then when in 1959 the recently elected Premier of the Bahamas appointed the first woman Bahamian to serve in the Senate, the Upper House of the

Bahamian legislature. For the very first time in the two hundred and thirty years of democracy in the ancient British Colony of the Bahamas, a woman occupied a seat in its legislature What was most remarkable about her appointment was the fact that it occurred before the enfranchisement of Bahamian women!

In 1968 Dr. Doris Johnson again made history when she became the first female member of the National Cabinet. Appointed to serve as Minister of Transport, she proved to be an able administrator. In this capacity, she was responsible for the execution of one of the largest building projects undertaken by the Government of the Bahamas - the construction of the multi-storied Post Office Building prominently located at the intersection of East Street and East Hill Street.

Now, the winds of political change continued to blow with increasing velocity during the formative years of the public service of Dr. Doris Johnson. Thus the Bahamas became an independent nation on July 10th, 1973 Dame Dr. Doris Johnson again made history when she was appointed as the first Bahamian Female President of the Senate -- serving with a competence based on years of experience as an educator and politically highly respected, achieving a "statesmanlike" status in the Bahamian community. Moreover, serving in this high office, she proved to be a "trailblazer". For, since that time several outstanding Bahamian ladies have done so, including Ms. Lynn Holowesko, Lady Sharon Wilson and The Hon. Allyson Maynard-Gibson, Dame Dr. Doris Johnson, then demonstrated that it was possible for women to succeed in the arena of politics, which traditionally had been regarded as the preserve of males, there can be no doubt that she has proved to be a role model and source of encouragement to many Bahamian women striving " to make their mark" in the competitive arena of "frontline politics"! Doris Johnson-courageous champion of social justice for Bahamian women. Now, Doris Johnson grew up at a time when Bahamian women were, indeed, "second class citizens" for women were not allowed to vote, could not serve on the jury and, in general were expected to be content to serve in domestic responsibilities. As an ambitious young lady, Doris Johnson certainly was not satisfied with this condition. Indeed, one of the driving forces which motivated her achievements in education and politics was her determination to bring about social justice for her fellow Bahamian females!

It was a cause to which she relentlessly dedicated herself throughout her career, utilizing to the fullest her legendary oratorical skills and vast knowledge.

Thus, in a stirring address to the Honorable Members of the House of Assembly, delivered early in her political tenure, January 12, 1959, she railed "women grieve and are deeply concerned when our sons and daughters, tried in courts of law, find always that they are faced by a male group of jurors. While, the barring of women to serve on the jury was a matter of concern, there was another issue of a more fundamental nature: The Right of Women to Vote and therefore to participate in the major political changes taking place in the Colony. Thus arose The Women's Suffrage Movement, led by stalwarts such as Mary Ingraham and Nettica Symonette, dedicated exclusively to achieve this most worthy goal. It "goes without saying" that Dr. Doris Johnson threw her full support behind them just as she had done in the formative years of the establishment of the PLP.

There was then, growing dissatisfaction on the part of progressive Bahamian women because of the prevention of women from exercising the right to vote. It reached "boiling point" when The Royal Commission appointed to bring about major political and social change in the wake of the General Strike did not recommend the enfranchisement of women. The rationale, according to Mr. Lennox Boyd was that Bahamian women had not demonstrated strong desire to be granted the right to vote. Now, it was not surprising that the rapidly growing number of members of The Women's Suffrage Movement deeply engaged in the struggle for social justice for Bahamian women, took grave exception to the position taken by the representative of the Colonial Office. Their concerns were very well expressed by Dr. Doris Johnson in a national address which has "stood the test of time". Manifesting strong conviction, the then budding Bahamian politician, began thusly "The Women's Suffrage Movement wishes to go on record as wholeheartedly supporting universal enfranchisement for men and women alike and the Secretary of State must be sternly reminded by the women of the Bahamas under the universal Declaration of Human Rights, set forth in the Charter of the UN, guarantees to all men and women, regardless of race, color or sex the fundamental right to vote!" Note, carefully that in this opening salvo, the principle is established that enfranchisement is the right of "men and women alike". Moreover, in the strong statement, totally disagreeing with the position of the British Secretary of State, Dr. Johnson invoked the powerful, universally recognized Charter of the United Nations on Human Rights, the Bahamian spokesperson for the Bahamian afraid of taking on the high ranking British Minister of Government. Turning then specifically to the enfranchisement of Bahamian Women, she continued:

"Today women have by force of circumstances taken on increasing responsibilities to ensure the proper development and growth of our homes, our children and our social structure. Bahamian women have risen to give outstanding leadership services in business activities, welfare work, home and school organizations, as well as the extension of brotherly love in 100 fraternal and benefactory organizations throughout the islands."

The rational here is crystal clear: It is unjust and totally unacceptable, to deprive Bahamian women, who have made and continue to make major contributions to the socio-economic, moral and spiritual development of the people of the Bahamas, of the right to vote! As distinguished Bahamian attorney-at- law, Peter Maynard has pointed out, the eloquent speech delivered by Dr. Doris Johnson on that momentous occasion contributed significantly to the enfranchisement of Bahamian women.

DORIS JOHNSON - BAHAMIAN WRITER/HISTORIAN

As has been occasionally observed, not many of "The Bahamians who made a difference" "put pen to paper". Indeed, in stark contrast to their contemporaries of the large Democratic nations of the North Atlantic, comparatively few of them wrote books sharing their thoughts and chronicling the events which transpired. Perhaps most of them were so "caught up in participating in these events rather than to the discipline of writing about them. As one young politician of that era put it, "We were so busy making history that we did not have time to write history!"

Now, Dr. Doris Johnson was amongst those Bahamians who did "put pen to paper". Logically, there was a real desire on the part of most Bahamians for an account of the events leading up to the attainment of independence in 1973. Thus Dr. Doris Johnson's major literary contribution, *presenting a "first hand" eye witness account of these events was widely circulated, becoming a Bahamian bestseller! Lucid, clear and very well written, it featured a paradoxical title, reflecting the brilliant educational background and wisdom of the writer - "The Quiet Revolution". For the word "revolution" immediately evokes images of violence, great conflict and even bloodshed!

In coining the expression "The Quiet Revolution", Dr. Doris Johnson subtly but vividly depicted the nature of these events in the case of The Commonwealth of the Bahamas. For whereas in many nations, the attainment of independence was manifested in violent revolution, "blood, sweat and tears", in the Bahamas there was no such violence. While there were times when tempers flared and occasions on which unpopular politicians were " booed" by the masses, there was no bloodshed, nor was there any loss of life during the years leading up to the attainment of the Independence of The Bahamas. It is submitted that there is no more apt and accurate description of the events leading up to the attainment of Independence by the people of The Bahamas—than Doris Johnson's "The Quiet Revolution!" A then famous Bahamian female political figure, who not only made history but also had the ability and found the time to write history!

DORIS JOHNSON - DEVOUT CHRISTIAN LADY

Dr. Doris Johnson, nurtured in a Christian family environment was throughout her life an active member of Bethel Baptist Church. At that time the Senior Pastor was the Rev. Dr. H.W. Brown, powerful preacher of the Gospel and prominent political and social activist. Dr. Doris Johnson served in various positions of responsibility in the church, taking a special interest in the operation of its educational institutions. An orator, gifted and eloquent, she managed to retain the rapt attention of her audience whether in the classroom, in Parliament, "on the campaign trail" in a political rally or...in the pulpit!

Thus, while serving as Pastor of Rhodes Memorial Methodist Church, the chronicler invited her to deliver The Divinely inspired message at a special service, she most graciously accepted this invitation to preach at a Church other than where she worshipped every Lord's Day. The large congregation assembled waited, with eager anticipation as Dr. Doris Johnson ascended to deliver the message from the pulpit of Rhodes Memorial Methodist Church. They were not disappointed. For, in a powerful forty-five minute sermon she dealt with a wide range of subjects of interest and concern to the nation. Indeed, you could hear a pin drop as she captivated the attention of the congregation in what could be truly described as "A State of the Nation Address from a Christian Perspective" or simply "A Christian State of the Nation" Sermon. Politics, Christian Nation Building, Crime and Violence, Education Home and Family Life were amongst the wide range of subjects.

Now, as expected, the officers of the Women's Suffrage Movement, deeply engaged in the struggle for social justice, took very strong exception to this position. Accordingly, Dr. Doris Johnson expressed their total disagreement in an outspoken address, which has stood "the test of time".

She began thusly: "The Women's Suffrage Movement" wishes to go on record as wholeheartedly supporting universal enfranchisement. Indeed, the Spirit of the Living God moved mightily as she delivered her inspiring message from the Lord. In retrospect, the chronicler can testify that he and many others who were present at that service were deeply inspired by the message delivered by Dr. Doris Johnson, and greatly assisted in our endeavor to follow Christ!

What, then, can we say about the legacy of Dame Dr. Doris Johnson? Well, she has certainly made a major contribution in the field of education. Indeed, the Government of the Bahamas, through the Ministry of Education has given strong recognition to her contribution by one of its major educational institutions in her honour. The exciting and inspiring story of how she rose from humble circumstances to become a leading educator certainly must be a source of encouragement to the many Bahamian women who serve in the teaching profession.

It is submitted, however, that Bahamian women in all walks of life can benefit from this truly outstanding Bahamian leader. For, growing up at a time when women were indeed "second class citizens" in their own country, Dr. Doris Johnson dedicated her resources to bringing about social justice. Indeed, she must be ranked with heroines such as Mary Ingraham, Nettica Symonette, Patricia Cozzi and Sylvia Johnson as a champion of social justice for women. Yet, despite the amazing strides made by women since the time of Doris Johnson, there are still many of the feminine gender who suffer from low self-esteem and so have fallen between the cracks. One thinks of promising young women, for instance, who face the challenge of coping with teenage pregnancy. Such young women can draw inspiration to continue life, to go on with their education inspiration from Doris Johnson as they "pick up the pieces", resume their studies and seek to fulfil the divine plan for their lives. Climbing the corporate ladder in the male-dominated world of business may be encouraged by the life of Doris Johnson. Indeed, all Bahamian women struggling "to make their mark" in whatever field of human endeavor they are led to choose, may find in Dr. Doris Johnson a role model challenging them "to be the best that they can be!"

Dame Dr. Doris Johnson,

Brilliant Educator,

Eloquent Orator

Pioneer Female Politician who attained statesmanlike Status

Courageous Champion of Social Justice for Bahamian women

Competent Bahamian Historian

Dignified Christian

Truly a "Bahamian Who Made a Difference!"

SOME QUESTIONS FOR GROUP DISCUSSION

1. Dr. Doris Johnson grew up at a time when Bahamian women was "second class citizens" in their own country. What steps did she take to bring about a change in this situation?

2. Why may Doris Johnson be described as "A Role Model" for Bahamian women?

3. Do you think that men and women are equal in every respect in the Bahamas today?

Write short notes on the following

1. The role of the United Nations on Human Rights

2. Why did one authority's assessment of Doris Johnson conclude "She had a habit of being first"

3. Dr. Doris Johnson is certainly regarded as a pioneer when it comes to women in politics.

Can you name three other influential Bahamian women who may be considered as politicians? Give reasons for your answer.

The Rev. Dr. Reuben Edward Cooper, Sr., B.TH. **J.P. D.D. M.B.E.**

PREACHER, EDUCATOR, NATION BUILDER

1913 -- 1980

"...And how shall they hear without a preacher?"

Romans l0:14, AV

"If life is worth living. It should be lived at its best."

-Reuben E. Cooper Sr.

"THROUGHOUT THE AGES"

Throughout the ages, "The Almighty, who at creation spoke the world into existence, has raised up men, especially endowed with the gift of prophecy, to bring about social, moral and spiritual reform!"[lxvii]

Thus, when Moses and his orator brother Aaron, stood before Pharaoh and demanded, "Let my people go!" the Exodus was initiated when the Lord delivered the children of Israel from Egypt, "their house of bondage."[lxviii] Likewise, the wiping out of the pagan worship of Balaam in ancient Israel began when the brave Prophet Elijah soundly condemned the corrupt King Ahab and his cunning Tyrian wife, the brazen Queen Jezebel.[lxix] It was the powerful preaching of John Knox in Edinburgh, which brought about the transformation of Scotland through the Reformation.[lxx] The preaching of John Wesley in England was for the purpose - "to reform the nation - more especially the church - to spread scriptural holiness throughout the land."[lxxi]

And the Rev. Dr. Martin Luther King Jr., certainly ignited the civil rights movement bringing about social justice for all the oppressed in the United States of America and, by extension the world, with his immortal proclamation, *"I have a dream of a time when all people will be judged, not by the color of their skin but by the content of their character!"* Yes, the spoken word can be very powerful, bringing about amazing transformation in every sphere of human endeavor!

Now, in the history of The Bahamas, there was a sermon which has proved to be of tremendous social, political, moral and spiritual consequence. It was that stirring message delivered at the service held on Sunday, July 8th, 1973, the eve of the Independence of The Bahamas, sponsored by The Bahamas Christian Council at Clifford Park, "Out West" in the island of New Providence. The preacher was none other than the President of The Bahamas Christian Council, The Rev. Dr. Reuben Edward Cooper Sr.

A very large, most attentive congregation was assembled at Clifford Park for that historic service, including Sir John Paul, last Colonial Governor and first Governor General of The Bahamas, Sir Milo Butler, Governor General designate and Lady Caroline Butler, Prime Minister

Sir Lynden Oscar Pindling and Lady Marguerite Pindling, the Chief Justice, Officers of The Bahamas Christian Council, many other dignitaries of church and state, and thousands of Bahamians "drawn from all walks of life."[lxxii] The members, then in that august congregation, eagerly looked forward to "a word from the Lord!"

The President of The Bahamas Christian Council delivered the sermon entitled, "You are a Chosen Generation," and he took as his text, *"But ye are a chosen generation, a royal priesthood, a holy nation, a peculiar people; that ye should show forth the praise of Him, who hath called you out of darkness into His marvelous light"* (1 Peter 2:9, Authorized King James Version).

Commencing his message on this optimistic verse, he called the Bahamian people to realize that they were, indeed, a chosen generation and a royal priesthood! 'Thus, he exhorted them to grasp the new exciting opportunities available to them as they transitioned from being subjects in the British. Commonwealth to becoming citizens of the fledgling Commonwealth of The Bahamas.

Speaking, then with prophetic authority, the eloquent Bahamian minister of the Gospel, urged all present to participate wholeheartedly in Christian nation building, thusly:

> "As members of this one generation, it's important that we must have a common concern for and an interest in human needs. The cries of our brothers across the world should reach us and find us in a heart of generosity for we are one generation. The man or woman in distress, regardless of where he or she is or what color he or she might be - we are all one, and we must have a concern for human dignity and

self-respect because *"If life is worth living, it should be lived at its best."*[lxxiii]

The preacher spoke with great conviction; for he deeply believed and lived by the principle that life should be lived at its best. Concluding amidst hearty "Amens!" from the large and varied congregation, he confidently proclaimed, "Independence through God will work."

What manner of man, then, was this who could deliver the Word of God with power and conviction to the thousands of Bahamians gathered at Clifford Park on the eve of the Independence of The Bahamas? What motivated him to speak in this persuasive way? What had brought him to this momentous occasion in his own life? Why is he recognized as one of the greatest ministers of the Gospel to come from The Bahamas?

It is our purpose here to answer these questions, especially for the benefit of "the younger generation" of Bahamians, many of whom know little or nothing about this outstanding Bahamian servant of God!

Born on 1913, Reuben Edward Cooper, Sr., rose from humble circumstances in Exuma to become and be acknowledged as a most eminent Preacher and Pastor, wielding tremendous influence in The Bahamian community. Nurtured in a Christian family background, Reuben Cooper, like prophets such as Samuel, Isaiah and Jeremiah of ancient Israel, was early in his life, conscious of a call to serve as a Minister of the Gospel. Indeed, it was this sense of a Divine Call which motivated him to serve effectively in ministry throughout his life.

Thus, after receiving his basic education in his native island, he as an ambitious Bahamian, like so many others who grew up in the Family

Islands, left home to study at more advanced stage in New Providence. Completing his studies at secondary level, young Reuben Cooper, in accord with his sense of call to the ministry, travelled to the United States to pursue studies at tertiary level. The young Bahamian then studied at American Baptist Seminary and Fisk University, both in Nashville, Tennessee, earning the Degree Bachelor in Theology. He remained in the USA and was ordained to the Ministry on May 22, 1939 at the Spruce Street Baptist Church in Nashville. Upon completion, then, of his theological education and ordination abroad, Reuben Cooper returned to his native land, embarking upon a long and distinguished career in the Christian ministry, grounded in a burning desire to serve his fellow Bahamians and in his great love for the Lord.

Now, Reuben Cooper certainly demonstrated an enthusiastic and buoyant approach to ministry. Never satisfied with mediocrity in any form whatsoever he threw himself wholeheartedly into the work of God. Both in his preaching and pastoral care, he served with an infectious and joyful spirit as manifested in the hymn, *"Come ye that love the Lord and let your joys be known."* In a sense most profound, he enjoyed ministry and those around him "caught the spirit" of his approach and themselves enjoyed serving as Disciples of Christ.

He was very determined and did not allow adverse circumstances to steer him from what he believed was the will of God for his life. The narrator vividly recalls him describing the circumstances under which he labored in laying the foundation for Mission Baptist Church. He toiled there for many years and until 1974 when the present imposing edifice located on Hay Street, was dedicated to the glory of God.

Now, the Rev. Dr. Reuben E. Cooper was, first and foremost, a preacher, one called by God to proclaim the Good News of salvation available to all who believe in Jesus the Christ. With prophetic power and authority, he preached the Gospel. His sermons, evidently well prepared, proved to be powerful and convincing and many souls were saved as a result of his faithful, forthright proclamation of the Word of God. Mrs. Cheryl Strachan, who held him in high esteem recalls that Dr. Cooper was able "to breakdown" a text, expounding powerful and complex biblical and theological concepts with profound simplicity so that all could understand and benefit from his preaching.[lxxiv] This eloquence as a preacher was certainly demonstrated at the memorable sermon on July 6th. When Bahamians celebrated the independence of their young nation gifted as preacher, a compassionate pastor by nature, Reuben Cooper was also a very competent church administrator. For, being charismatic as a leader, he was endowed with a number of gifts for ministry by the Holy Spirit (Eph. 4:1-16, 1 Cor. 12:1-9). As such his ministry and influence extended far beyond the Christian community of Mission Baptist Church.

It was not surprising, therefore, that he was elected President of the Bahamas Baptist Missionary and Educational Convention composed of most of the two hundred and fifty Baptist congregations in The Commonwealth of The Bahamas and as Vice President of the Caribbean Baptist Fellowship (composed of National Baptist groups to be active in the vast Caribbean region). Proud as he was of his Baptist heritage, Dr. Cooper was deeply interested and involved with Christians of all denominations in the region. In keeping with his development as an ecumenical churchman, he was a charter member of the Caribbean Council of Churches. In carrying out his administrative responsibilities, the Bahamian clergyman travelled extensively throughout the Bahamas, Turks & Caicos Islands as well as the Central and Southern Caribbean.

Dr. Cooper then, worked closely with ministers of many denominations especially those with whom he served upon his election as President of The Bahamas Christian Council. These included the Rev. Dr. Edwin Taylor of The Methodist Church, Bishop Michael Eldon and Archdeacon Williams Thompson of The Anglican Church. He seemed "completely at home" serving with these clergy persons of denominations other than his own and they all evidently were comfortable working with him. Accordingly, there can be no doubt that his election to serve as President of The Bahamas Christian Council (during the crucial years leading up to and including the celebration of the Independence of The Bahamas as a nation in charge of its own destiny under God (1972 - 1 975) was the crowning achievement of his ministry. For, it was in that capacity that he delivered that sermon "Ye are a Chosen Generation" which will go down in history as one of the major events of Bahamian history.

EMINENT BAHAMIAN EDUCATOR/COMMUNICATOR

Now, as we have seen, Dr. Cooper was keenly interested in education. He was constantly studying and was recognized for his achievements. Thus in 1966 he received the Doctor of Divinity Degree from the Florida Theological Seminary in Lakeland. Throughout his ministry, he "kept on reading," and as such his sermons and addresses were always marked by depth, freshness and relevance.

Coming, then from a small community in the Family Islands, and rising to the top in church administration and general education, Dr. Reuben

Cooper was acutely aware of the supreme importance of education. As such, not only did he ensure that his own children received the best in education, he was also keenly passionate about seeing that all children and young people who came under his care also received a good education.

This keen interest in education was demonstrated by the fact that The Government of The Bahamas appointed him a Member of its Committee on Secondary Education and that he was appointed liaison consultant in The Bahamas for Florida Memorial College.

There can be no doubt, however, that he made his major contribution in this field of human endeavor in secondary education. Thus, he served for many years as Principal of Jordan Memorial High School and on the staff of Prince William High School. Accordingly, he was on the Board of Governors of both these Baptist educational institutions. It was, therefore, not surprising that he was amongst those who were instrumental in watching over their development from cramped premises on Blue Hill Road opposite the headquarters of The Bahamas Electricity Corporation (now the Bahamas Power and Light Company) to a much more impressive campus located at Cowpen Road. Over the years, it has expanded greatly both academically and in the size of its student body. Providing education of a high standard, based on a Christian foundation, Jordan Prince William High School is recognized as a leading Bahamian institution of secondary education, thanks largely to the pioneering efforts of The Rev. Dr. Reuben Edward Cooper and others who fought to establish the Baptist Church as "a force to be reckoned with" in Bahamian educational community.

Now, as has been indicated, Dr. Reuben Cooper was multi-talented and most energetic. Thus besides serving in the pastorate, church administration and education, he proved also very effective in the field of Christian communication.

Thus, for several years he edited "*The Baptist Weekly*". This tabloid was dedicated to reporting events taking place in the Church as well as the publication of contributions on matters as varied as politics, socio-economic progress, moral and religious themes from a Christian perspective.

GOOD FATHER IN THE HOME, "FATHER FIGURE" OF THE NATION!

Now, The Rev. Dr. Reuben Cooper was truly "A Family Man", who despite his very busy schedule of activities in the Church and the Bahamian community, managed to devote quality time and effort to the care and nurture of his own family. For, he and his wife, "Mother" Florence Cooper (née Edgecombe) were the proud parents of ten children...a large Christian family! In keeping with his uncompromising conviction that education was a matter of top priority, the prominent clergyman and his faithful wife saw to it that all their children received the best in education that was available to them! Their children, then, were nurtured in an environment marked by a strong emphasis upon Christian principles and education. It is not surprising, therefore that they have all done well in life, with most of them having followed in his footsteps in active Christian ministry. These include The Rev. Dr. Reuben E. Cooper, Jr., who has succeeded his father as Senior Pastor of Mission Baptist Church, his elder sister The Hon. Rev. Ruby Ann Cooper, who contributes a weekly devotional article in "The Nassau Guardian" and younger sister, The Rev. Dr. Irene Cooper-Coakley, a professionally trained nurse, and a

Minister at Mission Baptist Church. Their siblings include Fanny Gardiner, John Cooper, Primrose Chase, Nathaniel Cooper, Bertha Cooper, and Carmelita Michelle Cooper. Truly, "The family that prays together stays together."

But not only was Dr. Cooper a good father in the home. He was a true Bahamian patriot, extremely proud of his homeland, a keen nation builder. Accordingly, he certainly was highly respected as a "Father-figure" in the nation, preacher, pastor, patriot, he was deeply interested in the socio-economic, educational and civic development of its people, his "fellow Bahamians", as well as in their moral and spiritual nourishment. As a long-standing Justice of the Peace, and Marriage Officer for the Commonwealth of the Bahamas, he was able to assist a considerable number of them in processing important documents, passports, birth and marriage certificates, property conveyances, etc.

He held tenaciously to the promotion of Tourism[lxxv] as "the engine of the Bahamian economy", and indeed, served as a Member of The Board of The Ministry of Tourism, the first Clergyperson to serve in such a capacity.

His influence, then, in the Bahamian community was enormous, intensive and extensive, impacting every aspect of life - religion, education, the economy, and politics. He believed strongly in Independence for the Bahamas, convinced that the Bahamian people," A chosen generation", were fully capable of running their own affairs. Accordingly, he took a lively interest and, indeed, participated in the political aspect of nation building. Thus, he served as the only non-Cabinet member of The Advisory Council to the Bahamas Secretariat for the Independence Celebrations. Thus, it was with great pride that it was his privilege to become bearer of the congratulatory message on behalf of the Bahamas Christian Council at the Installation of The First Bahamian Governor General of The Commonwealth of the Bahamas, Sir Milo Butler, August 1st, 1973.

In recognition of the major contributions to the physical, moral and spiritual development of the people of his native land, this outstanding Bahamian Clergyperson was awarded the honor of appointment as a Member of the Order of The British Empire (MBE) by HM Queen Elizabeth II in the same year. The Rev. Dr. Reuben Cooper, Sr., served for eleven years as President of the Bahamas Baptist Missionary & Educational Convention for eleven years and as President of the Bahamas Christian Council for three years.In keeping with his determination to serve whole-heartedly in any given responsibility, he resigned from both these ecclesiastic posts on being appointed Chaplain to HM Prison in 1974. He continued to serve in this capacity, with typical dignity, compassion and dedication until the end of his earthly sojourn, completing forty-six eventful, fruitful years as a Minister of The Gospel. Because of his tremendous appeal and widespread influence as a Preacher of The Gospel, his compassion as a Pastor, his competence as Church Administrator and Promoter of Christian unity, his exemplary manner as "Father in the home" and Father-figure in the Nation, and his dedication to the work of The Lord, The Rev. Dr. Reuben Cooper, Sr. must be ranked with Bishop Michael Eldon, Archdeacon William" Willie" Thompson, The Rev. Dr. H.W. Brown, The Rev. Dr. Charles Saunders, The Rev. Dr. Hervis Bain, The Rev. Dr. Philip Rahming, The Rev, Dr. Edwin Taylor, Bishop Paul Leonard Hagarty, The Rev. Joseph Perna, Msgr. Preston Moss, Bishop Brice Thompson, Evangelist Dr. Rex Major[lxxvi] and Pastor Hugh Roach as one of "The Spiritual Founding Fathers of the Commonwealth of the Bahamas!" For, it was directly through their influence, determination and contributions that the concept of Christian nation building is enshrined in the Preamble to the Constitution of our beloved Bahamaland!

The Rev. Dr. Reuben Eugene Cooper, Sr.:

Prophetic Preacher

Compassionate Pastor

Able Church Administrator

Eminent Educator

Christian Communicator Par Excellence

Ecumenical Churchman

"Family Man" /National "Father Figure" "Man of God!"

Truly a Bahamian Who Made a Difference!

Well may we all benefit by always bearing in mind and applying to our own lives the "motto" he coined and epitomized in his own life: *"If life is worth living, it should be lived at its best!"*

EXERCISES & QUESTIONS FOR GROUP DISCUSSION

1. Religion and Politics don't mix!" Discuss.

2. Is The Bahamas a Christian nation? Give two reasons for your answer!

3. Write short notes on three of the following: "The Baptist Weekly"; The Christian Council; Jordan Prince William High School; The Preamble to the Constitution of the Bahamas; The R.E. Cooper National Meritorious Service Award

4. The Rev. Dr. Reuben Cooper may truly be described as one of "The Spiritual Founding Fathers of The Commonwealth of The Bahamas". "Tell what you know about two other Ministers of The Gospel who may be described in this way. (250 – 300 words)

5. Why are not more Bahamian young people coming forward to offer to serve as Ministers of The Gospel?

FOR FURTHER READING

1). Booklet Published on The Celebration of the 53rd. Annual Founders Day , The Ninth Annual Presentation and Investiture of the R.E. Cooper Sr. National Meritorious Service Award, on Sunday, December 26, 1993 at Mission Baptist Church.

2). CD and Booklet "A Chosen Generation" Copyright the R. E. Cooper, Sr. Foundation, 2016.

3). Booklet "The R. E. Cooper National Meritorious Service Award at "A Chosen "Diamond Jubilee Kingdom Ball, Friday April 29, 2016.

Sir Cecil Vincent Wallace-Whitfield, **NH**

(March 30th, 1930 - May 9th, 1990)

"There is nothing to fear...but fear."

–President Franklin Delano Roosevelt

A. HIS ADVENTUROUS YOUTH!

INTRODUCTION --"A BORN LEADER!"

There is a tremendous amount of discussion about leadership "in the world today". This is evident in the many books written and seminars conducted on it. Moreover, it is certainly accentuated by the interest generated whenever the following questions are debated.

What precisely, is "leadership?" Is it a gift, endowed by The Almighty upon certain "charismatic" individuals, few and far between, and denied many; or is leadership an ability which anyone, who so desires, may acquire by training, i.e., reading books, attending seminars, etc., and exercise effectively? Concisely, are leaders born or made?

Now, whatever may be your answer to these questions, there can be not a shadow of a doubt that, in the long history of humankind, there have emerged certain individuals who have, indeed, demonstrated a natural ability to lead others. These are men and women who have been able to motivate and inspire others to act in particular ways and with enthusiasm.

People "in all walks of life" have gravitated towards them, attributing allegiance to them and expressing a willingness to follow when and where they lead. Appropriately described as charismatic leaders," "gifted leaders" or "born leaders" they have, in every generation and in every nation, contributed greatly to the progress of humankind!

Now, such a person was Cecil Vincent Wallace-Whitfield! For, it is submitted that it can be truly said that amongst the "Bahamians who Made a Difference," this remarkable "Son of the Soil" was "indeed a born leader!"

"WAIT FOR CECIL!"

Cecil V. Wallace-Whitfield was born to the late Oswald Whitfield and Mrs. Dorothy Louise Rogers née Wallace, both of New York (originally Bahamian by birth) on March 30, 1930 in the city of Nassau. During the formative years of his eventful life, this vibrant young Bahamian spent much of his time at the residence of close relatives on West Street, conveniently located next to that popular rendezvous of yesteryear "Strachan's Ice Cream Parlor." As such, he could truly be described as a "Hill Topper!"

Very significantly, or, prophetically, even in those early post-World War II years, he demonstrated that he was a young man endowed with the gift of leadership. For the narrator, then "a small boy in short pants," vividly recalls that Cecil was "A Big Boy," who somehow managed to wield a lot of authority amongst the young of the community. Thus, whenever a dispute erupted amongst them or on the verge of an altercation of some sort, the word would go out, "Wait for Cecil!" or "Wait on Cecil!" As this caution spread around, the young men would engage in no further activity as they patiently waited for Cecil.

Presently, to the relief of all concerned, Cecil, brimming with confidence, would arrive on the scene. Those involved in the dispute would explain their respective "side of the story" while Cecil listened intently. Then, they would, in turn, listen, and wait with rapt attention as he, demonstrating wisdom and maturity expected of a "grown man," would give his judgment. The matter was then settled as they all did what was required to bring about a resolution to the same "...Cause Cecil *say* so!" Thus, early in his life, Cecil Wallace-Whitfield epitomized the "Charismatic" ability to attract the attention of his peers and instill in them a sense of allegiance to himself and a willingness to accept his authority.

BRILLIANT STUDENT

A "bright boy" in every way, the young Cecil Wallace-Whitfield took full advantage of the opportunities afforded him for progress in his educational standard. This was evident in the fact that, after receiving his education at primary level at various private and public institutions including Ms. Wright's School and Western Junior School, he was successful in the highly competitive examination, which enabled him to continue his education, at secondary level at The Government High School. With comparatively few scholarships and fee-paying places (Ten pounds and ten shillings per annum!) available, only the most brilliant students gained entrance to that prestigious institution of education! The narrator recalls often "looking up to Cecil as a big boy," smartly dressed in his "blue and white GHS uniform, proudly making his way to school. Punctual and intelligent, he must have made an indelible impression upon his fellow students as well as upon his teachers. Indeed, young Cecil did very well at The Government High School, graduating in 1947. Moreover, that he was appointed to serve as a Prefect and Head Boy while there, clearly demonstrated that here was a young Bahamian destined for leadership in the land of his birth!

BUDDING CIVIL SERVANT

During the early post-World War II years, when tourism and financial services were just beginning "to pick up," opportunities for employment, especially for young black Bahamians, in the private sector were very limited. accordingly, most graduates of the Government High School Immediately went to work in the public service, or as it was then described, "The Civil Service--Government Departments" such as the Ministry of Education, The Princess Margaret Hospital, The Bahamas Electricity Corporation or "Telecoms." In this regard, young Cecil Wallace was no exception.

Accordingly, upon leaving Government High, or as some persons prefer to say "The Old Government High," he joined the ranks of those working as civil servants in Her Majesty's Customs Department. He remained there until 1956, when political aspirations made it necessary for him to resign from The Civil Service.

Indeed, young Cecil Wallace did very well at "The High School," participating fully in all aspects of school life-- academics as well as sports and extracurricular activities. Very significantly, while there he met young persons, who, like himself were most ambitious and who eventually proved to make major contributions to the progress of their homeland. These included Paul Adderley, A. D. Hanna, Orville Turnquest, Ruth Maycock (née Miller), "Mitch" Hanna, and Lynden Oscar Pindling! Amongst his peers he developed a reputation as a very keen debater, who held tenaciously to his opinion in the lively discussions which inevitably erupted when young ambitious people, especially those with political aspiration, came together.

He graduated from Government High School in 1947 just two years after "The War" (i.e. World War II, 1939-1945). Very significantly, that he had been appointed to serve as a prefect and head boy while there, he clearly indicated that there was a young Bahamian destined to make a difference in the land of his birth.

During those early post-World War II years, when tourism and financial services were just "beginning to pick up" as a result of the efforts of Sir Stafford Sands, opportunities for employment, especially for young black Bahamians, in the private sector were very limited. Accordingly, most graduates of The Government High School, immediately went to work in the public service, or as it was described then "The Civil Service" -Government Departments, the Bahamas Electricity Department or Bahamas Telecommunications.

In this regard, young Cecil Wallace was no exception! Accordingly, upon leaving the Government High School (or as some prefer to say "The Old Government High," he joined the ranks of those serving as civil servants as an officer of Her Majesty's Customs Department. He remained there until 1956 when political aspirations made it necessary for him to resign from The Civil Service.

ARDENT VERSATILE ATHLETE

Throughout his youth, Cecil Wallace, who enjoyed robust health and was most energetic, participated fully in sporting activities. These included basketball, softball and cricket, which, in those days were officially and, actually, the national sport of the Bahamas!

In this regard, however, it is germane to point out that it should not be surprising to learn that this young Bahamian enjoyed playing basketball.

You see, West Street in those days, in contrast to East Street, which was always very busy "day and night," was a quiet residential community, where many old distinguished Bahamian families lived. These included the Burnsides, Nashes, Taylors, Strachans, Wallace, Fountains, Moxeys, Virgils, Weirs and many others.

West Street, then was relatively quiet most evenings with the residents going to bed early. Yes, "All was quiet on the western front" except on those evenings when literally hundreds of young people, from all over the island, invaded the community to play and watch basketball at "The Priory". Most of the young people "growing up on West Street" joined them by either participating watching basketball on that well-lit basketball court on the level ground at the foot of the hill on which stood St. Francis Xavier Cathedral. There, under the watchful eye of Father Marcian Peters, "The Sporting Priest" they enthusiastically played basketball or supported their team with loud shouting and strong words of encouragement. They were most enjoyable times for the young people as senior citizens can testify. After the games, exhausted and thirsty, many of them returned to their homes but not without stopping at Strachan's Ice Cream Parlor for much needed refreshments - cold sodas and, of course, **delicious ice cream!**

Evidently Cecil, as a young man growing up on West Street" was amongst those who played basketball at the Priory, for, Mr. Frederick Taylor, who also grew up on West Street at that time, vividly remembers playing this exciting, fast moving game as a member of a team along with "Cecil". He claims that it was managed by this dynamic young Bahamian.

Tall in stature, erect in posture, endowed with a magnetic personality which attracted others to him, the youthful Cecil Wallace-Whitfield was the epitome of a confident, ambitious young Bahamian of his generation. And because he himself was so confident, he inspired confidence in others as a "born leader," brilliant student, budding civil servant and versatile athlete, he was, indeed, a remarkable young man, it was not surprising, therefore, that many who came into contact with him in these formative of his eventful life, were so impressed by him that they realized that here, indeed, was a young Bahamian destined for greatness!

B. HIS COURAGEOUS CAREER

The winds of political change blew, with increasing velocity during the year Cecil Wallace-Whitfield, served as an officer of HM Customs (1948 - 56). In this regard, there can be no doubt that the most significant development was the formation of the Progressive Liberal Party in 1953. With it objective of wresting political control of the Colony from the "Bay Street Boys," this political party grew very rapidly, attracting many young black Bahamians to join its ranks.

Now, Cecil Wallace-Whitfield as a young ambitious Bahamian with political aspirations certainly took notice of these changes. Thus, he joined the PLP, where several others known to him from his days at The Government High School, including Lynden Pindling and Arthur D. Hanna were already active. Thus in 1956 he resigned as a Customs Officer and entered the political arena as the PLP candidate in the Central Eleuthera Constituency in the General Election held that year. Moving rapidly, with typical energy and determination, "on the campaign trail" in Eleuthera, he adopted an aggressive reasoned approach, which appealed to many. Although Cecil was unsuccessful in winning a seat in Parliament, his loss by less than fifty votes clearly indicated that here was a young man with great potential in the political arena.

His defeat in his first foray into the competitive world of politics, however, did not deter the young Cecil Wallace-Whitfield. With the election and any prospect of becoming a career civil servant behind him, he went into business as a Customs Broker. Serving, however, in a routine, mundane capacity was too mediocre a prospect for such an ambitious young man, and so he decided to enter the legal profession, which was more challenging and in keeping with his political aspirations. Amongst those who had assisted him over the years was his Godfather, the proprietor of Strachan's Ice Cream Parlor, and his father, who gave him their full support.

It was during this period that the narrator, then a Civil Servant employed in the Audit Department, had a most interesting conversation with Cecil. As always, in speaking to young ambitious persons, the narrator added his quote of encouragement to this most promising young Bahamian.

Thus in 1958, he left his homeland to read law at .the University of Hull East Yorkshire, England. Here again, the academic brilliance which he had demonstrated while at The Old Government High School was evident and he earned the degree Bachelor of Law (LL.B) in 1961.

The winds of political change were continuing to blow rapidly when he returned home. Being "a political animal," he stood for election in the same constituency in the General Election of 1962 as he had done in that of 1956. Again, he was defeated!

Now most persons, after two consecutive defeats at the polls, would "throw in the towel" and give up battling in the challenging political arena. But not Cecil Wallace-Whitfield, who was truly a warrior when it came to political activity! Indeed, these initial forays into the political arena served only to whet his appetite for participation in politics!

> What was it that motivated this young Bahamian to continue in the field of politics after two defeats at the polls? What kept him going in the context of such disappointing "setbacks?" the answer is at hand - he had a genuine desire to improve the lot of his fellow Bahamians, to break down the barrier which impeded the progress of the men and women "Over-the-Hill". It was because of this commitment to improving the welfare of his fellow Bahamians, rather than any desire for personal gain or fame that he remained active in the political arena throughout his courageous career. For, just as his contemporary, the young Lynden Oscar Pindling, then growing up on East Street was deeply conscious of the challenge to end the domination of "The Bay Street Boys," so Cecil Wallace-Whitfield, growing up on West Street, was motivated by a similar desire to bring about the end of the socio-political power of this group and to establish the right of "the man on the street"!

Many years later, having served in Parliament and earned his place as a veteran politician, Sir Cecil Wallace-Whitfield, testified that

"From the time I was a very young man -- a student, I have been out there in the front line fighting for what I believe to be right!"

Explaining precisely what he meant by "what he believed to be right," the then mature politician continued:

"...And in the struggle for freedom from 1957 through 1967, when our people were fighting against one block of our population being discriminated against and victimized, Cecil Vincent Wallace-Whitfield was right there up front fighting for the people." (See article *Whitfield Publicly Answers 'Bully' Charges,* by Anthony Forbes, "The Tribune," Monday, August 31, 1987.

As we have seen, the young Cecil Wallace-Whitfield, despite failure to "win a seat" in the House of Assembly in two consecutive general elections, remained steadfast in his determination to pursue a career in the highly competitive Bahamian political arena. This bold objective was certainly evidenced by the stamina, vigor, organizational skills and dedication he demonstrated "on the campaign trail" in Eleuthera. There can be no doubt that recognition of these abilities "factored in" his election as Chairman of the Progressive Liberal Party in November, 1965. The confidence thus vested in him was vindicated by the major achievements and advances made by his Party in his two terms at its helm.

Most significant amongst them was the victory of The Progressive Liberal Party in the historic General Election held on January 10, 1967, ushering in Majority Rule. This was followed by the more impressive victory of The PLP in the General Election conducted a year later.

Acting with typical decisiveness in his capacity as chairman of the Progressive Liberal Party, the young dynamic Cecil Wallace-Whitfield was a "mastermind" behind the effective organization and strategic positioning of participants of The PLP in this most important event in the historical development of the people of the Bahamas. Official recognition of this fact was made in the Act of Parliament in

2014 AD, decreeing that henceforth January 10; "Majority Rule Day" would be celebrated as a Public Holiday.

That persistence "in the long run" inevitably results in success was certainly demonstrated in the courageous political journey of Sir Cecil Wallace-Whitfield. For, in the referenced 1967 General Election he was elected to The House of Assembly as the Representative of the huge St. Agnes Constituency. This was not surprising; for as indicated, he grew up on West Street, which geographically, was near to St. Agnes and where he was well-known and popular.

> He who had been unsuccessful in two attempts to serve his country as a Member of Parliament as representing Eleuthera, succeeded in doing so as a "Home Boy". Indeed, he was a member of the first Cabinet under Majority Rule and was selected by Premier Sir Lynden Pindling to serve as Minister of Works and Utilities. He served in this capacity until the General Election, after which, he was appointed Minister of Education & Culture.

Now Cecil Wallace-Whitfield was "a man of action," who tackled any assignment he was given with a tenacity and sense of urgency which were most remarkable. Like the Late Pastor Keith Albury, another Bahamian who accomplished much in a comparatively short life span he did not hesitate to act with decisiveness and promptness in carrying out his duties which he took very seriously.

Thus, as Minister of Works and Utilities, he immediately took note of the fact that many communities" over the hill," the most densely populated part of the colony, were without electricity...Grants Town, the streets and alleys off East Street, Wulff Road, etc. There were those who thought that he should carry out the process of the electrification of these communities gradually. However, he took the position that this should be done as expeditiously as possible, and so "he lit up Grants' Town" and other communities "over the hill," ensuring that electricity was available to virtually all residents of New Providence!

The same "no nonsense" productive approach shown in his capacity as Minister of Works and Utilities characterized his performance as Minister of Education and Culture. For, in this capacity, Sir Cecil was instrumental in the construction of two air-conditioned schools, again in "over the hill communities – Uriah McPhee Primary School on Kemp Road and Stephen Dillet Primary School on Wulff Road. The Minister of Education and Culture had taken the opportunity to observe the operation of air-conditioned schools in South Florida, and was so impressed by what he saw that he was convinced that " they could work" in the Bahamas with a similar climate. (The theory here is that children in the closed atmosphere of air-conditioned class rooms, without the distractions of outside scenery and influences would concentrate more on their studies and so perform better in their academic endeavors.)

Thus, in his two comparatively short terms in ministerial office, the newly elected Member of Parliament proved to be a strong, principled leader with a reputation for getting things done.

At least one thing can be said about Cecil Wallace-Whitfield, without fear of contradiction, - "he left his mark wherever he went!" He gave himself unstintingly and assiduously to whatever responsibility he was given and expected others to do the same. Concisely, all concerned soon realized that working with this human dynamo was anything but business as usual!"

It is certainly germane to mention here two other young Bahamian political rising stars, who worked along with The Hon. Cecil Wallace-Whitfield in the struggle for social and political justice during this turbulent era in the history of the Commonwealth of the Bahamas:

...The Hon. (later Sir) Arthur Foulkes and The Hon. Warren J. Levarity. Their respective contributions were complementary: for whereas the former was active, for many years, both in journalism and politics, the latter concentrated on the political arena! In this regard, the following observation of Sir. Arthur Foulkes is most illuminating:

> "Bahamian Times" contributed significantly to the historic victory in 1967. Warren was appointed Minister of Out Island Affairs and demonstrated that he was not only good at politics but was also an excellent administrator. *The work he accomplished in one year with the cooperation with his Colleague Minister of Works Cecil Wallace-Whitfield, contributed significantly to the PLP's overwhelming victory in the Out Islands in April of 1968.* (Sir Arthur Foulkes, "Tribute to Warren J. Levarity," "The Nassau Guardian," Wednesday, November 26, 2014. Words underlined by "the Narrator").

"FREE AT LAST!"

The years following the historic victory of the PLP in 1967 and more resounding triumph in 1968 at the polls, turned out to be extremely eventful as the winds of rapid political change blew furiously throughout the length and breadth of the Bahamian archipelago. With the United Bahamian Party (UBP) gradually waning in influence and political clout as manifested in its dwindling number of members in The House of Assembly, it might be expected that the Progressive Liberal Party would have moved forward, as a mighty united political party entity to govern the affairs of the Colony "with powerful leadership, but it transpired that such was not the case! Indeed, the seeds of dissension were germinating both amongst its member in the House of Assembly and the" rank and file" of the governing party in the community. Very significantly, perhaps predictably, the young ambitious Cecil Wallace-Whitfield played a leading role in these developments.

With tensions increasing and greater internal conflict, the hierarchy of the PLP, under the leadership of the Premier Sir Lynden Pindling, convened at Hope Bay, Andros, "to patch up their differences!"

This conclave was temporarily useful in alleviating the volatile situation, but "in the long run" proved to be little more than "political band aid," incapable of bridging the deep seated division brewing within the ranks of the governing party.

"Things came to a head" at its Fifteenth National Convention in October, 1970. In his capacity as Minister of Education and Culture, The Hon. Cecil Wallace-Whitfield was slated to deliver the crucial keynote address. He began in an appropriately conciliatory manner, touting the achievements of the Progressive Liberal Party, astutely "making light" of his own contribution. Then, like the weather, in that address delivered "at the height of hurricane season," there was a sudden change in the content and direction of his oration. Then, he launched into a litany of complaints and criticisms against the Government. What were these factors leading up to this position by the Minister of Education and Culture?

First, a major "bone of contention" was the relationship of the governing party to the principals of the rapidly developing city of Freeport, Grand Bahama, already known as "The Second City of the Bahamas"! For, from the signing of The Hawksbill Creek Agreement in 1955 the officers of the PLP had taken the position of the UBP, acting in accord with the initiative of Sir Stafford Sands, had been too generous in granting concessions to the Grand Bahama authority and its licensees. Moreover, "the powers that be" were still not satisfied that the Bahamians were being afforded the opportunities for employment in executive positions and participation in the fruits of prosperity they deserved; in "The Magic City".

Accordingly, The Premier Sir Lynden Pindling delivered the famous "Bend or Break" speech at the opening and dedication of the huge BORCO refinery on the largest industrial complex in the Bahamas, on Saturday, July 26, 1969. In this landmark address, he took the opportunity to express these concerns, boldly calling for a change to bring about a more equitable condition. There was very mixed reaction to it.

On the one hand, it was welcomed by many Bahamians, who gave the Prime Minister credit for opening up new opportunities for them. On the other hand, reception to it by many of the expatriate investors was rather cool, and there was an economic downturn as those who were not satisfied left the county or reduced their investments in "The Second City". There were then highly polarized "points of view" on the effects of "The dramatic 'Bend or Break Speech'," and this resulted in major implications for the destiny of the governing party. There were differences of opinion within its hierarchy on this matter. The presence of such tension and conflicting opinions continued, setting it on the path of open dissension.

Thus, according to noted authority on Bahamian History, Michael Craton: The split opened up in the debate on Freeport changes, when Warren Levarity and Maurice Moore, the two PLP representatives for Grand Bahama shifted their position to blame the recession on the actions of the government—if not side actually with the licensees and the Port Authority.

This act of the two PLP members representing Grand Bahama constituencies in the House of Assembly condemned by the hierarchy of the PLP "for siding with the enemy," was predictably, commended by the parliamentarians of the United Bahamian Party. Inevitably, the position taken by the two PLP Members of Parliament for Grand Bahama would affect the overall unity of the governing party.

There was another "bone of contention". According to his son, the Hon. Cecil Wallace- Whitfield, and those who supported him, were of the mindset that those in leadership of the PLP were straying from its basic principles. "These fellows are losing their way!" They were of the opinion that the leadership of the governing party was not consulting enough with the other members of the PLP in making decisions or engaging in a certain course of action, notably the "Bend or Break Speech". Indeed there were those amongst them who were of the opinion that their actions were moving in the direction of "totalitarianism".

Disagreement, then, with the manner in which The Hawksbill Creek Agreement was being administered, charges of self-interest rather than concern for the welfare of the people, and indeed, the perception that there was a general moving away from the basic principles of the PLP were the major concerns of Sir Cecil Wallace-Whitfield and those who were gradually siding with him against the leadership of the governing party. These were the matters about which the Minister of Education complained in delivering the key note address at the crucial Fifteenth National Convention.

Continuing, then, in this highly critical manner, the Hon. Cecil Wallace-Whitfield, with predictable flamboyance, dramatically announced his resignation from the Cabinet as Minister of Education and culture "effective immediately"! Concluding with an expression of liberation, made famous by the great American clergyman and civil rights activist Dr. Martin Luther King, Jr., he left the gathering, proclaiming "Free at last"

There can be no doubt that this speech, like the "Bend or Break" speech delivered by Sir Lynden Pindling, marked a "watershed" in the history of the people of The Commonwealth of The Bahamas.

"The die was cast"! The members of the PLP, both within the walls of the House of Assembly and in the community, were rapidly moving into two opposing factions – those loyal to the Premier Sir Lynden Pindling and those aligned with sir Cecil Wallace- Whitfield.

Events, then, followed the "Free at last" speech with breathtaking rapidity! This was epitomized in unforeseen resignation from the cabinet of Dr. Curtis McMillan. This must have taken many by surprise as he was perceived to be a strong supporter of the Pindling administration. Certainly, Dr. McMillan's resignation was symptomatic of the deep divide which had developed within the ranks of the governing party.

At the next meeting of The House of Assembly, Sir Randol Fawkes, sole member of the Labor Party, moved a vote of no confidence in the leadership of the Progressive Liberal Party; thereupon followed a twelve-hour marathon debate lasting from "dusk to dawn". This resulted in a pyrrhic victory for the governing party, which garnered nineteen votes compared to fifteen for those who were opposed to the Pindling administration. Seven Members of Parliament joined with Cecil Wallace-Whitfield, the leader of the Labour Party and six members of the United Bahamian Party in a coalition against the Government. These Members of Parliament, who came to be known as "The Dissident Eight," were subsequently suspended from the governing party at its Council Meeting:

They included:

The Hon. Cecil Wallace-Whitfield

The Hon. Elwood Donaldson

The Hon. Randol Francis Fawkes

The Hon. Arthur Foulkes

The Hon. Warren Levarity

The Hon. Dr. Curtis McMillan

The Hon. Maurice Moore and

The Hon. James Shepherd

The Hon. Cecil Wallace-Whitfield was the de facto charismatic leader of this group.

"The wheels were set in motion" then, for the emergence of a new political grouping to oppose the governing party, especially in view of the gradual decline of the United Bahamian Party. Such a political development was inevitable in the democratic form of government of the Bahamas.

Consequently, and predictably, the year 1971 turned out to be most eventful with major changes taking place in the political arena. "The Dissident Eight" were organized as "The Free PLP" and, naturally, Cecil Wallace-Whitfield was its leader. They were joined by various groups including the members of the United Bahamian party and the Bahamas Democratic Movement, and this merger led to the formation of The Free National Movement.

Elected Leader of The Free National Movement by a huge majority, Sir Cecil Wallace- Whitfield then was recognized as Leader of The Opposition.

He then embarked upon a new chapter in his most eventful political career. He offered as a candidate in the general election held in 1972, for the St. Agnes Constituency but was not successful. Indeed, all his other colleagues of the fledgling Free National Movement lost their seats in the august halls of Parliament.

For ten years, Sir Cecil Wallace-Whitfield remained "in the political wilderness" as far as representation in the House of Assembly was concerned. Indeed, during this period, he lost in two attempts to become a Member of Parliament.

But Cecil Wallace-Whitfield "did not give up" in his endeavor to enter again into frontline politics. Invited by The Hon. Warren Levarity "to come to Grand Bahama" as he was "bowing out of political activity," Cecil Wallace-Whitfield was, indeed very well received by the people of this Northern Island. He made his reentry into frontline politics when in 1982 he won a seat in the General Election. He was elected to the House of Assembly representing Marco City when "he polled more votes than any of the other 48 candidates in that election!"

Surely, it was "His finest hour" as a politician! Cecil Wallace-Whitfield continued to represent Grand Bahama for the rest of his political career. In his position as Leader of the FNM and as the Leader of The Opposition in Parliament, he wielded very wide influence in Grand Bahama, and as a result of his residing there he proved instrumental in firmly establishing the Free National Movement in that island.

Yes, Cecil Wallace-Whitfield was, indeed "a born leader".

Sir Cecil Wallace-Whitfield, Attorney-at-Law

Cecil Wallace-Whitfield's achievements in the political arena were so overwhelming that it is easy to underevaluate those he made in his chosen profession of Law. For, as we have seen, he was called to the bar in 1961. His brilliance in the legal field was matched only by his prowess in the political arena.

With his eloquence, tenacity and natural passion for justice, Cecil Wallace-Whitfield soon earned a reputation, throughout the Bahamas, as an outstanding defence attorney; for by temperament and training he was more suited for the atmosphere of the court than the more mundane and routine work of the chamber. This ability was certainly demonstrated in the protracted case of Mr. D'Arcy Ryan in his highly contested battle for citizenship of the Commonwealth of the Bahamas, which went "all the way to the privy council"! Eventually, Mr. Ryan won his appeals and was granted citizenship.

In recognition, then, of his sterling contributions in public life as a politician and elder statesman, and in private practice as an eminent defense attorney, Cecil Wallace-Whitfield was awarded a Knighthood (Knight Bachelor) by Queen Elizabeth II on July 25, 1989 at Buckingham Palace, London, United Kingdom. The proverbial saying "better late than never" proved to be most apt with regard to the bestowal of this crowning honor in the twilight of his sojourn through this transitory life.

Sir Cecil Wallace-Whitfield, at the time of his demise, was joined in matrimony to the former Naomi Rosetta Darville. This dignified daughter of long island in her inimitable manner earned the respect of all Bahamians (regardless of race, religion, or political affiliation), affectionately known as "Lady Whitfield-Wallace" or simply "Lady Naomi". As a result of this and his two previous conjugal unions, Sir Cecil Wallace-

Whitfield was the beloved father of eight children including:

Cecil Vincent, Jr.

Kenneth Gascoyne

Paul Andrew

Merle Nicolette

Justina Ann

Joseph (Joey) Alexander

Robert Christopher

David Godfrey

He proved to be a good father to them all, ensuring that they received an adequate education. In contacts with them, the narrator found them to be very fond of their father, whom they greatly loved. Moreover, his sons always spoke very highly of their father, whom they obviously admired as an excellent role model. It is, therefore, not surprising that two of them followed him by serving in the legal profession the land of their birth!

His Enduring Legacy

What then can we say, in summary, about the life and contributions of Sir Cecil Wallace-Whitfield? What lessons can we discern in them to help us in tackling the challenges we are bound to encounter in our own journey?

Well, first of all, we can certainly be reminded of the absolute priority of perseverance, of not giving up too quickly or easily, of being persistent in carrying out whatever task or responsibilities we are called upon to fulfill.

Remember that Sir Cecil Wallace-Whitfield failed in his first two attempts to represent his people in Parliament. And even after he was successful on the third attempt, there were three more occasions, in his political life that he failed to win a seat in The House. Despite these setbacks, Sir Cecil Wallace-

Whitfield never gave up. For, had he done so after any of these disappointing experiences, he would not have become the outstanding figure in the political history of the Bahamas that he eventually was. For, our overall achievements in life depend as much upon how we cope with our failures as how we handle success. As Kipling poetically put it, you can achieve greatness "If you can meet with triumph and disaster and treat both those imposters as the same." This leads directly to the second lesson we can learn from the life and contributions of Sir Cecil Wallace-Whitfield—the inestimable value of immediate action. This means being alert to discern the opportunities which come our way, and exercising the courage to take full advantage of them!

Indeed, those who can take full advantage of opportunities and act immediately upon them usually "rise to the top"; such a person was Sir Cecil Wallace-Whitfield. Always courageous, never afraid to act, he knew nothing of procrastination, or hesitation. The motto of the old Western Senior School, often repeated by the late T. G. Glover, was the Latin proverb, "Carpe Diem!" It really means "Grasp the opportunity!"

Like other great Bahamians—such as Sir Milo Butler and Rev. Edwin Taylor, Sir Roland Symonette and Pastor Keith Albury, Sir Cecil Wallace-Whitfield knew when opportunities came his way and how to use his God-given abilities in taking full advantage of them! There is much "food for thought here".

The late Dr. Myles Munroe, in his many sermons, speeches and books, consistently reminded us that God has a purpose for the life of each and every one of us. In the same vein, Bishop Laish Boyd of the Anglican Diocese of Nassau, The Turks and Caicos Islands assures, "God has a mission for you!"

It behooves us, therefore, to seek to discern what is God's purpose or mission for us, and then, using diligently the gifts with which he has enabled us, and the opportunities which come our way.

Let us, then, seek to discern what is in the Creator's purpose of mission for our life. Then, using the gifts and talents He has given us, and the opportunities which come our way, let us give ourselves, with passion and persistence, to attaining it for, this edifying goal as expressed in our National Anthem is treading the road which leads to God.

Now, it is germane to bear in mind that the virtues observed in the life of Sir Cecil Wallace-Whitfield—persistence and immediate action—are by no means unique. Rather, as we have seen, they may be discerned in some measure in the lives of all Bahamians Who Made a Difference. Indeed, they are among the virtues universally recognized as essential for effective leadership.

What then was the unique contribution of Sir Cecil Wallace-Whitfield which he accomplished for the benefit of his people using his peculiar gifts and opportunities? The answer to those questions becomes abundantly clear when upon careful examination of his political career. It certainly had to do with his ability to elicit the loyalty of others and to inspire them to work together for the common good. These charismatic abilities were consistently demonstrated by Sir Cecil Wallace-Whitfield in the turbulent years leading up to and immediately following his dramatic "free at last" blast.

Now, as well known, the United Bahamian Party was defeated by the Progressive Liberal Party in the general election of 1967, and more decisively, in that of 1968.

After these major setbacks and with the departure of Sir Stafford Sands and several other staunch supporters, it entered into a period of rapid decline. Indeed, with comparatively few seats in the House of Assembly, and unable to garner many votes due to the stigma of "'racism," it gradually ceased to perform as a viable opposition to the Progressive Liberal Party. But, since as it has been truly said, "Nature above a vacuum, an opposition began to emerge within the ranks of the governing party.

This resulted in, as we have seen, in Sir Cecil Wallace-Whitfield leading "The Dissident Eight" in leaving the PLP. In keeping with the theme of his "Free at Last" speech" they adopted the name "free PLP". The members of the United Bahamian Party, realizing that they could not continue in the way they did, joined with the Free PLP to establish the Free National Movement.

All the Members of Parliament known as "The Dissident Eight" were defeated in the General Election in 1972. Indeed, the fledgling Free National Movement went down to a crushing defeat in that election when the main issue was Independence for the Bahamas. Moreover, the FNM, defeated in one election after another, remained in the political wilderness or opposition until attaining a victory at the Polls in 1992, under the leadership of the youthful, decisive Right Hon. Hubert Alexander Ingraham.

Now, Sir Cecil Wallace-Whitfield did not live to experience this most important watershed in the political march of the people of his beloved Bahamaland, but there can be not a shadow of a doubt that it was largely through his relentless effort and strong leadership that it came about.

For, considering the diverse nature of those who came together to form it—dissident PLPs, members of the UBP, remnants of the Bahamas Democratic Party (BDP)—it might have been thought that the FNM, after so many defeats in general elections, might have fallen into disarray. But it was through the courageous leadership of Sir Cecil Wallace-Whitfield that it survived and eventually thrived in Opposition. He managed to hold together and inspire the various factions, to work together in adversity. Yet, he proved to be the master welder who bonded together the varied groups that came together to form the FNM. He was the human glue that made them into a cohesive political unit able to move from being H.M. Loyal Opposition to become the Government of The Commonwealth of the Bahamas.

Now, in retrospect, the contribution of Sir Cecil Wallace-Whitfield is hard to over- estimate. For in his successful effort to establish the Free National Movement into a viable opposition to the PLP, he contributed most significantly to the preservation of democracy in the Commonwealth of the

Bahamas. Indeed, no less an authority than veteran politician an Elder Statesman, a founding member of the PLP, Fifth Governor General of The Commonwealth of The Bahamas, on several occasions, paid high tribute to Sir Cecil for his part in ensuring that the Government of The Bahamas operated in the democratic manner.

For the democratic form of government posits the existence of the two-party system, in which there is a governing party, duly elected by all citizens, matched by a viable opposition party which monitors its activities and is capable also of governing the country.

This effectiveness of the two-party system (or at least two parties) has been demonstrated in the great democratic nations of the world over many centuries—the United Kingdom, the United States of America, Germany, France, Jamaica, India, the world's largest democracy based on the ancient principle (going back to Greece) that all citizens should be afforded the opportunity to participated in the government of their nation, it has been thus described by President Abraham Lincoln: "Government of the people, by the people, for the people." It is the reason why a Barak Obama, born in humble circumstances in Hawaii has been able to become President of the USA. Moreover, it is why the opposition party in the UK and nations which have adopted the Westminster form of democracy is known as Her Majesty's Loyal Opposition.

Sir Cecil Wallace-Whitfield, then, in establishing that there was in place a strong viable opposition party, did contribute most significantly to the preservation of the democratic form of Government in the Commonwealth of the Bahamas.

As Mr. David Wallace summed it up "The Greatest Contribution of Sir Cecil Wallace-Whitfield was the preservation of the two-party system of government." Indeed, if Sir Roland Symonette is justly called "The Father of the House," and Sir Lynden Pindling is known as "The Father of The Nation," then it is submitted that Sir Cecil Wallace-Whitfield may be most appropriately designated "The Champion of Democracy".

"Champion" is a term which may be applied, generally speaking to the life of Sir Cecil Wallace-Whitfield. Through his life he was engaged in many battles and he courageously dealt with them all. There can be no doubt that this was one reason why he was respected by all Bahamians. It can be truly said that he was greatly admired by many who were always, loyal to him. Such a person is Mr. Gordon Cooper, who used to serve as Sir Cecil's chauffeur on trips to Nassau, who proudly described himself as "a Free National!"

Besides his courage, there was another positive tract that he displayed—patriotism. While many Bahamians disagreed with him politically speaking, yet on the whole; they held him in high regard. Why? They sensed in him a genuine sense of identification to his native land. Yes, like Sir Roland Symonette and Paul Adderley, Sir Milo Butler and The Hon. Loftus Roker, he was at heart a fierce nationalist who dearly loved the people of the land of his birth. "Land of our birth we pledge to thee."

Yes, Cecil Wallace-Whitfield was a champion. "A warrior in every sense of the word -- yet warrior though he was, he succumbed to that formidable foe which has caused the demise of many of his fellow Bahamians—Cancer!

The extent to which his Christian faith informed the thoughts, actions and the general course of the eventful life of Sir Cecil Wallace-Whitfield is not too easy to discern. For, he was not vocal in expressing his religious convictions. Yet it can be asserted that his Christian faith was an important component of his life.

Like many "Hill Toppers" of his generation, he was an active member of St. Mary the Virgin Anglican Church. He served at the altar of what was truly a community church. Its Rector in those days was the diligent Parish Priest known by all as "Father Holmes". Serving then as a bearer of the Crucifix, young Cecil Wallace-Whitfield could be seen leading the procession of the congregation through the community at its annual Patronal Festival. Throughout his life Sir Cecil Wallace-Whitfield remained a faithful member of that congregation.

Now, in measuring the contribution of Sir Cecil Wallace-Whitfield, comparison is inevitably made with that of his major political counterpart—Sir Lynden Oscar Pindling. For despite the much touted and publicized differences and political banter between them, they indeed, had much in common. Very much! Note then that both were born in 1930, at dates not far apart, and grew up, on East Street and were strong respectively in the turbulent post-world war era.

Squadron Leader Lester Brown

December 2, 1915 – September 10, 1994

Super soldier in war...Super salesman in peace!

INTRODUCTION

The annals of humankind are replete with the exploits of those where great military leaders, men of tremendous fortitude and valor, who excelled during times of war. Such were Tiglath Pileser of Assyria, Emperor Julius Caesar of Rome, and Admiral Horatio Nelson of England, Napoleon Bonaparte of France, and General Dwight Eisenhower of the United States of America. On the other hand, there were those who have made their major contributions, and have excelled during peace time. These include people of the caliber of Hippocrates "Father of Medicine"; Cicero, legal luminary; the Rothschilds, Jewish bankers; Helen Keller, blind heroine, and clergyman and civil rights advocate Martin Luther King, Jr.

Here and there (very rare), however, there have arisen those multi-talented geniuses who have managed to excel in both the military and civilian spheres of human activity. Such an extraordinary personality was proud son of Bahamian soil...Squadron Leader Lester Brown, World War II hero and successful realtor!

"THE CALL OF DUTY"

Lester Brown was born into an old distinguished Bahamian family, renowned for its prowess in maritime exploits! His father Captain Willard Brown was the patriarch of a large, happy, and closely-knit family including his wife and their children including Geoffrey and Anton.

In a sense most profound and "prophetic," his birth during World War I was no mere coincidence, but a harbinger of one destined to play a significant role in the unfolding of the momentous events of World War II![lxxvii]

Young Lester, who was nurtured in the Christian faith at Ebenezer Methodist Church, received his education, at both primary and secondary levels at Queen's College, a Methodist foundation.

Now, the youthful Lester Brown grew up at a time when dark clouds of tension were developing in Europe, exacerbated by the rapid ascendency of the infamous Adolf Hitler to power in Germany. Endowed with an adventurous spirit by the Almighty, Lester Brown delighted to taken on new challenges. It was not surprising, therefore, that when, at the onset of World War II, Great Britain made an appeal to all the able bodied men of its then extensive empire to participate in combat, he was amongst the first five Bahamians to volunteer to serve in this way. They were known as ".The Gallant Five," the others being Fane Solomon, John Mills, Ivor Thompson and John Maura.

Thus at age twenty-four, Lester Brown left the Bahamas to embark upon a military career, which was to prove most remarkable!

SUPER SOLDIER IN WAR

Like most Bahamians who responded to the call of military duty in World War II, Lester Brown elected to serve in the Royal Air Force. Evidently, with his natural adventurous spirit, the challenge of the operation of aircraft appealed greatly to him. It is germane to bear in mind that the aircraft industry was still in its infancy as all planes were propeller driven, requiring much more in terms of human skill and courage than the highly computerized jet liners flying around the world today.[lxxviii]

During his training in England, Lester Brown demonstrated a special aptitude in flying. This proved to be a real advantage; there was a great demand for trained pilots as the war escalated both in intensity and extent. Indeed, the combat spread throughout Northern and Central Europe into Italy and even North Africa!

Immediately upon completion of his training, the young Bahamian pilot was engaged in military combat "in the sky". The highlight of the early period of his outstanding military career was participation in the bombing expedition, which resulted in the expulsion of the greatly feared German General Rommel from North Africa!

The energetic pilot, then moved rapidly through the ranks eventually being promoted to the post of Squadron Leader. In this capacity, the crowning achievement of his eventful life, he led squadrons of up to twenty-four wings in bombing expeditions over Germany and France.

By this time, Squadron Leader Brown had been abroad engaged in military combat for nearly four years. And as a patriotic Bahamian, he no doubt, had a desire to return home. Fortunately, there was a major war-time project in the Bahamas, which facilitated this move back home.

As we have seen, the escalation of military activity during World War II called for the training of many pilots to "man" the rapidly growing fleet of military aircraft. However, the unpredictable, rainy weather of "The Mother Country" severely limited the number of days available for training the urgently needed pilots. On the other hand, the Bahamas with its warm subtropical climate with warm sunshine virtually every day of the year, proved ideal for this purpose. Accordingly, the Royal Air force established a huge base for the training of its pilots. It is noteworthy that this, and other military installations built by the United States proved to be the economic mainstay of the Colony after the sudden collapse of the sponge industry.

Now, Squadron Leader Lester Brown, as a Bahamian war hero was most certainly the ideal person to serve as Commander of the Royal Air Force military facility in the Bahamas. Duly installed in this post, he served with distinction and great competence. His prowess in this capacity was demonstrated by the fact that he proved to be as adept in instructing experienced pilots as "raw recruits" in the intricate control of comparatively primitive aircraft of World War II.

SUPER SALESMAN IN PEACE

After the end of World War II on November 11, 1945 (at the 11th hour of the 11th day of the 11th month! World War II hero, still a young man, faced the challenge of re-adjusting to civilian life. Concisely, he was ready "to settle down"...to get a job..., get married and raise a family.

Accordingly, in 1950 he married Mary McPherson. Consequently they became the proud parents of two children, Deborah and Ian Lester.

With regard to civilian employment, the young Bahamian war hero had served as manager of the Shell Oil Company in Bermuda, where he had resided for three years. He then returned home where he served in a similar capacity.

His real "breakthrough" in the private sector, however, came when he resigned, and entered into partnership with his father-in-law in the lucrative real estate market. When the real estate company McPherson and Brown was established, the Bahamian economy was riding the crest of a post-World War II economic boom. Largely through the efforts of Sir Stafford Sands, the Bahamas was becoming a major tourist destination and financial center. Many wealthy persons, some fleeing from the cold climate, others avoiding the high taxes of the developed nations of the North Atlantic, were flocking to the warm tax free Isles of June. This influx of affluent residents resulted in a great demand for expensive properties. The firm of McPherson & Brown flourished by catering to this niche market. For more than thirty years, then, Lester Brown remained as a major, highly effective sales executive in the flourishing Bahamian real estate industry. Thus, this great Bahamian, who began and pursued his adventurous career as a bold, invincible pilot in combat in the air abroad, ended it as a very successful businessman during peace time... "At home!"

Squadron Leader Lester Brown, despite his many years of service in the commercial business world, never really severed his ties with matters military. For, he was at heart a military man, obviously extremely proud of his achievements in that most challenging and exacting field of human endeavor.

For instance, during "the war" His Royal Highness the Duke of Windsor, appointed him as The Military ADC to the Royal Governors of the Bahamas, a post he held for twenty-two years. Then, as a well-recognized war hero, it was "with pride and joy" that he participated in the annual observance of Remembrance Sunday at The Cenotaph, conveniently located on the grounds of The Nassau Public Library. The writer vividly recalls how impressed he was to see one whom he admired as a hero of World War II at one of these ceremonies at The Cenotaph. There he stood, erect as a lamp post, smartly attired in his khaki Royal Air Force uniform complete with all his colorful military decorations including:

Distinguished Flying Cross

Air Crew Europe Star with France and Germany clasp

North Africa Star with 8th Army Rosette

Burma Star

Defense Medal

Victory Medal

Squadron Leader Lester Brown, truly "A Bahamian Who Made a Difference"...in war and in peace!

QUESTIONS FOR GROUP DISCUSSION AND EXERCISES

1. Squadron Leader Lester Brown is well-recognized as a hero of World War II. Name two other Bahamians who may be described as war heroes. Give at least two reasons for your answer.

2. Tell what you know about three of the following:

   The Royal Air Force; The British Legion; "The eleventh hour of the eleventh day of the eleventh month; military decorations.

3. "Let there be peace on earth, and let it begin with me!" What practical steps can you take to promote or bring about peace "in your community"?

Mary "May" Ingraham

July 30, 1901 – March 26, 1982

Founding President of the Bahamas Women's Suffrage Movement

"**M**ary Ingraham was a strong-willed and intelligent woman. These were the very attributes that enabled her to complete the work destiny had assigned to her in the Women's Suffrage Movement. "May", as she was affectionately called, was born on July 30, 1901 in New Providence. A housewife, she became actively involved in politics in the late 1940s when her husband, Rufus, was a Member of the House of Assembly for the Crooked Island and Acklins Districts. In the 1949 General Election, her husband lost his seat; and he attributed his loss to the fact that women were not allowed to vote. He felt that most of the males who were eligible to vote did so only in exchange for materialistic things such as alcohol or cash, which his opponents were able to supply. The experience of her husband impressed upon Mary the need for women to be able to vote. She had been agitating the powers-that-be for some time to give women equal voting rights with men, but she had been unsuccessful, until she joined forces with some other strong-willed and intelligent women."[lxxix]

"In 1950 Mrs. Mabel Walker, wife of PLP Parliamentarian C. R. Walker and a long time close friend of the family, approached Mrs. Ingraham on behalf of a young women's group wanting to know how to go about getting the vote for women. Mary was willing to work with them to bring about this change. The women formed a committee, the Women's Suffrage Movement. Mary already had some experience in the fight and was made chairman; Georgiana K. Symonette, later chairman of the Women's Branch of the PLP, was made vice chairman; Eugenia Lockhart was its secretary; and Althea Mortimer, Mabel C. Walker, and Muriel Eneas were members. Most of these women held influential positions in various female organizations of that period: Mabel Walker had established the Teachers Union and was working to get recognition for it; and Mrs. Ingraham was a Past Daughter Ruler of the Elks of the World and Past Matron of the Order of Eastern Stars.

"The committee evolved in structure, size, and effectiveness between 1950 and 1962. In 1958 Doris Johnson joined the Movement as spokesperson and mobilized the movement into a fighting force. Following two Petitions, an executive meeting with Lennox Boyd, an epochal speech by Doris Johnson on the moral imperative of universal adult suffrage to members of Parliament, and a visit to the Secretary of State for the Colonies in London, Mr. Stafford Sands tabled a Bill "to enable women to have and exercise rights of registration as voters and of voting similar to those accorded to men....' The Bill passed Parliament in February 23, 1961. It came into effect on June 30, 1962; and women 21 years or older voted for the first time on November 26, 1962."

A Brief History of the Women's Movement in The Bahamas

1929 September	•Return of Mother Francis Butler from the United States and the founding of the Mother's Club. (Mother Butler, Mrs. Violet Chase, Mrs. Winifred Mortimer and Mrs. Blanche Thurston)
1942 June	•The Burma Road Riot
1948	•The beginning of the Women's Suffrage Movement. Women began to agitate for the right to vote. •Mrs. Mary Ingraham was the president and founder of the movement. (Mrs. Georgianna K. Symonette, Mrs. Mabel Walker, Mrs. Eugenia Lockhart, Dame Bertha Isaacs, Mrs. Grace Wilson, Mrs. Mildred Moxey, Mrs. Ethel Kein, Mrs. Gladys Bailey and the support of thousands other Bahamian women).
1951	•Mrs. Mary Ingraham and Mrs. Mabel Walker attended a sitting of the House of Assembly. They resolved that women should be able to be allowed to vote equally with men.
1952	•Dr. C. R. Walker presented a Petition to the House of Assembly demanding that women have the right to vote. Mr. A. F. Adderley did likewise in the Legislative Council.
1952-57	•Alignment with the new and emerging political party - the Progressive Liberal Party.
1958	•The General Strike.
June	•The Federation of Labour pledged its support to the Women's Suffrage Movement in recognition of its contribution to Trade Unions. •Sir Gerald Cash supported by Sir Milo Butler presented another petition to the House of Assembly. •Emergence of the National Council of Women. •Dame Dr. Doris Johnson returns from University abroad and joins the Movement. •The Women's Suffrage Movement petitioned the Colonial Secretary to present their plea for enfranchisement to the British Government.
1959 January 20	•Dame Dr. Doris Johnson led a demonstration, presented a petition to the House of Assembly and demanded that women have the right to vote. In an impassioned speech, she also asked for the inclusion of females on juries and as members of boards and committees and called for the end of sending delinquent girls between the ages of 8-11 to jail and for the appointment of female Justices of the Peace. •The following day the movement led by Mrs. Mary Ingraham attended Government House and demanded that the law be changed.
1959	•The General Assembly Election Act was passed, granting universal suffrage to males of 21 years of age. IT DID NOT INCLUDE THE RIGHT OF WOMEN TO VOTE.
1960	•Bye-election the PLP championed the right of women to vote. •Dame Dr. Doris Johnson, Mrs. Eugenia Lockhart and Sir Henry Milton Taylor (then Chairman of the PLP) go to England to present a petition to the Secretary of State for the Colonies.
1961	•A report was laid before the House of Assembly giving women the right to vote but effective January, 1963. This was unacceptable. An act was passed for the enfranchisement of women with effect from June 1962.
June 23	•Mrs. Mary Ingraham in radio broadcast addressed the nation urging all women to register to vote.
July	•Women began to register to vote.
November	•Women in The Bahamas voted for the first time.
1962-67	•Women became actively involved in the political campaign of the Progressive Liberal Party.
1967	•Majority Rule - The first black Bahamian Government. •Dame Dr. Doris Johnson appointed the first Senator and Cabinet Minister (without Portfolio). She was later appointed Minister of Transport.
1968	•The Appointment of Dame Dr. Doris Johnson as the first female President of the Senate.
1982	•Mrs. Janet Bostwick elected as the first female member of the House of Assembly.
1997	R. Italia Johnson was the first female Speaker of the House of Assembly (268 years).
2000	•Umbrella - National Organization Of Women's Association in The Bahamas (NOWAB).
January 2002	Dame Ivy Dumont was confirmed first female Governor-General.
May 2002	The Honourable Cynthia A. Pratt was appointed Deputy Prime Minister and Minister of National Security.

Bishop
Michael Eldon
(August 8, 1931—February 7, 2011)

"Then the word of the LORD came unto me, saying, 'Before I formed thee in the belly I knew thee, and before thou camest forth out of the womb I sanctified thee a prophet unto the nations,'"
Jeremiah 1:4-5, AV

"But each of us was given grace according to the measure of Christ's gift. Therefore it is said, 'When He ascended on high He made captivity a captive; He gave gifts to His people.' The gits He gave were that some would be apostles, some prophets, some evangelist, some pastors and teachers, to equip the saints for the work of the ministry, for the building up of the body of Christ, until all of us come to the unity of the faith, to the measure of the full stature of Christ."

Ephesians 4:7-8, 11-13, NRSV

"To whom much is given, much is expected." – The Master

Many and varied are the ways in which, and the seasons of life, that the call of God to ministry comes to His servants. For instance, there have been (and continue to be) those devout men and women, who, like the First Apostles and St. Paul, received and responded to the call as mature adults then, there are those, like the boy Samuel and the Prophet Isaiah who responded to the call of God while "in the flower of youth" or even childhood. Moreover, there have arisen in every generation those rare men and women of God, who, evidently, have always been aware of the call and claim of God upon their lives, who, like the prophet Jeremiah, "from womb to tomb", have proved to have been mightily used of God *"According to His purpose."* (Rom. 8:28) Such a servant of Christ was Michael Hartley Eldon, affectionately known by Bahamians of all ethnic and socio-economic groups and all religious persuasions simply as "Bishop Eldon". For as Bishop Gilbert Thompson observes "For as long as anyone knew Michael Eldon, he wanted to be a priest."[lxxx]

"Growing up on Delancey Street"

Michael Hartley Eldon was born August 8, 1931, into an old Bahamian family.

His father, The Rev. Sidney Eldon, was, in every respect, a pioneer, who, in several ways, did "make a difference!"

A very competent and highly respected civil servant, he rose "through the ranks" to become Comptroller of HM Customs, being the first Bahamian to serve in this very important and prestigious office!

An active and devout churchman, who with his family (including his faithful wife, Rowena, Michael and his younger sister, Keva) every Sunday at St. Mary's Anglican Church, he was amongst the first company of Bahamian Lay Persons to be appointed a Diocesan Permanent Deacon.

lsの،

These pioneering achievements must have been harbingers of "things to come" as both his children proved to be outstanding citizens of their homeland achieving a number of "firsts" in their respective careers.

Now, the Rev. Sidney Eldon was a disciplinarian "from the old school." Accordingly, he and his wife, brought up their children, in a highly disciplined home on Delancey Street, then, very significantly, a well-recognized venue of Bahamian education! Thus, like many other Bahamians of his generation who became distinguished law abiding contributing citizens of our beloved Bahamaland, Michael Eldon was, indeed, "A Hill Topper"!

The Eldons, in common with all ambitious Bahamian families of their generation, placed very high priority on education, and saw to it that their children received the best education available! Nurtured in such an environment, it should not be surprising that young Michael Hartley Eldon grew up to contribute major achievements in those two very important closely related, but clearly distinguishing from each other disciplines religion and education.

Compassionate Bahamian Priest and Prelate

Michael Hartley Eldon was admitted to Queen's College, then one of the premier institutions of education in the Bahamas, at the tender age of six and continued there until he completed his education "at home". As Bishop Thompson observes:

> "Having gained entry Michael displayed superior academic brilliance and athletic prowess by dominating his contemporaries with brains and brawn. He graduated as

Head Boy and obtained a first class Cambridge School Certificate."[lxxxi]

The young Bahamian, then, entered St. Catherine's College, Cambridge University, where he earned a Bachelor of Arts degree. At that time when "one could count on the fingers of one's hands" the numbers of Bahamians who had earned academic degrees, his obtaining of a degree from the most prestigious Cambridge University, certainly made a tremendous impact upon the entire Bahamian community. Indeed, the narrator vividly recall that a picture of him along with a "write up" appeared on the front pages of the local media. In keeping with his priestly vocation, he then continued his studies at St. Stephen's College, Oxford University concentrating on preparation for the General Ordination Examination.

In common with a number of Bahamians who made a difference, young Eldon was gifted with a "photographic memory enabling him to achieve much in the world of academia. It is no small wonder that he excelled in general and theological disciplines at the two leading British institutions of tertiary education.

Concisely, at a comparatively young age, he was well prepared to serve the Lord in ministry amongst the people of his homeland He, therefore, returned home in 1954 and immediately embarked upon a most active ministry, which was bound to affect the lives of many.

Thus, on July 22, 1954, Michael Hartley Eldon was made a Deacon, and on August 10, 1955 he was ordained to the sacred priesthood. The impressive Ordination Service took place at Christ Church Cathedral, the Rite of Ordination being administered by Bishop Spence Burton.

After serving in several parishes in Nassau, the young priest was assigned to serve in the Island of Grand Bahama. Youthful and energetic, he managed to serve very well in the Anglican churches in one of the largest islands in the colony. Greatly beloved by the people of that island, he developed a reputation of being a compassionate priest, who knew all his members very well. Thus, in 1967 he was appointed rural dean for the Northern Bahamas. His gifts as a pastor were matched by his ability as an ecclesiastical administrator.

He, therefore, moved rapidly through the ranks of the priesthood and it was evident that he was bound and with his many gifts and talents, backed up by academic brilliance, it was evident that the young priest "was destined for greatness".

At that time, the winds of political change were blowing throughout the Caribbean and the peoples of these colonial territories were seeking to gain independence. At the ecclesiastical level, this was manifested in the promotion of native clergy to serve in the episcopal level of ministry. Jamaica, for instance already had its first native born Bishop in the person of the eminent Bishop Percival Gibson. There can be no doubt that a similar move towards the elevation of indigenous clergy to the Episcopate was beginning to impact the life of the church. Very significantly, indeed, providentially Bishop Bernard Markham was conscious of this "movement of the Spirit" and identified the Rev. Michael Eldon as well qualified to serve in episcopal office. Accordingly, he nominated Him as his Suffragan Bishop in 1971.

Events then, moved rapidly as the Anglican community in the Bahamas eagerly anticipated the advance of Michael Hartley Eldon to the top ecclesiastical post in the Diocese. It was not long in coming. For, as Thompson recalls:

> Bishop Markham having prepared the Anglican Church for a black Bishop announced his retirement from the Diocese with the sense that he had played the role of a predecessor or herald. At this time Bishop Eldon was nominated a priest and seconded by a lay person as a Bishop of the Diocese on April 20, 1972.[lxxxii]

Thus, when Michael Hartley Eldon was enthroned at Christ Church Cathedral, it was, therefore, "A Red Letter Day" for the church in the Bahamas when on May 28, 1972, Michael Eldon was enthroned as Lord Bishop of The Diocese of The Bahamas, Turks and Caicos Islands. And while Anglicans rejoiced at the elevation of this popular priest to the Episcopate, there can be no doubt that all Bahamians, whatever may have been their religious persuasion, felt a deep sense of pride when at long last "a son of the soil" was called upon to serve in the highest ecclesiastical post in these islands.

Under the dynamic and energetic leadership of Bishop Michael Hartley Eldon, the Anglican Church in the Bahamas, Turks & Caicos Islands made tremendous progress in every respect. Here it is germane to pause and reflect on what may be described as the three major stages in the development of Christianity in the colonial territories, or churches established by missionary boards or societies of Churches in the developed Christian nations of the North Atlantic. These include:

1. **A Mission Church**

   At this stage the local church is almost entirely dependent upon the Mission Board of "The Mother Church. Missionaries, then do most of the pastoral work. Grants supplied by the mission board provide funds for the operation of the church.

2. **A Self-supporting Church**

   While missionaries continue to serve, the local congregations gradually are able to provide funds to provide stipends for those in ministry. The training of local clergy takes place as more and more of them take up positions in the church and the missionaries gradually depart.

3. **Church with a Mission**

   At this stage, the Church is in a position to provide funding for the ministry and the building of new churches. At the theological level, local clergy write books and contribute to the theological development of the church. There are now more than enough locally trained ministers to fulfil the needs of the church and it now send some of them to serve as missionaries abroad.[lxxxiii]

   Utterly crucial for movement of the church from the first to the second and eventually third stages is the training of local clergy to serve alongside the missionaries, and eventually to take full responsibility for the operation of the Church.

   Now, in the case of the Anglican Church, movement from the first to the second stage began as early as 1839 when the Rev.

William Kensal Duncombe became the first Bahamian to be ordained to the priesthood This remarkable evangelical priest served at Harbour Island where he established a theological seminary, which indeed led to the training of more Bahamians. This process, however, of attracting more Bahamians to serve in the priesthood was rapidly "a stepped up" during the ministry of Bishop Michael Eldon. There were several reasons for this trend.

In the first place, the very presence of Michael Eldon as a Bahamian, who had moved through the ranks of the ministry to become Bishop was an incentive and encouragement to other young Bahamians to serve in the priesthood.

More pertinently, however, was the fact that Bishop Eldon himself passionately pursued a policy of recruiting and encouraging young, and not so young Bahamians to serve in the ministry. As Archdeacon Harry Bain, Rector of the Cathedral of Christ the King stated, Bishop Eldon was very interested in recruiting indigenous clergy.[lxxxiv] Accordingly, many Bahamians did come forward and responded to the call of God to serve in the ministry of the Church during the ministry of Bishop Michael Eldon. Indeed, men were ordained to the priesthood.

The record, then, of Bishop Eldon here is impressive. Many men were ordained to the priesthood during his ministry.

The financial viability of the Church also was greatly enhanced by Bishop Michael Eldon A greater emphasis was placed upon Christian stewardship as members were challenged to devote more of their material resources to the work of God this increase in income placed the Diocese in a stronger financial position and there was no need for grants from abroad. Companion relationships, however, were developed with congregations in the USA in terms of what was known as MRI, Mutual Responsibility and Independence. This called for a mutual sharing of resources rather than the "mission church" receiving support from the Church in the developed nations.

There was rapid expansion of the Church with new congregations being established especially in the rapidly growing communities in the Southern and South Eastern sections of New Providence. All in all then the Church did grow rapidly under the leadership of Bishop Eldon. Indeed, it moved from the second to the third stage becoming not merely a self-supporting church but a church with a mission with a number of Anglican clergypersons serving in other dioceses in the region of North America.

Now, throughout his ministry, Bishop Eldon travelled extensively in the Bahamas, Turks and Caicos Islands. Indeed, according to some who knew him well, he was more "at home" in the Family Islands and the Turks & Caicos Islands than he was in New Providence, where he was nurtured in the Christian faith and spent his formative years. He made it a point of duty, therefore, to get to as many churches in the Family Islands and the Turks & Caicos Islands as he possibly could in any given year. The people of the remote Family Island settlements, especially certainly appreciated the interest he demonstrated in them and in turn were greatly loved by them. This was well expressed by His Grace Bishop Laish Boyd, who eulogized him thusly:

> "Michael Eldon was a popular, beloved, gentle people's person. He had a deep faith in God and high hopes for people. He was passionate about improving people and their lot. He loved the Church, loved being in church and loved the worship of the Church."[lxxxv]

EMINENT EDUCATOR

Such, then were the achievements of Michael Hartley Eldon when serving as Lord Bishop of The Bahamas, Turks and Caicos Islands. It has to be pointed out, however, that his accomplishments in the field of education were no less impressive and far-reaching.[lxxxvi] For, throughout his ministry, he placed very high priority upon education in keeping with his background growing up on Delancey Street in a home where education was valued.

Interestingly enough, he was the first Bahamian to serve as a teacher on the staff of St. John's College. He had a short stint there in 1947 before going to study in England and upon his return he taught for a year in the field of Mathematics. As has been pointed out, when this young Bahamian earned his degree from Cambridge in 1950 there were very few Bahamians who had reached such a stage in their education. Thus, when St. John's College was established in 1947 virtually all the members of staff were white expatriates. Michael Eldon, then, was the first Bahamian to serve on the staff of St. John's College. It was to prove to be the first of several "firsts" of his eventful career.

Bishop Michael Eldon's major contribution in the field of education, however, was his many years of public service as Chairman of the Board of The College of The Bahamas. He was appointed to serve in this capacity at its inception in 1975 and he served, for twenty years. Taking into consideration that this was a post in the educational sector which was entirely under the control of "the powers that be", it must be concluded that he served in a very competent manner. With a rapid succession of principals/presidents especially in the early years of the existence of The College of The Bahamas, his long tenure as Chairman of the Board provided an element of stability and continuity which were crucial in the ongoing operation of this most important Bahamian institution of tertiary education.

The contributions of this remarkable man of God in the field of education have not gone unrecognized.

Thus, in Grand Bahama, the main educational institution operated by the Anglican Church has been renamed in honour of Bishop Eldon. Then, a modern new complex at the College of the Bahamas has also been named in recognition of the contribution of this remarkable Bahamian clergyman to education.

Bahamian Patriot

His Grace the Rt. Rev. Michael Eldon served at the helm of the Anglican Church at a time of rapid political change.

When he returned to serve at home in 1954, the winds of political change were blowing through the Bahamas. During the year of his service in the priesthood events such as "Black Friday" and the attainment of Majority Rule certainly indicated that the people of the Bahamas were moving towards Independence. And very significantly, consecrated Bishop of the Bahamas, Turks and Caicos Islands—a matter of months before the Bahamas became independent on July 10, 1973.[lxxxvii]

Bishop Eldon, like his contemporaries in ecclesiastical office, including the President of the Bahamas Christian Council and the Bishop of the Catholic Church the Rev. Paul Leonard Hagerty, was supportive of the people of the Bahamas in moving in their direction. Just as the Catholic Bishop released Father Joseph Perna to serve as Secretary of the Bahamas Christian Council during this period, Bishop Michael Eldon appointed Archdeacon William Thompson to represent the Anglican Church in that then most influential ecclesiastical body.[lxxxviii]

This should not be surprising for as has been intimated, Bishop Eldon loved the Bahamian people and was concerned for their advancement in every way. Without entering into politics Bishop Michael Eldon, certainly supported the people of the Bahamas in their quest for Independence. According he was, indeed, present at Clifford Park along with other religious leaders on that historic night July 9th when the Rev. Dr. Reuben Cooper, Sr. preached that earth shattering sermon "To Save A Nation" and when the Union Jack was lowered, even as the black, gold and aquamarine flag was raised signalling the birth of a new nation the Commonwealth of The Bahamas.[lxxxix]

Man of Great Ability…Greater Humility!

That Michael Hartley Eldon was a very gifted person there can be no doubt. For, besides being a compassionate Pastor and competent Church Administrator, he was a brilliant theologian who served the

Church not only in the Bahamas but throughout the region. According to peruse carefully any document, grasping the salient points with great facility. By the same token, he could absorb much information about people and thus knew his parishioners by name.

Remarkably humble, Bishop Eldon never boasted about his gifts and abilities, leaving others to draw attention to them. The narrator recalls a conversation with his sister, Dr. Keva Bethel, past President of The College of The Bahamas, in which she reminded him that "Michael is quite a theologian!"[xc]

With his alert encyclopaedic mind, and impeccable academic qualifications as a young man being a graduate of a leading Bahamian institution of secondary education and also of England's two most prestigious institutions of tertiary education – Oxford and Cambridge Universities, he certainly was well positioned to pursue a teaching ministry at a university or seminary abroad. However, he elected to return to his homeland to serve as a parish priest and prelate. For besides being humble, Michael Eldon was a patriot who greatly loved his fellow Bahamians. As such, being gifted and privileged, it was his sincere desire to share what he had received with others. It was this desire which motivated him in encouraging young Bahamians to offer to serve as priests and which was the reason he served for many years as Chairman of the council of the College of The Bahamas. Thus he was instrumental in offering encouragement and making available opportunities for young Bahamians to serve in the Church and state.

Now, many Bahamians have made major contributions in the field of education By the same token, a considerable number of them have proved to be very active and influential in the religious and spiritual life of our young nation. However precious few have managed to make major contributions in both these most important spheres. It can, therefore, be confidently asserted that no Bahamian so far has more significantly impacted both the religious and educational advance of the people of the Commonwealth of the Bahamas than...Michel Hartley Eldon. Charles Spurgeon, that great nineteenth century Baptist preacher, echoing the teaching of Christ,[xci] declared:

> "The rich believer should be thankful for the talent entrusted to him but should not forget his large responsibility, for where much is given much will be required."[xcii]

This great Bahamian minister of the gospel, a giant in every respect—physically, intellectually, morally and spiritually – certainly was given much. In a sense most profound he gave back...more![xciii]

Conclusion

Bishop Michael Hartley Eldon

- Compassionate Parish Priest

- Competent Prelate

- Brilliant Scholar

- Eminent Educator

- Bahamian Patriot

- "Man of God"

Truly, "A Bahamian Who Made a Difference!"

Questions for Group Discussion

1. Do you think that at least one Minister of the Gospel should be named a National Hero of The Bahamas? Give three reasons for your answer.

2. Two Ministers of The Gospel are included in this contribution on "Bahamians Who made a Difference!" The Rev. Dr. Reuben E. Cooper, Sr. and Bishop Michael Eldon. Give the names of at least two clergypersons whom you consider to be worthy of recognition as "Bahamians Who Made a Difference!"

3. What is the difference between "A Mission Church" and "A Church with a Mission"?

   Or

   "What steps did Bishop Michael Eldon take to enable the diocese in the Bahamas, Turks & Caicos Islands to move from merely being a self-supporting Church to becoming "A Church with a Mission"?

4. Michael Hartley Eldon was the first Bahamian to serve as prelate of the Diocese of The Bahamas, Turks and Caicos Islands. Give the names of two Bishops who served before Bishop Eldon

5. Bishop Eldon was most interested indeed passionate about recruiting candidates for the ministry. Are many young people today willing to serve in the Ministry? Why is this the case? What can be done in order to encourage more of them to offer for the full time ministry of The Church?

Recommended for Further Reading/Study

Gilbert Thompson, <u>A Godly Heritage</u>, A Concise History of the Diocese of the Bahamas and the Turks and Caicos Islands, Nassau: Avenue Graphics 2011.

The Archives of the Diocese of the Bahamas, Turks & Caicos Islands,

"Bishop Eldon: Pastor, Carer and Listener", Article published in "The Tribune", Vol. 107 Number 64, Nassau, Bahamas, Tuesday February 8th,

Richard Frederick Anthony Roberts

(May 12, 1932 – July 4, 2005)

**Trade Unionist Politician
Diplomat...Priest**

"For God's gift and call are irrevocable."

Romans 11:29, NIV

INTRODUCTION – GROWING UP PIGTAIL ALLEY

We human beings are, as the Bible says of the ancients Israelites, are indeed "a peculiar people." For the expression "many and varied," when applied to human kind is no cliché, but a profound, insightful recognition of the fact that The Almighty, in His infinte wisdom, has created each of us as unique, endowed with our own gifts, talents, choice, idiosyncrasies etc.

Nowhere is this phenomenon more patently obvious than in the manner in which we present or promote: - ourselves: to others you see, at the one extreme are those who are obsessed with selfagrandisement! They never get tired of boasting of their achievements – of telling you how educated they are, how hard they worked and the sacrifices they made to get where they are in life. How many rich and famous people they know (or who know them, bla, bla, bla!) their personal motto seems to be: *"Blow your own trumpet; for no one else will blow it for you!"*

At the other extreme of the spectrum are those who are most modest, yea reluctant, in promoting themselves, hardly ever mentioning or highlighting their accomplishments. For, rather than boring you by perpetually speaking about themselves, they let their deeds speak for themselves. Concisely, they work diligently, achieving much without fanfare or boastful self recommendation.

Now, such a person was Richard Frederick Anthony Roberts. Born on May 12, 1932, he was the second son of a distinguished, highly respected Bahamian family – The Roberts of Pigtail Alley.

Now, it is instructive and inspiring to reflect upon the fact that this most remarkable family, in three generations, has given to The Commonwealth of The Bahamas, some of its most gifted, progressive, and patriotic citizens. This list, which reads like a mini Bahamian "Whose Who", includes: the inimitableEnoch Pedro Roberts (a.cc. E.P Roberts), patriarch, pioneer in technical education. Mrs. Gladys Raine Roberts (née Archer), matriarch, Gerald Roberts, who followed his father in the technical field of service, Dorothy Wisdom, one of "the gallant eight," Sylvia Johnson, dedicated social worker. Pedro Roberts Jr., leading pharmacist, Patrick Roberts, eminent physician, mostly for treatment of sickle cell anemia, Rosamund Williams, matriarch of the Da Costa Williams Family, Italia Johnson, first and only female to serve as Speaker of the 293 year old House of Assembly, and Daniel Johnson, physician and politician. Gerald Wisdom, sports orator.

Anthony Roberts himself had a most outstanding and versatile career, making major contribution in fields of human endeavours as varied as trade unionism, politics, diplomacy and, yes religion. Despite these most significant achievements, very little is said about him and it would appear that the memory of his deeds is being allowed to slide into oblivion. Indeed, asked about him, many young Bahamians may simply respond, "Anthony who?"

Our purpose, here then is to tell the most interesting and encouraging story of the life of this fine Christian gentleman, truly an "unusual hero," worthy of admiration and emulation by Bahamians "in all walks of life."

Now, a little known fact about Anthony Roberts is that, early in life, he gave serious consideration, and indeed began preparation for becoming a Minister of the Gospel in the Methodist Church!

Yes, the narrator still vividly recalls that, when in the early 1950's he embarked upon a course in theological studies for the Methodist ministry, he met another young Bahamian who was pursuing the same objective – Anthony Roberts.

It is futile, after so many years to speculate as to why he did not continue on this course of action. The reason for this is that he himself hardly ever mentioned it. For, Richard Frederick Anthony Roberts was not a person who looked back at the past with regrets but to the future with its opportunities. In this regard there is much for us to learn from the sterling example of this fine Christian gentleman. For, too often in our sojourn through life we encounter those pathetic figures, who allow themselves to become so bitter about past hurts and insults, so defeated by past set backs, or so frustrated by past failures that they fail to grasp present opportunities! Not to mention bright hopes for the future!

Pioneer Bahamian Trade Unionist

Now, the tremendous contribution that the young Anthony Roberts to the fledgeling trade union movement in the Bahamas can hardly be over-stated! For, when during the formative years of his eventful life, the winds of socio-economic and political chances were blowing, manifested in the cry of working for social justice, he always stood in full support of them!

Such was the case that when serving in the aviation industry, he became painfully aware of "the cries and job pains of the airport workers." Anthony, together with Caldwell Ambrister responded by establishing the Airline Workers Union, the first Bahamian organized union in 1953. Consequently its name was changed to the Airport and Allied Workers Union (AAAWU) and Anthony Roberts became its first president. In this capacity he fought valiantly for improving working condition for the worker, endowed with a calm confident approach by the Almighty, well trained and skilled, he piloted the AAAWU through the turbulent period of industrial unrest culminating in the General Strike of 1958.

Here it is germane to emphasize that Anthony Roberts was the first formally trained trade unionist in The Bahamas! As the country's representative at the headquarters of the prestigious powerful International Confederation of Free Trade Union, he had the opportunity to attend conferences and training seminars in France, Holland, Luxemburg, Switzerland and England.

Anthony Roberts, then, proved to be a very strong advocate of social justice for the working classes of The Bahamas. In private encounters he was quiet, reserved, polite and dignified. The narrator does not recall him ever lifting his voice or losing his temper! Yet when it came to fighting for the rights of workers he approached his responsibilities with a tenacity and courage which most certainly moved both the worker, and employers to take action.

Whence came his passion for social justice? The answer is at hand – his deep religious faith you see, brought up in a Christian home, engaging in study of the scripture, he had a special interest in the teaching of the 8th century prophets of the Old Testament, especially Amos, Micah and Isaiah of Jersusalem. These prophets were uncomprimising in their srong condemnation of the oppression of the poor, calling for social justice for all in the name of the Lord (See Amos 5, Isaiah 1-2, Micah 6:8).

Following then in the footprints of their strong advocates of social justice, Anthony Roberts in his own calm, dignified manner courageously championed the cause of Bahamian workers.Indeed, throughout his outstanding contribution to national socio-economic development as a pioneer Bahamian Trade Unions, he epitomized the profound truth of the proverbial statement: " Meekness is not weakness." Accordingly, it is submitted that Anthony Roberts, must be ranked with Sir Randol Fawkes, Sir Clement Maynard, Mrs. Adena Burrows and Dr. Thomas Bastian as a giant of the Bahamian Union Movement.

EMINENT POLITICIAN

Now in the Caribbean region, there had developed a tradition of a close relationship between politics and trade unionism. It was not surprising, therefore, that the youthful Anthony Roberts, having "made his mark" as a pioneer trade unionist leading ventures into the competitive arena of party politics, fully aware of the wings of political change,he was steadfast in his commitment to the concepts of Majority Rule and the Women's Sufferage Movement thus accordingly was an active member of a dynamic organization of progressive young Bahamians – The National Committee for Positive Action (NCPA).

Mr. Anthony Roberts then joined the Progressive Liberal Party, quickly becoming a charter and national council member. Accordingly, he travelled to every major island to proclaim the liberating message of the Progrssive Liberal Party and to campaign for its candidates.

He approached the inevitable challenges of party politics with typical quiet determination and great courage. Thus defeat in his initial attempt to become a Member of Parliament (contesting the seat of "the city" occupied by the then powerful incumbent Sir Stafford Sands), did not discourage him.

He continued to serve as an active council member of the PLP, and in 1968 was elected to the honourable House of Assembly as the

THE REV. DR. JOSEPH EMMETTE AUGUSTUS WEIR, OM JP

Representative of the Centerville Constituency. As in other fields of human endeavour, The Hon.R.F. Anthony Roberts moved rapidly through the ranks as a parliamentarian. Thus he received cabinet appointments, serving as Minister of Agriculture and Fisheries and Local Government, Minister of Home Affairs, and occasionally as acting Minister of Education. Well-respected and acknowledged as an administrator, he was very active in helping to prepare the people of the land of his birth for the attainment of its independenceas a sovereign state in charge of its own destiny, under God, on July 10th, 1973.

Always a peacemaker, he was a leader amongst those who laboured valiantly to bring about reconciliation when a split developed within the PLP camp. These attempts to reunite the groups, however, were unsuccessful, resulting in the formation of the Free National Movement (FNM) not long afterward, The Hon. R.F. Anthony Roberts, gracefully retired from frontline party politics.

DIPLOMAT *PAR EXCELLENCE!*

There can be no doubt that The Hon. Anthony Roberts made a significant impact as a politician. However, it can be confidently asserted that with his naturally mild temperament, his dignified demeanour, and his reputation as a person offering wisdom and calm leadership, he was more suitably qualified to served as a diplomat and or elder statesman!

It was not surprising, then, that after his retirement from politics, the Prime Minister, The Rt. Hon. Sir Lynden Pindling, himself an astute judge of human ability, appointed The Hon. R.F. Anthony Roberts to the prestigious post of The Bahamas High Commissioner to The

United Kingdom. Thus, he and his family took up residence in London in 1977. The diplomatic sphere of human endeavour proved to be one for which he was, in every way well prepared. Moving rapidly through its ranks, he gained recognition as Caribbean Senior High Commissioner and The Commonwealth Senior High Commissioner. Then in 1984 he was elevated to the highest rank of acting Doyer Diplomatic Corps. Among his notable achievements as The Bahamas' High Commisioner was the officiating at the commissioning and launching of the first vessel of the fledgeling Royal Bahamas Defence Force.

In the midst of his many and varied responsibilites; including representing his country at international conclaves, meetings with executives both in government and commerce and extensive travelling, he always found time and made the effort to make Bahamians feel "at home." Such was the experience of the narrator and his family while on study leave in The United Kingdom.

DEVOUT PARISH PRIEST

Now, as we have seen, Anthony R.F. Roberts was a very religious man. Throughout his life he found time to engage in diligent study of the Bible and theology, and whenever he went he was steadfast in his witness to Christ as Saviour and Lord. With St. Paul he could truly testify, "I am not ashamed of the gospel, for it is the power of God unto salvation to everyone that believes to the Jew first and also to the Greek." (Romans 1: 16–18)

Thus, after he and his family took up residence on Carmichael Road, he invited Anglicans in that then rapidly expanding community to worship at services held at the back patio. This led to the establishment of St. Gregory's Church, conveniently located on Carmichael Road where he served in a leading role for many years.

Taking into consideration his deep faith in God, and his pastoral approach in dealing with other people who knew Anthony Roberts well were not surprised that upon completion of his remarkable tour of duty as a diplomat, he entered into full time ministry of the Gospel. Accordingly, he pursued theological studies in The United States of America including Princeton University Mercier School of Theology and The General Theological Seminary, New York. He began his ministry as a deacon at St. Barnabas in 1987 and was ordained to the priesthood in 1988.

The Rev. Anthony Roberts then served simultaneously as Assistant Priest at Christ the King Anglican Church and Chaplain to the Royal Bahamas Police Force. He then was appointed to serve as Priest in Charge at St. John's Anglican Church in Harbour Island with pastoral responsibility for St. Paul's in the Bluff and St. Joseph's in Upper Bogue, Eleuthera.He spent the latter years of his very productive life assisting as a "retired priest" at St. James Church in that old Bahamian community dating back to the days of slavery.

ADELAIDE

As a Minister of the Gospel, Fr. Anthony Roberts proved to be a devout servant of Christ, always demonstrating a deep pastoral concern for the mature and spiritual welfare of all the members of the consultative committee to his charge.

Now, throughout the ups and downs, the trials and triumphs of his eventful career, Anthony Roberts, fortunately received full cooperation of the once and only love of his life... a fine Bahamian beauty called Melvern.

Evidently, Anthony and Melvern, daughter of Mr. Edgar Bain, prominent and influential black businessman of yester-year, knew each other from childhood. For, the Roberts' homestead, at Pigtail Alley was "easy walking distance" from that of the Bains coveniently located on Blue (Baillou) Hill Road!

Their relationship blossomed from friendship into courtship. Consequently, Anthony and Melvern were united in holy matrimony on June 29, 1960. This happy marriage was blessed with four grown children including: Wayne and Brandon Roberts, Hollis Sherman and Tanya Roberts.

In the midst of his busy schedule of activities, Anthony Roberts always found time, quality time for romantic moments with his beloved Melvern and for the Christian nurture of their children. Moreover, he always demonstrated a keen interest in the physical, moral and spiritual development of Bahamian youth and serving as an officer of the Boys Brigade, and later of the Boy Scouts! Versatile and well rounded, he was an inventor and his hobbies included cricket, fishing, woodwork, cooking and entertaining family and friends.

CONCLUSION

What, then can we say,summarily, about the life and contribution of this fine Christian gentleman? It is submitted that, more than anything else, he demonstrated the profound truth of St. Paul's doctrine that the call of the ministry is irrevocable . Once it takes hold of a person, it nevers leave them. Thus, His Excellency the Rev. Fr. R. F. Anthony Roberts, who began his career with the aim of becoming a Methodist minister, after brilliant performances as a trade unionist, a significant tenure as a politician and a most impressive tour of duty as a diplomat, completed it as an Anglican priest!

What was most remarkable, then about Anthony Roberts was the fact that he excelled both in the secular and sacred sphere of human endeavor. As such he earned the respect and admiration of people "in all walks of life" both at home and abroad. This was very well expressed by his long time friend and colleague in ministry, The Rev. Fr. James Moultrie, "I am honoured to follow every step Fr. Roberts walked. He was a true decent human being and a dedicated child of God!"

Richard Frederick Anthony Roberts, trade unionist, politician, diplomat, priest, a "Bahamian Who Made a Difference" in ways more than three. Absolutely!

NOTES

1.) See Genesis 1:26-29; Ephesians 4:1-16

2.) The source of much of the content of this contribution is biography of R. F. Anthony Roberts prepared by his sons, Wayne and Brandon Roberts.

3.) "Pigtail Alley" is a narrow lane being the connection between Blue Hill Road and Hospital Lane. Like other similar roads in New Providence (e.g. Dog Flea Alley) it has an unusual name. The narrator's father, Gasper Emmette Weir, highly respected Bahamian land surveyor, wrote an unpublished book outlining the interesting history of the names of the streets of New Providence.

4.) This list is by no means exhaustive, as there are many outstanding members of this remarkable large Bahamian family. As such it is necessarily arbitrary as they are too numerous for mention here.

5.) Because he served as Deputy Prime Minister and Minister of Tourism during the administration of The Rt. Hon Sir Lynden Oscar Pindling, Sir Clement Maynard is remembered mainly for his sterling contribution in politics. However, early in his eventful life, Sir Clement was very active in the Trade Union field, and indeeed, was a pioneer trade unionist. See his autobiography, *"Put on More Speed."*

The others cited are all recognized as prominent trade unionists.

6.) See contribution on the life of Sir Stafford Sands.

7.) As we see, The Hon. R. F. Anthony Roberts was very active in the events leading up to the attainment of Independence of The Bahamas on July 10th, 1973. It was, therefore most appropriate that he should be called upon to serve in what was regarded as the most senior post in The Bahamian diplomatic service.

8.) The narrator studied at the University of Aberdeen Scotland, United Kingdom,from1978-1981. While there he and his family were warmly welcomed to the UK by the High Commissioner of the Commonwealth of The Bahamas.

9.) Mr. Edgar Bain was a proclaimed successful black Bahamian businessman, he was amongst those prominent citizenwho provided much needed financial and influential support to the PLP in the early years as a fledgling political organization.

10.) The Rev. James Moultrie who served for many years in dedication and administration before ordination to the priesthood, following a career path in many ways, similar to that of the Rev. Anthony Roberts.

QUESTIONS AND EXERCISES FOR GROUP ACTIVITY

1. EITHER

   What steps did Anthony Roberts take, as a young man, to improve the working conditions of Bahamian crafts people?

   OR

   Why may Anthony Roberts be recognized as a pioneer Bahamian Trade Unionist?

2. Discuss the reason why some trade unionists later became politicians.

3. Write short notes on three of the following: E. P. Roberts, Pigtail Alley, The role of Anthony Roberts in the preparation of The Bahamas Independence High Commission.

4. "More of a statesman than a politician," discuss in relation to the life and contribution of R.F. Anthony Roberts.

Sir Randol Francis Fawkes

(20 March, 1924 – June, 2000)

Eminent Lawyer, Courageous Labour Leader, Literary Luminary

INTRODUCTION

Early Days and Education

There can be no doubt that one of the most enjoyable and popular holidays on the Bahamian calendar is the first Friday of June. For, on this day, thousands of workers representing virtually every sector of the Bahamian economy join in massive parades. Traditionally celebrated as Labour Day it is now known as Sir Randol Fawkes Labour Day in honour of the great Bahamian who made such a tremendous contribution to the advance of the Trade Union Movement in the Commonwealth of the Bahamas!

Who then was Randol Fawkes? What motivated him to devote his life to the socio-economic progress of the working people of the Bahamas? What lessons can Bahamians "in all walks of life" apply to their own lives as they reflect on his many achievements? These questions certainly merit most careful attention.

Born in Nassau, Randol Francis was the youngest of a well-respected dignified old black Bahamian family—the Fawkes of Fort Fincastle. Its patriarch, Edward Fawkes a gentleman as sturdy in physical stature as sterling in character, was a disciplinarian "from the old school". A builder by profession, he toiled hard in order to care for his family and to ensure that all five of his children received the best education available, instilling in them the importance of a good education, high self-esteem and the dignity of labour. Its matriarch was a fine Christian lady, a prayer warrior, who made sure that their children were brought up, "in the nurture and admonition of the Lord!" There can be no doubt that these positive influences of his formative years--highest priority upon education, industry and religion—played a major part in the eventful life Randol Francis Fawkes.

It was not surprising, then, that on completion of his education at primary level at institutions operated by the Board of Education (now the Ministry of Education) Randol entered the Government High School for studies at secondary level. He was always a diligent reader and as such proved to be a brilliant student.

II. Brave Young Lawyer!

Now as we have seen, Mr. Edward Fawkes was a gentleman who did his best to provide his children with a good education. With the encouragement of his father, young Randol decided to become a lawyer. According upon graduation from the Government High School, served as an articled student in the Chambers of one of the two leading black lawyers in the Bahamas early in the Twentieth Century.

For six years the young Bahamian studied under the tutorship of 'Lawyer Toothe'. His efforts proved successful, for early in July, 1948, Randol Francis Fawkes was called to the Bar Council of the Bahamas.

It was indeed 'with pride and joy' that the members of the family gathered at the Supreme Court to witness this major event in the life of Randol. For, in those days when there were very few lawyers in the Colony, entrance into the legal profession was, indeed, recognized as a major achievement!

Always creative, Randol Fawkes embarked upon his responsibilities as a lawyer with the typical determination and zeal. By his own admission, he had a special interest in the plight of the poor and oppressed of society. He gained a reputation as a very good defense attorney. The narrator recalls a friend who advised, "If you ever get into trouble with the law and you need someone to plead for you, get Lawyer Fawkes." He did tend to be on the side of the oppressed. Moreover, he was not afraid to challenge those in authority on the fine points of the law. However, his approach did not 'sit well' with the powers that be and after just a few years in practice, he was like "a prophet who was without honour in his own country!" Accordingly, along with his young family, he left the Bahamas and spent two years in the USA, where he was able 'to make a living' and care for them. He, however, kept in touch with family and friends in the Bahamas. Being well informed of what was taking place, and it was not surprising that after his two year sojourn abroad, he returned to his homeland for, Randol Fawkes was at heart a patriot, who greatly loved his beloved fellow Bahamians!

III. "A Mighty Meekness!"

When the young Randol Fawkes and his family returned to the Bahamas in May, 1955, the winds of political and socio-economic change were blowing with ever increasing intensity!

Indeed, two major developments had transpired while they were abroad. These included the formation of the Progressive Liberal Party to be formally established in the colony and the growth of the Trade Union Movement. With a plethora of small craft unions being formed amongst the workers. Fired by a burning desire to make a significant contribution to the political and socio-economic advance of the people of the Bahamas, it was inevitable that the dynamic young Bahamian lawyer would make an impact in both these areas of human endeavor.

Thus, not long after his return, he joined the fledgling Progressive Liberal Party. And, at that time, when the colony was preparing for a general election, he immediately took a most active part in its advancement! For, Randol Fawkes never approached any challenge in a half-hearted, lukewarm manner. For him, it was 'all or nothing!'

Accordingly, along with his plunge into the swirling pool of party politics, he took the initiative by assuming a leading role in the struggles of working people for social justice. Concisely, although he grew up in a middle class family background, he made a conscious and deliberate decision to identify with the oppressed workers of the Colony, in this regard, he was very much like Moses. For, bear in mind that Moses, who was adopted by Pharaoh's daughter, was 'groomed to be an Egyptian Prince with all its privileges and 'perks'. But he made a conscious decision to identify with his Israelite brethren who were slaves at that time, boldly confronting Pharaoh with the rallying cry, "Let my people go!" (Exodus 9:1-7)

It is no wonder, then, that the workers spoke of him as 'Moses' and were willing to acknowledge him as a leader in their struggle for social justice. By contrast he was not so favourably received by all Bahamians. Thus, he recalls that:

> "The small black professional class," who sought acceptance by the elitist society, thought it impolite to be seen in my company, truth to tell, the only people really happy about my return from exile were the working classes in the ghettoes of 'Masons' Addition' and 'Grant's Town', the longshoremen, the vendors on Prince George Dock and the street sweepers and garbage collectors. As I moved among them I prayed: 'Lord, open my eyes that I may see what you have in store for me.'"

Undaunted, the determined Randol Fawkes continued with his endeavours to improve the lot of the workers of the then British Colony. Thus, he established an employment agency to assist them taking advantage of job opportunities. Then he was instrumental in organizing the many small craft unions into one huge labour organization: The Bahamas Federation of Labour, for it was realized that 'in unity there is strength.'

Thus, in the famous General Election of 1956, Randol Fawkes, with the strong support of the Labour Movement became one of the 'magnificent six' candidates of the Progressive Liberal Party who were elected to serve as Members of The House of Assembly.

After the election, as a Member of Parliament, Randol Fawkes continued to build the Bahamas Federation of Labour. Thus an impressive headquarters building was constructed on Wulff Road. While significant progress was made by the workers, there remained matters which caused much discontent, especially with regard to opportunities for economic advance.

It was not surprising, therefore, that there was a growing desire on the part of the workers for a larger share of the economic pie. This was evident when the taxi drivers took action because they felt that they weren't getting their fair share of the benefits of providing transportation in the lucrative tourist trade. Thus in December, the Taxi Cab Union organized a blockade of the newly constructed ultra-modern Windsor Airport.

Industrial Action was greatly accelerated when Clifford Darling, President of the Bahamas Taxicab Union requested the assistance of the Bahamas Federation of Labour in their struggle for social justice. As a result, many workers in the Tourism industry joined in supporting the taxi cab workers. By early January, the strike had spread like wild fire to include workers in all segments of Bahamian society. The narrator, then, a clerk in the Audit Department vividly recalls the long parades of the workers as they gathered on Bay Street to protest working conditions. With the rallying cry 'Not a sweat!' The workers put down their tools and joined in the General Strike. Randol Fawkes and Lynden Pindling went from one hotel to another rallying the workers and encouraging them in their endeavours, for three weeks the workers refused to serve.

As the news of the unrest spread abroad, the British Government sent in troops, of the Royal Worcestershire Regiment 'to keep peace' and to operate the utilities. While there was concern about the possibility of violence, it was kept at a minimum. The Alabama bus boycott were urged not to respond to violence. Thus, it was described as 'A Mighty Weakness' or 'The Quiet Revolution'.

Providentially, the British soldiers didn't have to do much in terms of putting down violence, while most of them left on the completion of their assignment in the Bahamas, a few of them remained, married and settled down in the Bahamas. Amongst these was John Philpott, who made major contributions especially in the promotion of the Boy Scout Movement in the Bahamas

Now, as a result of the General Strike, the Hon. Lennox Boyd, Colonial Secretary, visited the Bahamas and was involved in bringing about major reforms including provision for a Labour Department, the abolition of the company vote, the franchise being granted to all males over the age of twenty-one and the addition of four more seats in the House of Assembly to represent the rapidly growing population of New Providence.

Now, during the General Strike, Randol Fawkes and other Labour Leaders addressed the striking workers at Windsor Park, East Street. Night by night they gathered to draw inspiration by listening to their leaders. As a result of statements made at the 'University of Wulff Road, Windsor Park,' Randol Fawkes was charged with sedition. The case in the Supreme Court presided over by Chief Justice Sir Guy Henderson galvanized the attention of the entire Bahamian community, and indeed attracted attention at the international level with brilliant Jamaican attorney the Hon. Vivian Blake, Q.C., Randol Fawkes was acquitted. There was great celebration amongst the workers on his victory in this celebrated case.

After being acquitted, Randol Fawkes continued his lifelong endeavor to improve the lot of the Bahamian workers. By this time, he was gaining the support of the entire Bahamian community. Thus, in 1961 he piloted through the Legislature of the nation the Bill for an Act establishing the first Friday of June as "Labour Day", an official public holiday of the Bahamas. Henceforth, it became the law and custom for the workers of the Bahamas to have a holiday on the first Friday of June, a day set apart for all the people of the Bahamas to acknowledge, appreciate and, indeed, celebrate the contribution of workers to the development of our young nation!

There can be no doubt that this was the crowning achievement of the long and dedicated service rendered by Sir Randol Fawkes for the welfare of workers. It became the event for which he was most remembered and, indeed could be described as; "his finest hour." Having achieved this major victory, Randol Fawkes continued for the rest of his life to work for the cause of the small man. This is precisely why he came to be known as "The Father of Labour!"

IV. Randol Fawkes, Pioneer Bahamian Writer

Not many of the great "Bahamians Who Made a Difference" produced literary works recording events of the exciting history of their homeland, and sharing their thoughts and opinions, and reflections on them. The reason for this phenomenon need not detain us here. It is sufficient to ponder the testimony of a dynamic young Bahamian politician then totally involved in the struggle for social justice in the early years of majority rule which are at once insightful and illuminating.

"We were so busy making history, we did not have time to write history." It can confidently be asserted, however, that this observation cannot be applied to Sir Randol Fawkes! For throughout his life, he was a prolific writer, contributing articles in the print media, poems, songs and several books. Indeed, even before he was recognized as a prominent

Labour Leader, Randol Fawkes had already distinguished himself as a leading Bahamian author. For he published his first book in 1949, its arresting title being "Know Your Government." The narrator, "then a school boy in short pants" vividly remembers the great interest, even excitement, generated by this particularly literary achievement. For at a time when most publishing works, especially text books, were produced in London, New York, Toronto and in other cities of the industrialized nations of the North Atlantic, here at last was one written and published by a Bahamian in the Bahamas for Bahamians! For the book proved most useful, precisely because it presented important historical facts about the development of the Government of the Bahamas then still a small colony of the vast British Empire! Accordingly, young Bahamians were encouraged by teachers, librarians and mentors to read this book so that they may gain knowledge as to "how the Government works."

Now, one reason why the young Randol Fawkes proved to be an informative writer was his lifelong habit of keeping a diary! He reveals he developed this positive habit after hearing a sermon on "Christian Stewardship" by eminent Minister of the Gospel, Dr. Brown Pastor of St. Andrew's Presbyterian Kirk, he challenged the members of his congregation to make the best possible use of the time allocated to them by the Creator. Thus, when writing a Letter to the Editor, an article or a book, he was able to record events accurately and in vivid detail simply by reviewing his record of same in his diary.

Now when it comes to his literary works, there can be no doubt that "pride of place" must be attributed to his autobiography "Faith that Moved the Mountain". It has proven to be very useful precisely because (as pointed out above) it tells us much about others. Thus one learns much about other great Bahamians, including Dr. C. R. Walker, Sir Lynden Pindling, Sir Stafford Sands, Sir Milo Butler, Sir Roland Symonette and many others. Moreover, major events in Bahamian history, including "Black Tuesday", "The General Strike", "Majority Rule", and all described with the vitality and freshness which are the hallmarks of an eyewitness account. This book which has been published in a new edition, was produced by his daughter Rosalie Fawkes, very competent Bahamian educator.

For the reasons cited, there can be no doubt that it is a valuable resource of Bahamian history. In addition, Sir Randol wrote poems and songs, including a favorite of Bahamian Trade Unions "Bahamas, Glorious Homeland".

The versatile Randol Fawkes, was not only a leading trade unionist, he was also a literary luminary. For he has bequeathed a rich literary and historical legacy to Bahamians of coming generations; precisely because while busily involved in making history he somehow found time to write history!

V. Sir Randol Fawkes, Family Man *Par Excellence*

Early in his eventful life, the youthful Randol Fawkes met and married "the one and only" love of his life, the charming, vivacious Jacqueline

Rosalie Bethel of West End, Grand Bahama. Both nurtured in large well-respected Bahamian families residing at the time in the Fort Fincastle community. They did have much in common. Thus it was not surprising that they were joined in Holy Matrimony on June 3, 1951 at St. Agnes Church. The narrator recalls being present with his younger brother Roger at the magnificent reception held following this impressive ceremony.

There can be no doubt that, Archdeacon William "Willie" Thompson was right in describing their marriage as "made in Heaven". For it was the beginning of a forty-nine year conjugal relationship marked by fidelity, felicity and a freshness which made it a perpetual honeymoon. This happy union produced four well-disciplined, productive offspring: Rosalie, David, Francis, and Douglas.

Now sometimes those involved in the struggle for social justice become so "caught up" in pursuing this, admittedly most worthy cause, that they neglect their domestic responsibilities. Concisely, they become so busy helping others that they don't have enough time and energy to adequately take care of their own. But not Sir Randol Fawkes!

For, despite his extremely busy schedule as an attorney, Trade Unionist, politician and social activist, he found it possible to find quality time to fulfil his domestic responsibilities. Indeed, his children all always spoke of their father with great affection and nostalgia. Thus, he led in family devotion. As a father he made sure that they did their homework. Respect for teachers was expected of them. Moreover, he encouraged them to develop their talents, especially music. He returned from trips abroad with music books for them. No wonder, two of them, Rosalie and Francis, became accomplished musicians.

Sir Randol Francis Fawkes, a faithful husband and loving, encouraging father could be truly admired as a family man *"par excellence!"* The Father of Labour at the natural level was a loving father in the home.

VI. "The Faith that Moved the Mountain"

Now, Sir Randol Francis Fawkes, was a deeply religious layman, whose faith profoundly impacted every aspect of his life. This tremendously significant fact was demonstrated by the very high priority that he placed on the life and teaching of Christ, as encapsulated in the text:

> *"Verily, I say unto you, if ye have faith, and doubt not, ye shall not only do this which is done to the fig tree, but also if ye shall say unto this mountain, be thou removed and be thou cast into the sea, it shall be done." (Matt. 21:19)*

A study of its context reveals its tremendous relevance here. Here you see, Peter and the disciples had expressed great astonishment because the deceptive fig tree, cursed by Jesus, had withered. The Master's terse reply was unequivocal and challenging! For rather than his miraculous power, He in a not so veiled rebuke, assured them that they too could do mighty works if only they were prepared to exercise faith in God. Indeed, such bold faith could remove mountains!

Now, it was precisely this challenge of the Master to his disciples in all ages, which had such appeal to Sir Randol. This text proved very meaningful to him.

Indeed, that this particular text had tremendous comprehensive significance for him there can be no doubt! As such, it proved to be the spring of his passion for social justice, the source of his strength in times of challenge, his solace in experiences of sorrow and in moments of despair his hope. Moreover, as we have seen, it informed both the title and content of his major literary contribution: "The Faith that Moved the Mountain." Accordingly, this text of the Gospel of St. Matthew, may be truly described as the personal motto of Sir Randol Francis Fawkes.

It is noteworthy to observe here that Sir Randol Fawkes, was nurtured in a home where high priority was placed on Christian virtues and prayer, "generally speaking". He enjoyed a good, positive relationship with the members of the clergy. Indeed there were those among them for whom he had great respect, often soliciting their counsel especially in times of crisis. Prominent among them were Archdeacon William "Willie" Thompson (Anglican), the Rev. Dr. R. E. Cooper, Sr. (Baptists) and the Rev. Fr. Brendan Forsythe (Catholic) who euphemistically describes him as "A Man for All Seasons."

Sir Randol Fawkes was a Christian gentleman who demonstrated his faith not so much by his participation in the church as by seeking to apply the principles of Christ in his participating in the struggle for social justice for all God's children in the Commonwealth of the Bahamas!

VII. Sir Randol Francis Fawkes, "Bahamian National Hero!"

Randol Francis Fawkes, despite his many outstanding achievements and personal sacrifices for the welfare of all his fellow Bahamians, was not without his critics amongst them.

For as we have seen, he was a middle class Afro-Bahamian who made a conscious, deliberate decision to identify with black Bahamians from "Over the Hill" in their struggle for social justice. Now, this approach did not "sit well" with some members of the black middle class community. Then during the General Strike there were those of the business community who were highly critical of him, accusing him of trying to wreck the tourism based economy of the nation.

Thus, in the senior years of his eventful life, he suffered isolation. None were more painfully aware of this ostracized condition than the members of his own tightly-knit family!

In retrospect, however, it may be discerned that the eulogies at his passing marked the development of a great appreciation of the major contributions of this great Bahamian. For, "In the fullness of time" they did record due recognition by the people of the Commonwealth of the Bahamas.

Accordingly, there can be no doubt that the highlight of his career was the bestowal of the Knighthood by Queen Elizabeth II.

Then on the first Friday of June, in the year of Our Lord 2006, for the very first time the traditional annual Labour Day Holiday was celebrated as the Sir Randol Fawkes Labour Day. Thus he became the first and only Bahamian to have a public holiday named in his honour.

Finally, on the tenth of July, 2020, the forty-seventh anniversary of the Independence of the Commonwealth of The Bahamas as a sovereign state in charge of its own destiny under God it was announced that Sir Randol Francis Fawkes had been recognized as a Bahamian National Hero. Thus he was posthumously inducted into that prestigious panoply, including Sir Milo Butler, Sir Roland Symonette, Sir Lynden Oscar Pindling, Sir Cecil Wallace Whitfield, judged worthy to receive the highest and most distinguished honour which can be bestowed by the Government and people of the Bahamas on one of its citizen!

It is submitted that the eventful life and legacy of Sir Randol Fawkes with its trials and triumphs, its, "ups and downs", yea all its vicissitudes, has demonstrated once and for all the profound truth of the old Bahamian Proverb: "You can't keep a good man down!"

Sir Randol Francis Fawkes, eminent attorney, outstanding labour leader, writer, family man, man of "The Faith that Moves the Mountain," Bahamian National Hero. Truly "A Bahamian Who Made a Difference" in ways more than one.

Assignments and Questions for Group Discussion

1. Why do you think that Sir Randol Francis Fawkes is recognized as a Bahamian National Hero? Give two reasons for your answer.

2. Give the names of the other Bahamian National Heroes. List the main contributions of any two of them.

3. What steps did Sir Randol Fawkes take in order to bring about social justice for the workers of the Bahamas?

4. Write short notes on three of the following:

   The General Strike of 1958

   Sir Guy Henderson

   "The Gallant Six"

   Trial for Sedition

   "Know Your Government"

5. "Sir Randol Fawkes not only made history, he also wrote history." Discuss

Sylvia Ethlyn Johnson

(August 12th, 1928 – August 2000)

"The hand that rocks the cradle rules the world."

William Ross Wallace

"Her children will rise up and call her blessed." (Proverbs 31:28)

INTRODUCTION

WHAT IS GREATNESS?

Greatness, "how magnetic in its attraction, yet how mysteriously elusive is this amazing attribute!

Aspired to by many, desired by more, acquired by few, it remains forever tantalizing, challenging us "to aspire to be the best that we can be! For, in the annals of humankind, there have been those who set out to become great, but never reached near this goal. And others, who never really sought to attain greatness, but merely sought to do their best and, "in the process of time", were recognized by their compatriots to have been great. Indeed, in a sense most profound, their greatness has existed and consisted in their contribution to the greatness of others. There can be not a shadow of a doubt that such a person was Mrs. Sylvia Ethlyn Johnson née Roberts, a fine Bahamian matron, who, because of how very much of herself she poured into others, merits a place amongst "Bahamians Who Made a Difference!"

A Mother in the Home Par Excellence

Born on August 12th, in the Year of Our Lord 1928, Sylvia Ethlyn Johnson was the third child of Mr. E. P. Roberts (Enoch Pedro Roberts) 1894 – March 2, 1976, famous Bahamian educator and his wife Gladys Raine Johnson née Archer.

Both her parents hailed from the island of Abaco (her father from Green Turtle Cay and her mother from Marsh Harbour) coming from families with a strong Christian heritage and deep faith in God. Nurtured, then, in a disciplined home in which high priority was placed on Christian virtues and education, the young Sylvia Johnson applied herself diligently to her studies. Indeed, throughout her life, she demonstrated a keen interest in education, not only for herself, but also for that of her family and extended family throughout the length and breadth of the Commonwealth of the Bahamas. She received her education at primary and secondary levels at the Western Preparatory and Western Junior and Senior Schools and the prestigious Bosfield -Johnson private high school.

An ambitious young lady, she pursued education at tertiary level at The University of The West Indies, Cave Hill Campus in Barbados, where she was awarded a scholarship by the United Nations to pursue a course in Social Studies dealing with children and elderly persons residing in urban areas. Moreover, she continued studies in this area of social work at the University of Eastern Michigan.

With her bright sparkling eyes, sharp aquiline nose, perfect posture, always appropriately and tastefully attired, the youthful Sylvia

Roberts was, indeed, a Bahamian beauty! Well educated, polite, petite, "polished" and, most articulate, impeccable in character, she was blessed with an alert mind and an essentially optimistic approach to the challenges which came her way.

Endowed with such attractive attributes, she captured the attention and captivated the heart of a young enterprising printer and budding politician Oscar N. Johnson. Consequently, they were united in matrimony in 1951. Having already had some experience in the printing industry, the now Mrs. Sylvia Johnson was able to work efficiently with her husband in the operation of the family business – The Craftsman Press conveniently located on Crawford Street in the Oakes Field Community.

As a young mother she did her best to raise her own children as she had been nurtured. They were brought up in accord with Christian principles. Thus, nurtured, as we have seen, in a home where high priority was placed on education, she, along with her husband, worked hard, making the necessary sacrifices involved in ensuring that all six of their children received quality education, in accord with their respective aptitudes and abilities at primary and secondary levels at home, and at tertiary level "at home and abroad".

Accordingly, it should not be surprising to the reader that all of them grew up to become law abiding, competent, contributing citizens of our beloved Bahamaland. They are:

Mrs. Cora Cooper, Educator, who served for many years at Kingsway Academy,

Miss Italia Johnson, an insurance executive by profession, who followed her father by entering the political arena, becoming the first

Bahamian lady to serve as Speaker of the ancient House of Assembly with its history dating back to 1729,

Mrs. Kathleen Hassan, noted Bahamian Attorney at-Law

Mrs. Gladys Sands, prominent Bahamian Psychologist

Mr. Oscar Johnson Jr., Attorney-at-Law and

Dr. Daniel Johnson, second Bahamian to qualify as a Podiatrist (physician who specilizes in healing diseases of the feet), who also pursued a career in politics, now serving as a Member of Parliament being the Minister of Youth and Sports. His youth and enthusiasm with regard to sports make him well qualified to serve in this capacity as evidenced by the major progress made by the Bahamas in this competitive field of human endeavor in recent years!

In contacts with these brilliant young persons, the Narrator noted that they have always spoken very highly of their mother. It is evident that they are greatly appreciative of the love and concern that she showered upon them during her lifetime. Indeed, the words of the wise writer of The Book of Proverbs may be truly applied to her: *"Her children will rise up and call her blessed!"* (Prov. 31:28)

Mother Figure in the Bahamian Community

Throughout her life, Mrs. Sylvia Johnson devoted herself not only to the nurture of her own children but also to the children of others, especially children who did not have the opportunity to have been raised in a model home, where they had parents who cared for them in every way, physically, mentally, morally and spiritually. Her studies in social work and her own unselfish character enabled her to serve well in this capacity. A social activist, she became a member of the Mothers Club and also of the Red Cross, where she helped with its "Meals on Wheels" Programme.

She was elected President of The Mothers Club and it was in this capacity that in 1981, she embarked upon the major project of her eventful life. For in that year she and the members of The Mothers Club took it upon themselves the challenge of reopening of the Children's Emergency Hostel which had been closed for many years. The hostel located on McKinney Drive was originally established by a group of prominent Bahamians who were concerned for the welfare of children from early infancy to childhood. Amongst them were Dean William Granger, Mr. and Mrs. John Hedden, Major Thomas Brooks and Pastor William Nairn. The Kiwanis Club of Nassau built this facility which consisted of two cottages with accommodation for 36 children, Administration block, library, kitchen, sanitary facilities, etc. This was indeed a very challenging undertaking. Led by Mrs. Sylvia Johnson, a very energetic and determined person, the Children's Emergency Hostel was revived. Much of her time, then in the senior years of her life, when she had successfully raised her own biological children, was spent at this institution where she diligently and dutifully raised children who did not have homes of their own. On visits to the Hostel to take gifts for the children, the Narrator was deeply impressed by the manner in which Mrs. Johnson cared for the children there.

In 1982, then, she was appointed Matron of the hostel, a position she held until 1992. She then served as Director of Business and Public Relations. In this capacity she served with dedication and was able to garner much support for this institution from both corporate and individual citizens. She was not afraid "to beg for this worthy cause" and generally speaking, the response from the general public was generous and encouraging! All this she did because of her love for the underprivileged children. As such, Matron Sylvia Johnson was not only a mother *par excellence* in her own home but also a foster mother and mother figure to many children of the Bahamian community.

Social Activist and Behind the Scenes Political Activist

Mrs. Sylvia Johnson was certainly a multi-talented person, who managed to participate in the socio-political development of the Bahamas along with her domestic and social responsibilities. For, as has been intimated above, she was a very influential person, whose advice was respected by all with whom she came into contact. During the eventful years leading up to the establishment of Majority Rule in (1967) and the coming of Independence in (1973) her husband was active in the political arena having been elected to represent Cat Island in the House of Assembly. Her brother, Mr. Anthony Roberts who later was ordained to the priesthood was active in the Trade Union Movement. As such, Mrs. Sylvia Johnson née Roberts took a keen interest both in politics and the Trade Union Movement. The Narrator recalls that she attended the political rallies of the PLP on the Recreation Grounds during that turbulent era. She certainly demonstrated a keen interest in the political development of the nation and was, of course, in full support of the concept of Independence for the Commonwealth of the Bahamas. Working, then "behind the scenes", giving her full support to her husband in politics and her brother in trade unionism, Sylvia Johnson, then, did play her part as one of the many, many "unsung heroines" In bringing about what her contemporary Dr. Doris Johnson (no relative!) accurately and aptly described as "The Quiet Revolution"![xciv]

"Devout Woman of God"

While, however, she did not attain national fame by being featured in "the headlines" in the media, the efforts of Mrs. Sylvia Johnson to care for the welfare of her fellow human being, especially its children did not go unnoticed and unrecognized. For, in an impressive and most inspiring service held at Mission Baptist Church, Hay Street, she became the ninth recipient of the distinguished R. E. Cooper, Sr. National Meritorious Service Award. The service, which took place on Sunday, December 26, 1993, was conducted, most appropriately by the Rev. Dr. Reuben E. Cooper, Jr.

In reflection upon the life and contribution of Sylvia Ethlyn Johnson née Roberts, it can be truly said that her greatness consisted not so much in what she did as in how much she contributed to the achievements of others. For, it is impossible to estimate the extent of her influence upon the lives of others, not only in the careers and achievements of the eminent members of her family, but also upon the eventual accomplishments of the many underprivileged children who came under her influence while serving in the Red Cross and the Children's Emergency Hostel.

She was, indeed, the epitome of that rare combination of physical beauty, moral integrity, mental alertness, deep spirituality, a sense of duty to the care of family and patriotic loyalty to the land of their birth, which enabled the women of her generation to contribute so richly to the overall advancement of all the people of our young nation. As

THE REV. DR. JOSEPH EMMETTE AUGUSTUS WEIR, OM JP

such she became a Bahamian lady worthy of emulation by the Bahamian ladies of "the younger generation"!

What, then, motivated this outstanding Bahamian woman, with six children of her own, to spend so much quality time and expend so much energy to the nurture of the children of others? Why did she not complain then that because "she had her hands full" and so she could not help others? The answer is at hand, her deep Christian faith. For, she was a devout Christian lady, an active member of Transfiguration Baptist Church, who believed in the power of prayer and the imperative to demonstrate love in action in accord with the life and teaching of the Master (Matt. 5 -7, Mk. 12: 28-32; Luke 10. 25-27; Jn. 13:34).

Now, as we have seen, The Rt. Rev. Michael Hartley Eldon, Bishop of the Anglican Diocese of Nassau, and the Turks & Caicos Islands, eulogized His Excellency Sir Milo Boughton Butler, first Bahamian Governor General, as "a deeply religious man and he left us no doubt that this was the motivating force of his life."[xcv] In retrospect, no less can be said of Mrs. Sylvia Johnson! Indeed, the positive indelible effects of her life and contributions were encapsulated in this most insightful observation, which has proved prophetic in every way.

She has unselfishly promoted God's redeeming love in our abandoned and neglected children and she has nurtured their tender and impressionable minds, molding them into productive citizens who, if given the opportunity, will prove to be future leaders of our nation and the world.[xcvi]

It is worthy of careful attention that it speaks of her concern for the physical, moral and spiritual nurture of our abandoned and neglected children. Here, we are reminded that the welfare of all the children of our community (not just our own biological children and those of near relatives!) is the sacred responsibility of all of us who are citizens of our beloved Bahamaland, a nation which includes in the Preamble to its Constitution the concept of Christian nation building. This is in line with the teaching of Isaiah who realized that he *"dwelt amongst people of unclean lips"* (i.e. he identified with all his contemporaries!) and the teaching of Christ, (Isa. 6:5 ; cp. Mark 10:45; Phil. 5:1-11).

Taking into consideration the course of events since then, notably the increase in the rate of crime and violence, especially on the part of youth it is a statement most relevant and one we should all take most seriously as we seek to make our own contribution to the physical, moral socio-economic, moral and spiritual growth of the citizens of our beloved Bahamaland!

Sylvia Ethlyn Roberts Johnson, "Unsung Bahamian Heroine"

Diligent daughter of distinguished Bahamian educator E.P. Roberts and Gladys Raine, his wife,

Loving spouse of Oscar Nathaniel Johnson Sr., Printer/Politician,

Beloved mother of Cora, Italia, Kathleen, Gladys, Oscar Jr., Daniel,

Dear sister of Gerald, Dorothy, Anthony, Pedro, Rosamund and Patrick,

Esteemed "mother figure" to many,

Devout "Woman of God",

Truly "A Bahamian Who Made a Difference"!

Questions for Group Discussion & Exercises

1). How would you define "greatness?" Give the names of two persons who you consider to be great in support of your definition.

2). *Some are born great. Some achieve greatness. And some have greatness thrust upon them."* William Shakespeare. To which of these categories do you think Mrs. Sylvia Johnson may be assigned. Give reasons for your answer.

3). Mrs. Sylvia Johnson may be described as an unsung heroine, that means that her name is not found in Bahamian history books and did not appear in the headlines during her lifetime!) Give the names of at least three other ladies who may be described in this way. Write a paragraph on each of them to explain the reasons for your choice.

4). *"The hand that rocks the cradle rules the world."* Discuss.

5). Tell what you know about two of the following (200 – 500 words)

The Red Cross

The Children's Emergency Hostel

The Ranfurly Home for Children

Sir Stafford Lofthouse Sands

(1913–1968)

"...zero tolerance for mediocrity!"

INTRODUCTION

Sir Stafford Sands and the Renewal of the Bahamian Economy

The Bahamas (then a small colony of the mighty British Empire reputed to be so extensive that the sun never set upon it!) teetered, at the end of World War II (1939 – '45) on the precipice of intense economic challenge!

For, the sponge industry, which had sustained its fragile economy during the earlier part of the twentieth century (after the bubble generated by prohibition burst!) was obliterated by a marine disease just before the beginning of the war. During the war, the economy of the colony had been sustained largely, by the construction maintenance and operation of military bases for the training of pilots and crew of the airplanes of the Royal Air Force and other military installations. Now, with the inevitable reduction in employment and revenue caused by the gradual "down-sizing" of these military facilities in the wake of the end of the war, the need for the taking of new bold initiatives, directed to the sustenance, diversification and expansion of the Bahamian economy was urgent!

It was, in the context of this unique socio-economic crisis, that there emerged a young, brilliant Bahamian attorney, demonstrating the aptitude for, and tremendous interest in the development, of the economy of his homeland - Stafford Lofthouse Sands! For, his impressive achievements, which were, "many and varied," impacting virtually every aspect of Bahamian society, were all, in some measure, related to its economic development.

Now, the young Stafford Sands rose to prominence in the lively debate in the House of Assembly on The Report of The Royal Commission appointed by The Governor His Royal Highness the Duke of Windsor in the wake of the historic 1942 Burma Road Riot. Amongst its progressive recommendations were the enactment of advanced labour legislation directed to recognize the rights and improve the working conditions of employees; the reduction of the length of a legislative term of the House of Assembly from seven to five years; the imposition of income tax and the implementation of universal adult suffrage, based on the principle: "one man one vote."

Sir Randol Fawkes, Labour Leader and literary luminary, who was present in the House of Assembly on that historic date, September 10, 1942, gives us this vivid moving "eyewitness" account of its proceedings:

> The principal actor that night on the legislative stage was a young politician/lawyer/businessman of 29 years known as Stafford Lofthouse Sands. He moved with Teutonic

thoroughness to demolish the progressive recommendations of the Governor's Riot Commission.

On the agenda there was a motion for a Select Committee 'to take into consideration all matters relating to, connected with, and arising out of the June 1st disturbance with a view to preventing a recurrence thereof with power to send for persons and papers.'

As Mr. Sands rose to speak, an aura of silence descended upon the house. Every head was turned in his direction, so great were his histrionic powers. Sands had only one good eye, the other was made of glass but among those pompous Cyclops, the one-eyed giant was king.

That he, speaking on the most crucial contemporary "burning issue" could command the rapt attention of all the members of the most powerful legislative body of the colony, clearly indicated that here indeed was a brilliant young white Bahamian ... destined for greatness!

Now, the contributions of Sir Stafford Sands, like those of Sir Lynden Pindling (with whom, "in the books of some authorities" he shares the distinction of being amongst the greatest Bahamians of the twentieth century) were four-fold. They include:

1. The establishment of Tourism as a "year round" industry, becoming "The engine of the Bahamian economy,"

2. The establishment of Nassau as a principal center of finance and banking, the second pillar of the Bahamian economy

3. The revaluation of the Bahamian Dollar placing it on par with the U.S. Dollar precisely when many other countries were devaluing theirs in the wake of the devaluation of the Pound Sterling , the currency of world trading.

Taking the initiative in the, drafting of the   resulting in the development of Freeport, Grand Bahama as "The second city of the nation."

As indicated, these all had to do with the renewal of the economy of the Bahamas after World War II. Let us, proceed, then by examining each of these measures in detail.

II. The establishment of Tourism as a year round industry, "The engine of the Bahamian economy."

There is a popular Bahamian (Goombay) song, often heard on the local radio stations, which begins with the intriguing question:

"If the good Lord did not go on holiday,

Tell me why He created the Bahamas?"

The underlying thought here is that the Bahamas, known as "The Isles of June," with its delightful sunshine every day of the year climate, its beautiful beaches and its multi-colored "seascape," is an ideal place for the development of tourism! And so it is!

Thus, throughout its long history, stretching back to Columbus arriving at San Salvador in 1492, people from abroad, especially the United States, Canada and Great Britain, have been coming to these isles to take advantage of their warm climate, beautiful scenery and enchanting beaches. Moreover, Bahamians, for the most part, are very accommodating to visitors to our young nation. Tourism, then, as in a sense most profound, has always been an important segment of the economy of the Bahamas.

Tourism, however, was seasonal in nature. Most of the tourists came for vacation during the winter season when it was cold in the nations of the North Atlantic - from late November to mid-April, or "from Thanksgiving to Easter." The hotels, then, remained open for just these four months and were closed during the rest of the year!

As a result, Bahamians in the Tourism Industry worked only during "the (winter) season" and tried their best to "make ends meet" during the lean summer months as they waited eagerly for the next "season" to begin. The saying, "Look out or the gullies will get you!" indicated how tough it was for the average Bahamian to survive during the summer months. Tourism, then, was a rather informal four months of the year "feast and famine" industry! Clearly "the way forward" for the Bahamas was to make Tourism into a year-long activity.

Accordingly, the Government of the Bahamas took the initiative in pursuing this objective.

In this regard, the observation of Allan Murray (who taught Bahamian history at St. Andrew's school for many years) is most illuminating:

> Soon after the War, i.e. World War II, 1939 - 45) a special government department was set up led by a farsighted Bahamian to make tourism a year round business. The Development Board, the forerunner of the Ministry of Tourism, had been operating since 1937. But in 1950 a new

chairman was appointed, the brilliant lawyer and financier Stafford Sands, now recognized as "The Father of Tourism." Allan G. Murray, *Bahamian History Highlights*, Nassau: Media Publishing, 1999, p. 87).

The transformation of the economy of the Bahamas began when Stafford Sands as Chairman of the Development Board, took definite steps to make tourism a year round economic activity. This initiative proved successful, with the number of tourists visiting reaching a million in 1968. Now Stafford Sands, the determined lawyer, politician, businessman, buoyed up by these initial achievements in tourism, held tenaciously to the position that at least one new bold initiative was essential for the development of tourism as a year-round viable industry - the introduction of casino gambling! True legislation had been passed providing special incentives and tax breaks to attract investors to build hotels. But Sands was convinced that the introduction of casino gambling was the next logical step in this process. This was due to the fact that largely through the influence of mainline Protestant Churches, casino gambling was illegal in many of the Southern States of the USA. So Sands and his associates felt that the availability of casino gambling would give the Bahamas a distinct advantage in promoting Tourism as a year round economic activity.

Accordingly, in 1959, Sands applied to the House of Assembly for the grant of a license to operate casinos at hotels in Grand Bahama. Applications from other corporate bodies were soon added. Clearly it was necessary that this matter should be fully debated.

There followed, therefore, a long period of national debate on the matter of casino gambling. The narrator vividly recalls discussion by members of the Methodist Church, which was strongly opposed to casino gambling. The Rev. R. P. Dyer, then Principal of Queen's College was abruptly taken off the air" when in a sermon broadcast over ZNS, he was highly critical of the move to bring about casino gambling. Indeed, the whole Christian Council was strongly opposed to the introduction of casino gambling holding that it was unscriptural and would result in an increase in crime!

Now, Sir Stafford Sands' strong advocacy of casino gambling brought him into conflict with the Premier, Sir Roland Symonette. As a Methodist Sir Roland was strongly opposed to gambling, and indeed, attended an anti-casino gambling rally organized at Clifford Park by the Bahamas Christian Council. Along with the Methodists, Baptist Pastor Charles Smith, then Pastor of Zion Baptist Church, also opposed casino gambling.

Sir Stafford Sands realized that there was no way he could get legislation passed calling for the legalizing of gambling, accordingly, he applied, not for the legalizing of gambling but that his clients should be granted a Certificate of Exemption from the law, the Lotteries Act?

After much debate in the House of Assembly, the application of Sir Stafford was granted. Thus, casino gambling was introduced into the Bahamas and has remained in operation. It is significant that, despite many changes in government since that time, casino gambling continues under the terms granted to the clients of Sir Stafford Sands.

During the tenure of Sir Stafford Sands, who was the first Minister of Tourism of the Bahamas, tourism increased exponentially. Over the forty years that led to the celebration of Independence in July, tourism continued to grow as the engine of the Bahamian economy.

Over the years, several outstanding Ministers of Tourism, including Sir Clement Maynard, the Hon. Brent Symonette and Senator the Hon. Vincent Vanderpool-Wallace have emerged to lead in this most important segment of the Bahamian economy. Thus, in July, 2013, on the occasion of the Fortieth Anniversary of Independence, with the Hon. Obediah Wilchombe serving as Minister of Tourism, it was reported that:

There were 5.8 million visitors to the Bahamas in 2012:

That Tourism comprised more than fifty percent of the Gross National Product.

It is germane to point out here that other Caribbean territories which were reluctant to develop tourism as a viable industry "in the early days" have since totally changed their position and, indeed, have repositioned themselves as rivals to the Bahamas in this now highly competitive field of human endeavour. Concisely, Sir Stafford Sands' contention that Tourism could become a stable year round industry, "The engine of the Bahamian economy" has been vindicated!

III. Establishment of Nassau as a major international centre banking and financial services

During World War II, the Government of the United States, and indeed, other nations of the North Atlantic, had to raise huge amounts of money to finance the expanding military pursuits. Accordingly, taxes, both at the individual and corporate level, were greatly increased. Then, in Great Britain, the Labour Governments which came to power in the post war years imposed heavy taxes in the form of "Death Duty" on the wealthy land-owning classes of "The Mother Country."

It was in the context of very high taxation in the nations of the North Atlantic, home of many investors, that Sir Stafford Sands and other young attorneys realized that there was tremendous financial potential in the promoting of the Bahamas as a tax free haven.

Wealthy individuals and corporate bodies were, therefore, encouraged to establish companies in the Bahamas which could be the recipients of funds which were not subject to taxes in their home countries. Fawkes describes "Stafford Lofthouse Sands *as 'The originator of that growing institution--The Suitcase Company'."* The narrator vividly recalls walking along Bay Street, almost daily, being fascinated by the many large signboards covering the outside walls of the Chambers of Sir Stafford Sands, representing wealthy individual and corporate citizens drawn from every corner of the globe.

In advising wealthy individuals on "ways and means" of taking advantage of tax benefits in the Bahamas, Sir Stafford Sands formed partnerships with prominent American attorneys specializing in this aspect of Law. In time, international corporate bodies established branches in the Bahamas employing many locals at higher salaries than they could earn elsewhere. Prominent amongst these was United States Steel which established Navios Corporation. The higher wages and benefits of these companies led to an increase in the standard of living for many middle class Bahamian families. The growth of these "suit case" and local branches of international corporations inevitably led to an increase in the demand for financial services. There was, therefore, need for more attorneys and accountants to assist wealthy clients in managing their funds and this, in turn led to the setting up of more Trust Companies and Banks. While, then, Sir Stafford Sands was the pioneer in developing the financial services; indeed, many more law companies, banks, trust companies and accounting firms were established in the Bahamas especially during the latter part of the twentieth century. According to an article in "The Tribune," the banking and financial services industry in the Bahamas "grew like wildfire," .i.e., spontaneously and most rapidly without much supervision and planning.

At the time of the celebration of the Fortieth Anniversary of Independence, banking and financial services provided employment (well-paying jobs) for over 3,000 Bahamians and accounted for as much as 15% of the gross domestic product, ranking second only to Tourism within the framework of the Bahamian economy.

IV. The Revaluation of the Bahamian Dollar, placing it on par with the U.S. Dollar

Ever since the dawn of the Industrial Revolution early in the Nineteenth Century, the Pound Sterling, had dominated world trading and commerce. For, because of the huge amount of trade generated by this paradigm shift in the World Economy (moving from an agrarian based to an industrial base) it proved most feasible for nations to use the Pound Sterling in their transactions. Thus, the currencies of most nations with the exception of the U.S. Dollar) were measured in relation to this powerful currency of the British Empire. Trade, at that time, was based on the export of manufactured products from the industrial nations of the North Atlantic to the developing nations of the Third World, which, in turn supplied the latter with their raw products.

After World War II, however, the Pound Sterling was subject to severe economic pressure making its products very expensive "on the world market"! Drastic action was required to reverse this disturbing trend. Accordingly, in 1965 Sir Stafford Cripps, the then Chancellor of the Exchequer, took the unprecedented step of devaluing the Pound Sterling. This action sent shockwaves throughout the entire vast international business world. Not to be out—done, or disadvantaged, other nations, including the countries of Europe such as France and Germany, the major trading nations of the British Empire and many nations "in the developing Third World, also devalued currencies. Indeed within a week of Sir Stafford Cripps' bold initiative, many nations had devalued their currencies in order that their products might remain competitive "on the world market"!

Now, it might have been expected that the Bahamas, being a small colony of the British Empire, would have followed suit" by devaluing its newly minted currency—the Bahamian Dollar. But, such was not the case! By, no means! For, the Bahamas, under the innovative leadership of Sir Stafford Sands (the other Sir Stafford!) its brilliant Minister of Tourism and Finance, revalued its currency, the Bahamian Dollar placing it on par with the U.S. Dollar.

It was, indeed, an unprecedented masterstroke of fiscal genius, unmatched in the three hundred and fifty year economic history of the Bahamas! For, in so doing, Sir Stafford Sands moved The Bahamas

317

from the Sterling bloc into that of the American Dollar. It was bold, creative, visionary, and indeed, prophetic. For, the devaluation of the Pound Sterling marked the end of its dominance in the world economy and the emergence of the U.S. Dollar as the principal currency of world trade! Yes it demonstrated vision. It epitomized brilliance. It took guts!

Here, the question certainly comes to mind, "How did, The Bahamas, manage to re-value its currency upwards, when other much bigger nations, with much larger populations and immensely more natural resources such as France, Holland, Trinidad and Tobago, Nigeria and Jamaica) found it necessary to devalue theirs in the wake of Sir Stafford Cripps decision to devalue the Pound? The, answer is at hand - it was precisely because the Bahamas, by that time, had a viable economy based on "invisible exports"--Tourism and Financial Services--not on tangible products on which most countries in the Third World depended for their economic survival. As a prominent Bahamian Civil Servant put it, "We export sunshine!" Simply stated, the Bahamas did not have to devalue its currency when other nations found it necessary to do so because its economy was based not on the money generated by the export of products, but on revenue resulting from the spending of tourists and that generated by the provision of financial services to the wealthy, spending of tourists and the investments revenue generated by its Financial Services Industry.

The far reaching consequences of this bold step can hardly be over-evaluated. Being on par with the U.S. Dollar has worked much to the advance of Tourism as visitors do not have to resort to complicated mathematical calculations in order to do shopping. It makes it convenient for investors. And it certainly has made it most convenient for Bahamians when they engage in "shopping sprees" to Miami, Ft. Lauderdale and other cities in nearby Florida.

Moreover, the significance of the revaluation of the Bahamian Dollar becomes readily evident when it is compared with the rate of exchange of the currencies of neighboring countries of the Caribbean and the North Atlantic region.

Nation	Currency	Ratio to the US Dollar
The Bahamas	BAH Dollar	1
Canada	CAN Dollar	0.81
Cayman	Caymanian Dollar	1.20
Dominican Republic	Dominican Peso	0.018
Eastern Caribbean	EC Dollar	0.37
Guyana	Guyanese Dollar	0.0048
Haiti	Haitian Gourde	0.0099
Jamaica	JA Dollar	0.0065
Mexico	Mexican Peso	0.049

Moreover, it is salutatory to bear in mind that no Bahamian Minister of Finance (whether PLP, or FNM) since Sir Stafford Sands has attempted to alter, in any way, the status of the Bahamian Dollar as being on par with that of the U.S. Dollar. Indeed, such a move has not been seriously contemplated. It is a tribute to the vision, foresight and courage of Sir Stafford Sands that the position of the Bahamas as a currency on par with the U.S. Dollar more than fifty years after it revaluation by him, remains intact.

V. Participation in the promotion of the Legal Foundation of the development of Freeport as "The Second City of the Bahamas"

Now, as we have seen the Bahamas faced intense economic challenge at the end of World War II. It is germane to observe that the lumber industry proved tremendously important to sustaining the Bahamian economy during this struggling transitional juncture before Tourism and Financial Services were effectively developed.

Naturally, it flourished in those islands which had large pine tree forests--Andros, Abaco and Grand Bahama. Here the principal figure was an American venture capitalist--Wallace Groves.

For, as Murray points out,

> "In 1946, Mr. Wallace Groves purchased the Abaco Lumber Company, which had rights to timber on Grand Bahama. By 1951, it was steadily exporting lumber to Britain."

The cutting, processing and export of the products of the sturdy Bahamian Pine Tree--lumber, turpentine, pit props and pulp-- created employment for many Bahamians and from the Turks & Caicos Islands. This industry centered around the boom town "known as "Pine Ridge." Its prosperity however was short-lived, evaporating with the gradual"down-sizing" of the lumber industry. Dr. Havard Cooper, prominent Freeport businessman and Pastor, in his biography, "My Story, His Glory" vividly describes the rise, rapid development and equally rapid demise of Pine Ridge , now a "ghost town."

Accordingly, the visionary Wallace Groves sold out his interests in the lumber industry and turned his attention to the concept of an exciting "Freeport" type development. In pursuit of this vision, he established The Grand Bahama Port Authority.

Now, it was Sir Stafford Sands who served as his attorney, providing him with sound legal advice in executing these complex transactions. Thus, as Barratt rightly observes, it was natural that he should look to Sir Stafford for the legal expertise to conceive his bold plan: The development of a "Freeport Community" in the pine barren island of Grand Bahama."

It was, therefore, not surprising that Sir Stafford Sands occupied "pride of place" amongst those who witnessed the historic signing of the Hawksbill Creek Agreement on August 4th, 1955 by the Acting Governor, the Rt. Hon. A. G. Gardener-Brown, representing the Government of the Bahamas and Mr. Wallace Groves, representing the Grand Bahama.

Included in this 99-year Agreement were provisions for the dredging of a deep-water harbour, the development of Freeport as a city designed to attract industrial enterprises which were enabled to import duty free (bonded) raw materials for manufacturing products for local consumption and export; but there would be Customs Duty on "consumable stores;" granting the Grand Bahama Port Authority the right to sell real estate, supply utilities to all residences and industrial and commercial enterprises and to exact a fee from its licensees.

Licensees were to be granted the right to employ expatriates where suitably qualified Bahamians were not available, though it was expected that Bahamians would be trained to serve in such capacities. In exchange the Government sold 50,000 acres to the Grand Bahama Port Authority at a nominal price. This was later increased to over 200,000 acres; known as the Port Area, it is larger than New Providence, site of the Capital, Nassau.

> "So began a new city, Freeport, which has become the second largest city in the Bahamas."

Thus, Sir Stafford Lofthouse Sands was most actively involved in all the major measures to bring about the revitalization of the Bahamian economy during the post-World War II era. These, as has been demonstrated were:

> The development and promotion of Tourism and Financial Services as the principal pillars of the Bahamian economy, the revaluation of the Bahamian Dollar placing it on par with the U.S. Dollar and the implementation of the Hawksbill Creek Agreement.

Reviewing the progress of the Bahamian economy over the past half-century, it is evident that, despite various efforts at its diversification, "The Stafford Sands Model" still obtains, as Barry Malcolm, President of the Grand Bahama Chamber of Commerce reiterates, Tourism, and the provision of financial and marine services are the main means by which we make a living!"

Accordingly, it is submitted that Sir Stafford Lofthouse Sands, brilliant attorney and financial genius, may be justly described and acknowledged as "The Architect of the Modern Bahamian Economy!"

Now, Sir Stafford Sands, during that interlude in the history of our Bahamaland, when the UBP reached the zenith of its existence--its crushing defeat of the PLP in the General Election of 1962, and the eventual victory of the PLP in that of 1967--wielded tremendous political authority and economic power. For, as Minister of Finance and Tourism he controlled the purse strings of the colony, while firmly in control of the expansion of Tourism, which, by then, had become "the engine of the Bahamian economy"! Admired by some, hated by others, he was, nevertheless, respected by all! Such was his stature in the Bahamian Community in the "hey day" of the UBP!

Occasionally he walked along the main thoroughfare, proudly looking around as if saying to himself, "I am master of all I survey!" He was a tall man, standing "head and shoulders" above most people, and from the vantage of that exalted posture, he appeared to look (through his one good eye!) condescendingly upon them! It is recorded in The Bible that some of the Israelite spies felt themselves "like grasshoppers" upon encountering the giants dwelling in Canaan, the Promised Land (Numbers 13:33). Likewise, this Bahamian "Goliath's" presence was such that were it not for the grace of God, might have unwittingly exerted a similar reaction upon the narrator, then a humble Grade IV Clerk in the Colonial Civil Service, and his fellow employees!

Yet, for all his greatness, Sir Stafford Sands was painfully lacking in an essential cardinal virtue - humility! For, when the Progressive Liberal Party won the General Election in 1967, Sir Stafford, bitterly disappointed, left the Bahamas, never to return again "in the flesh." Unlike Sir Roland Symonette, who continued to serve his country in opposition, Sir Stafford Sands evidently could not bring himself to the point where he could serve in any other position than as a ruler!

Thus he died a year later in self-exile in Spain, a foreign land far away from his home land! This was a tragic demise for one who had not long before, wielded tremendous political clout in his homeland.

Now, Sir Stafford Sands' action of going into voluntary exile after the defeat of his political party (The UBP) at the polls in 1967 was the subject of much lively discussion. For, there were many who were strongly of the opinion that he should have remained to continue his contribution to the development of the land of his birth in opposition.

Here it is germane to observe that "un-regenerate human nature being what it is," those who easily adjust from being in a position of dominance to one of being in subjection in life, are, indeed, "few and far between"! Concretely, many who have sampled the addictive pleasure of "lording it over others" do find it very hard to turn around and we are inclined "to hold on to power as long as we possibly can"! Retired boxers, who return to the ring only to be disgraced by younger, stronger opponents; public servants who stay on the job long after the age of retirement, sometimes blocking the upward mobility of young aspirants to higher office; Ministers of religion who "hold on" to pastorates long after they have passed their prime are all examples of this all too common propensity to retain power and authority.

Moreover, the annals of the long history of humankind are replete with the tragic stories of political potentates who held on tenaciously to their positions of power until forced to surrender same - by resignation, abdication, exile or assassination!

As Lord Acton acidly accurately asserted: "Power corrupts! Absolute power corrupts absolutely!"

Providentially, however, there have been those having exercised great power and influence, who have demonstrated enough humility to surrender same...graciously. Here, pride of place must be attributed to John the Baptist, Patron Saint of the Anglican Diocese of Nassau, the Turks & Caicos Islands and a favourite biblical character of the narrator!

You see, "for a season" John the Baptist, proved to be extremely popular, attracting multitudes from throughout the Holy Land, who flocked to hear him preach, calling them to repentance and moral renewal! But when Jesus the Christ began his earthly ministry, John, in an act of supreme humility, graciously "bowed out," exhorting his disciples "Behold the lamb of God who taketh away the sin of the world"! With grateful resignation, confessing, "He must increase; I must decrease." (John 1:19-30; 3:26-30).

"Historically speaking," however, few, indeed, of the leaders of humankind, who have tasted of the addictive fruit of wielding great power, have, like John the Baptist, been willing to relinquish same.. gracefully! The haughty Stafford Lofthouse Sands was not one of them!

VI. "Zero tolerance for mediocrity!"

Despite the many criticisms leveled against him, the inevitable controversies evoked in discussion about him, and indeed, his own human failings and weaknesses, it is submitted that there is at least one positive lesson we can all learn, and greatly benefit from, by careful reflection upon the life and contributions of Stafford Lofthouse Sands.

It gradually becomes abundantly clear when we consider questions such as "Why was he able to accomplish so much? How did he manage to establish tourism and financial services as the major components of the Bahamian economy, a situation which has remained virtually intact for more than a half century?

Now, that Sir Stafford Sands was a man of great ability, there can be not a shadow of a doubt. Indeed, like many other brilliant Bahamians, such as Timothy Gibson, Michael Eldon, E. Clement Bethel, and the narrator's brother, Dr. Roger Leslie Weir, Rev. Charles Sweeting and Mrs. Ruby Bethel-Nottage, Attorney-at-Law; he was gifted with a photographic memory--that "computer-like" rare ability to peruse any document, rapidly grasping its salient points and retaining them for instant recall whenever required! But "the secret of Sir Stafford Sands' success was more than this ability. What was it then? The answer is at hand--he was a man, who in his own lifestyle epitomized excellence, and as such demanded the same high standard of performance by all who came into contact with him! Concisely, he was a perfectionist who was never satisfied with "second best." This was evident in the manner in which he dressed, the way in which he operated His law office, the manner in which related to his associates and the way in which he treated those whom he employed.

Physically a giant (300 hundred pounder!), Sir Stafford, neatly attired in his custom tailored suits, his ever present glasses without frames, complete with his mirror-shined ebony shoes, always appeared to be dressed like he was on his way to a banquet!

It is said that the late Five-Star General Colin Powell, former top ranking military officer of the United States of America, was the kind of person who made you make the effort to look your best when you have an appointment to meet him. Such a person also was Sir Stafford Sands. In the atmosphere of dignity and formality which surrounded him, you felt it necessary to make sure that your hair was properly combed, all buttons in place and that your shoe laces were properly tied!

As a pioneer in corporate law, the chambers of Sir Stafford Sands set the pace in proficiency. Those who worked therein: junior attorneys (no place for partners!) secretaries, receptionists, or messengers - knew that "the boss" was a person who demanded very high standards.

Thus secretaries were given a specific amount of time to complete the typing of the many important documents that passed through his chambers. According to the late Arthur Barnett and other educators of mathematics, "speed and accuracy are the absolute requirement for success in math exams. Speed and accuracy were expected of the secretaries who worked for Sir Stafford Sands, with emphasis on the latter. Sir Stafford Sands, then, carefully examined the manuscripts by the typists.

That he only had one good eye proved absolutely no impediment to the precision of his exacting scrutiny. Any signs of slipshod work, "typos," and poor spelling, and/or bad grammar, deviations from instructions were simply not tolerated. (Bear in mind that, in those days before) "spell-check," much more depended upon the skill of the typists then than today! Those who worked for Sir Stafford Sands knew that if they did not measure up" to the high standard demanded by him, they would (in the words of Donald Trump hear, "You're fired!" or more likely, they would not have gotten to be hired...in the first place. Excellence was the hallmark of all documents emanating from the chambers of Sir Stafford Lofthouse Sands, Attorney-at-Law!

It is now; abundantly clear (to use a favorite expression of Mr. Yarn Middleton, former Principal of Queen's College, and Nassau, Bahamas) that Sir Stafford Sands had a passion for excellence and efficiency. Not sparing any effort to attain the best, he demanded the same dedication to duty of the rest! Concisely, Sir Stafford Sands had "... zero tolerance for mediocrity!"

Assistant Commissioner of Police, Emrick Seymour, stationed in Freeport, often emphasized that the Royal Bahamas Police Force has "zero tolerance for crime!" by the same token, it may be asserted that the contributions and lifestyle of Sir Stafford Sands epitomized "zero tolerance for mediocrity!"

It is, indeed, most instructive for us to pause here to reflect profoundly upon the meaning of this particular word. In the Oxford Dictionary "mediocrity" is defined thusly:

1. The state of being average in quality.

2. A person of average ability and lacking in flair or imagination.

The compilers of this well recognized authority in the field of the meaning of words in the English language might well have added "lacking in ambition." For, you see, mediocrity has more to do with effort than achievement! It's more about being consistent and conscientious than about being successful. It has to do more with a journey than a destination. Mediocrity, therefore, is most destructive to human achievement precisely because it's being satisfied with "second best." It has caused a countless number of persons to fail to realize what Dr. Myles Munroe liked to describe as their God-given potential. Concisely, it is being satisfied with less than your best when you know that you are better than the rest! And while mediocrity is detrimental and stifling in all fields of human endeavor, it is especially devastating in that of education.

In this regard, there can be no doubt that one reason why we are not getting the results expected in our educational endeavors is simply this--there are far too many of our students who are prepared just "to get by" or "just to pass." They are satisfied to continue along the path of mediocrity (being average), which is not good!

Mediocrity, then in the classroom is being satisfied with attaining "a Passing Grade C, when you really are capable 'with a little more effort' to attain a 'B" or even 'A'"! It is deliberately attaining a lower grade than that of-which you are capable--in order "to please your pals" (known as 'dumbing down' the bane of many of our male students!) Or, perhaps, just not to be considered a nerd.' It is precisely for this reason that leaders in the field of education constantly exhort their students to rise above mediocrity and to strive to do their best.

Thus Timothy Gibson, eminent educator, composer of the Bahamian National Anthem, constantly called upon his students to reject mediocrity by striving "to be the best that they can be!" This, indeed, is well expressed in the opening words of our national anthem: "Lift up your heads to the rising sun, Bahamaland!" Moreover, in 2014, our Minister of Education, the Hon. Jerome Fitzgerald has, on many occasions, taken the opportunity to make a clarion call to all Bahamian students steadfastly to reject mediocrity by striving for excellence.

This call to reject mediocrity, may be applied to all whether, you are a student in a primary or secondary level, an undergraduate at college or a research scholar preparing for your PhD., you must take full advantage of the opportunities afforded you to improve your educational standard by ruthlessly rejecting mediocrity as you strive to excel by developing your God endowed talents to the best of your ability.

This call to eschew mediocrity, i.e., "getting by" rather than "aiming high" may be applied to people "in all walks of life." Whether, you are serving in government, commerce, banking, tourism, the administration of justice, education, the church or Industry--you can, indeed, prove to be most effective and greatly benefit from "taking a leaf out of the book of Sir Stafford Sands by consistently and uncompromisingly exercising "zero tolerance for mediocrity!"

What, then, can we say, summarily and unequivocally about the life and legacy of Sir Stafford Sands? The answer is by no means easy and straightforward. For, idolized by some, vilified by others, Sir Stafford Sands was, arguably the most controversial figure ever to emerge on the Bahamian political scene. Now, nearly a half-century since his demise in exile, the mere mention of his name can provoke lively highly polarized debate "in some circles"! Taking into consideration these developments, is it too much to suggest that as far as consensus with regard to the life and legacy of Sir Stafford Sands are concerned, "the jury is still out?" The narrator thinks not!

positively, however, there can be no doubt that the successful, most effective measures that Sir Stafford Sands initiated and executed in order to renew the economy of the Bahamas after World War II, his ability and stickability to get things done and his " zero tolerance of mediocrity" must be considered, in retrospect, commendable and worthy of emulation.

On the other hand, his condescending attitude, arrogance, lack of humility and abandonment of his homeland in the wake of the defeat of his party in the General Election of 1967 constitute reasons why there remain many in the Bahamas today who find themselves unable, honestly, to attribute to him a measure of respect, but by no means admiration!

Like every other human (created in the image of God, endowed with freedom), he had his strengths and weaknesses, virtues and vices, talents and temptations. As Mr. Prince Smith, retired police officer of the Royal Bahamas Police Force and amateur Bahamian historian, who has "vivid memories of encounters with Sir Stafford Sands," put it, "There was some good in him...and there was some bad in him!"

Many and varied, therefore, are the opinions of Bahamians with regard to the life, contributions and legacy of Sir Stafford Sands. It is not certain when or whether consensus will be reached on this still much debated personality. There can be not a shadow of a doubt, however, that all would agree that Sir Stafford Lofthouse Sands,"

Architect of the Modern Bahamian Economy was, indeed "A Bahamian Who Made a Difference--a big difference!"

Lillian Gloria Weir-Coakley

Librarian, Community Builder

(February 10, 1925 – July 27, 2002)

INTRODUCTION:

Whenever the word "Library" or "Library Science" is mentioned or discussed in any context in the Bahamas, there is one name which inevitably comes to mind—Lillian Weir Coakley. For she was a pioneer who rendered many years of quality service as a Librarian. Despite her major contribution, little is known about her. The purpose of the contribution is to tell the story about this remarkable Bahamian lady!

"PULLEY" GROWING UP IN NASSAU

Lillian Gloria Weir-Coakley was born on February 10, 1925 to Charles Hilton and Jenny Weir (née Foulkes), Nassau, Bahamas. Being the youngest of six children, she was greatly beloved in the family including her parents, elder siblings, and her aunt Lily Weir, after whom she was named. A diligent, intelligent child, she was affectionately known as "Pulley" by members of the Weir clan and close friends.

Now, the young Lily was very intelligent and most studious, demonstrating special interest in reading the many books available in her home, then a stately two-story mansion located on Blue Hill Road, opposite the extensive grounds of Government House. Her interest in reading and love of books were harbingers of a career dedicated to acquiring knowledge and imparting it to others. Librarian Pulley, although small in stature, robust in health was by no means a bookworm, confined to the home or classroom. Athletic and physically attractive, she was an avid player of lawn tennis and an able swimmer. In many ways she was a bridge personality, a connecting link between the older Weirs and those of the younger generation of Weirs including the narrator, his siblings and their cousin, Leo Roberts. Indeed the narrator vividly recalls occasions when Pulley took him and other youngsters swimming at Long Wharf. She always had a keen interest in helping others to develop to the best of their ability whatever field of human endeavor they were engaged.

Tutored at primary and secondary levels at schools operated by the Board, now the Ministry of Education, nurtured in the Christian faith at the family church, Grant's Town, Lillian developed into a Christian young lady of fine caliber. Indeed, she was groomed in and certainly demonstrated Christian principles and virtues in her daily living, notably discipline, good manners, respect for elders, the priority of education and dedication to excellence--virtues which really proved to be very important in her life of service in the land of her birth.

LIBRARIAN PAR EXCELLENCE

Interestingly enough, the young Lillian Weir had no intention to become a professional librarian, for it was her initial aim to become a social worker. To this end, she pursued studies at tertiary level at Hampton University, Hampton, Virginia. When she graduated from that prestigious institution with her Bachelor of Science degree in social work in 1947, it was probable that one could count on one's fingers the number of Bahamians who had earned academic qualifications at institutions of tertiary education abroad. Always ambitious, she later earned a Master's Degree at Atlanta University.

Now, with such impeccable academic qualifications, there can be no doubt that she could have remained in the USA with its many opportunities for lucrative employment at institutions there. However, being deeply patriotic, she elected to return home to serve her Bahamian people. Yet despite her high academic standard or, some would say, because of same, she was unable to find employment in the Bahamas in her chosen field of human endeavor. In a sense most profound, she was a prophet or prophetess "without honour in her own country."

Undaunted by this disappointment, she embarked upon a project providing education for persons who were desirous of improving their academic qualifications. It was during this period that she met and was joined in matrimony to the love of her life, Bruce Coakley, who was a musician, being saxophonist in the then very popular Lou Adams Band.

Then, an event occurred, which decisively proved to be of tremendous significance, a turning point which was destined to decisively influence the course of her sojourn through life. Mrs. Ruth Russell, Librarian at the Southern Public Library resigned. "There was no librarian to replace her and Mrs. Coakley was encouraged to take over this responsibility. With typical confidence, discipline and determination, she embarked upon her responsibilities as Librarian.

Very fortunately, the academic skills—research methodology, compiling and classifying data acquired at tertiary level abroad, greatly facilitated her entry into a new, challenging field of human endeavor. Accordingly, she diligently and persistently sought to qualify herself as a professional librarian by attending seminars and training courses, and of course, by extensive reading and research about Library Science.

Then, for thirty-eight years she served with diligence and dedication at the Southern Public Library, which she often referred to as "The Library," Mrs. Coakley was by no means a nine to five o'clock watching civil servant! Rather, she continued, consistently over her many years of service working for long hours every day, often going far beyond the call of duty!

'Bahamians in all walks of life' benefitted greatly from her service at the Library. As a strict disciplinarian 'from the old school', she carefully garnered students from the schools in the community, who came in great numbers to use the facilities of the library. She soon earned their respect and admiration. Thus, those who were inclined to be noisy and boisterous, suddenly became quiet and studious the moment they entered the Library! They all knew that they were expected 'to behave themselves' while studying at the library under the watchful eye of "Miss Coakley." Well-known and highly respected in the community, she would not hesitate to contact the parents of any students who misbehaved or forgot their manners while at the library...and they knew it! For, you see, during the early years of her service, a considerable number of the homes 'over the hill' were not electrified so, some students from such homes would do their homework at the library, often remaining until closing time late in the evening! In later years, after the establishment of the College (now University of the Bahamas) and other institutions of tertiary education, she assisted students in carrying out research and other academic skills required for study at advanced level. Indeed, this Librarian recalled that she was even called upon by politicians, who came to the Library when preparing speeches for delivery at political rallies at the adjourning Southern Recreation Grounds!

Fully cognizant of the fact that she had been afforded opportunities for educational advancement beyond the scope of the vast majority of her fellow Bahamians, she sought to 'give back' to the community by imparting to them as much as she could!

Now, in accord with her well-earned reputation as leading Librarian, she was very active in the Bahamas Library Association, serving for several years as its Vice President.

Moreover, she was a founding member of "The Friends of Archives," being most keenly interested in all aspects of the extensive and ever expanding field of Library Science.

Assessing the sterling contributions of Mrs. Lillian Weir-Coakley to the progress of Library Science in the Bahamas over many years, from the perspective of the teaching of Dr. Myles Munroe, it may be confidently concluded that, in so doing, she was acting in accord with the "divine purpose" for her life!

COMPASSIONATE SOCIAL WORKER

Now, as has been demonstrated, Mrs. Lillian Weir-Coakley, originally prepared herself for a career, not in Librarianship, but as a social worker. So, in addition to her tremendous strides in the library service, her lively life-long concern for the welfare of others led her to engage in many activities which may be truly described as 'social work'; these were done on a purely voluntary basis, motivated by a strong desire to serve the Bahamian public.

Accordingly, she served for many years as a member of the Juvenile Panel. It was in this capacity that she became acutely aware of the challenges of many of the young Bahamians who found themselves on the wrong side of the law. Indeed, she demonstrated a special concern for the socio-economic, moral and spiritual development of those young Bahamian males who, being unable to cope with the challenges of academic studies, became engaged in anti-social behavior. It was for this reason that Mrs. Coakley rendered much voluntary service to other youth organizations, including the Girl Guides and the Young Women's Christian Association, commonly known as "The Y"!

SERVICE IN THE CHURCH

Now, there can be no doubt that the motivating factor in Mrs. Lillian Weir-Coakley's sacrificial service in the Bahamian community was her deep Christian faith! For, as has been indicated, she was nurtured in Christian principles at Wesley Methodist Church, Grants Town, Nassau, Bahamas.

There, her father, Charles Hilton Weir, "Uncle Charley," had served for many years as Director of the choir. An accomplished musician, he participated enthusiastically in divine worship. Accompanying the vigorous singing of the congregation blowing his ever present cornet. Also very active in the church was his sister, Miss Lily Weir. Affectionately known as "Aunt Lilly" by all, she was the highly respected Sunday School Superintendent, who taught music during the week.

Brought up in a Christian atmosphere, little Lily made her commitment to Christ early in life. She remained faithful to it, serving the Lord for life as a Sunday School Teacher, class leader and Prayer Group Leader.

She participated, with deep devotion, in church services, always most attentively to the proclamation of the Gospel by the preacher. And just as she disciplined children in the Library, she instructed them 'to be quiet and respectful' while attending services in the church! For as we have seen, she placed very high priority on the nurture of youth.

In recognition of and appreciation for her many years of dedicated service in the church and community, Mrs. Lillian Weir-Coakley was honoured by the women of the Methodist Church at a testimonial luncheon which was held on Sunday, January 20th, 2000. This gala ceremony was held under the distinguished patronage of the Rev. Dr. Raymond Neilly, then Superintendent Minister of the Nassau Circuit and Mrs. Neilly, at Breezes Super Club, Cable Beach. It was a most appropriate and well-deserved gesture of appreciation. For, she was indeed, a fine Christian lady, whose robust faith was manifested in all her activities!

Thus, in a manner, at once creative and effective, Mrs. Coakley blended her profession (Librarianship) and her passion (social work/community service) in making her unique contribution to the intellectual, moral, social and spiritual development of the people of her beloved Bahamaland! For, this disciplined Christian lady never ever missed the opportunity to impart positive Christian values to others, especially 'those of the younger generation'! This verse from a song, which was very popular in the Bahamas during her youthful years, sums up, most poignantly, her contribution to the Bahamian society:

"To love someone more dearly every day

To help a wondering child to find his way

And smile when evening comes,

And smile when evening comes

...This is my task!

HER ENDURING LEGACY--DRAMATIC IMPROVEMENT IN BAHAMIAN LIBRARY SERVICES!

When Mrs. Lillian Weir-Coakley took up the challenge to serve as Librarian at the Southern Public Library, the provision of library facilities was by no means a priority of 'the powers that be'. As a result, she served in that capacity at great personal sacrifice receiving very little in terms of financial compensation. Indeed, when the time came for her to retire, a special Act of Parliament had to be passed to ensure that she should receive a well-deserved pension.

Instrumental in this process was Dr. Cleveland Eneas, a long time member of the Board of this Library.

Now, a report issued at that time included the statement that:

> "A matter of concern of this dedicated woman of little physical stature, who has championed the cause of Librarianship for over thirty-seven years continues to be that Library Service in the Bahamas has received only 'lip service' when it comes to funding and providing adequate facilities. This is unfortunate but it is Mrs. Coakley's hope that library and library services will be perceived as an important element in the educational, economic and social development of the Bahamas."

Now, there can be no doubt that Mrs. Coakley herself did much to realize this goal in her own many years of dedicated service. Thus due recognition was afforded to her by a grateful community. Accordingly she received honours and awards including:

1984 Awards from the Zonta and Kiwanis service organizations

1984 The British Empire Medal (M.B.E.) bestowed upon her by Queen Elizabeth II

1989 Wesley Methodist Church for faithful service

1991 Exemplary Leadership and Outstanding Award by the Bahamas Law Guild

1996 Zeta Phi Beta Sorority Award for Outstanding Community Service and Lillian Coakley's Scholarship in Library Science

1999 The Bahamas Order of Merit

2004 On July, the Government of the Bahamas, in an act of supreme appreciation and recognition of her sterling contribution to the development of Library Science in the Bahamas renamed the Southern Public Library "The Lillian Weir-Coakley Library."

At that impressive, well-attended ceremony, several prominent personalities, including the Hon. Allyson Maynard-Gibson, MP and the Hon. Alfred Sears, MP; testified that they had benefitted from the wise counsel of Mrs. Coakley while studying at the library!

Then a few years later, the Ministry of Education made a major step forward by appointing a full-time Director of Library Science.

Another development in this area was the establishment of the ultra-modern Moore Library at the University of the Bahamas.

The dream, then, of Mrs. Coakley that Library Service should become an important element in the Bahamian community is gradually being realized.

Its fulfillment can only be of tremendous benefit to all the people of the Bahamas in the years ahead. When the gathering, classification and imparting of information is expected to become a matter of top priority in the educational and social and socio-economic progress of humankind. In keeping with this trend, the Hon. Jeffrey Lloyd, Minister of Education (2017- Sep.2021) had announced an ambitious plan to computerize all the documents in our schools including the resources in the libraries providing all students with the latest in technology as they seek to acquire more knowledge. This was very encouraging, for as it has been truly said, "Knowledge is power!" As such, it is a key to success in life.

There can be no doubt that Mrs. Lillian Weir-Coakley would have certainly approved these advances in education for they are in keeping with her vision for the land of her birth.

Lillian Gloria Weir Coakley, Librarian par excellence, social worker, and pacesetter...truly "A Bahamian Who Made a Difference!"

Questions and Exercises

1. What steps did Mrs. Lillian Weir-Coakley take to improve Library Service in The Bahamas?

2. Why was she successful in this undertaking?

3. Would you consider becoming a Librarian? Give three reasons for your answer.

4. "Knowledge is power." Discuss.

5. Write short notes on three of the following:

   Library

   Library Science

   The use of technology in obtaining knowledge

   Historical Research

Rev. Charles Christopher Curry
1915 – 1980

Intimate Spirituality, Family Man, Pastor and Missionary

Introduction

An Overview of His Life and Background

Rev. Charles Christopher Curry was born in 1915 to his parents Mr. Bruce Curry and wife, Mrs. Branhilda Curry née Sawyer, at New Ply, Green Turtle Cay, Abaco, Bahamas. Charles was the eldest of five children, his siblings were Robert and Paul his brothers, and Cynthia and Marion his sisters.

Charles' childhood and youth was exposed to all that life had to offer the inhabitants of the Abacos at that time. Key influences upon his life were his family, the church, and school. Growing up in a small close-knit community, he had the opportunity to watch and be nurtured by toiling and harvesting the soil and the sea. Migration and immigration was normal in Green Turtle Cay with families going and coming from other Family Islands and the USA. Culturally, Green Turtle Cay, a settlement known today for its fastidiousness in maintaining clean and well-kept homes and gardens, is a community rich in history.

Born into a Methodist family, Charles was baptized as an infant in the local Methodist Church and matured through the Methodist catechism of Christian formation and discipleship. He was a Sunday School pupil, confirmed as a member of the church, became a Sunday School teacher and a local preacher. He was regarded as the pillar and stalwart of the church for many years before leaving for theological training.

Educationally, Charles attended the Green Turtle Cay All Age School and after completing the required classes he matriculated and became a school monitor as a young teenager. A position he held for a number of years.

Later, Charles, while still in the civil service, became a police officer and served the community in that capacity with distinction until he entered the Methodist ministry.

Charles married a native of Green Turtle Cay, Miss Enid Moncur, in 1935 and this union produced 16 children: Edwina, Eudene, Faye, Christopher, Zorene, Patricia, Leonard, William, Charles, Adel, Colon, Eugene, Pedro, Mary, Angela, John and Calvert...

Charles' deep desire in life was to be a Methodist minister. This was his career choice, goal and vocation. It is recalled that he shared the effect that the gospel had upon his life, as he sensed God impressing upon him the need for ministry which penetrated his life. The call to enter the ministry at this time, had to be divinely inspired. It was a challenge from many perspectives for a young black man with a growing family. For many it appeared irrational and

346

impossible. Yet, Charles' pursuit of this ministerial ambition was remarkable. It was a great personal and family sacrifice to pursue this calling. However, Charles' persistence and success was culturally uplifting and inspiring.

The Strong influence of Methodism in The Bahamas

The Methodist Church began in the Bahamas about 1783 when Joseph Paul, a free black former slave from America came to the Bahamas. Mr. Paul first settled in the Abacos with other loyalists from America and later moved to Nassau. Mr. Paul was identified as the one preaching outdoors at Augusta and Heathfield Streets under a spreading tree. Mr. Paul later started the first schools for black people (the descendants of slaves) in the Bahamas. The first Methodist trust was incorporated, the first parcel of land purchased and the church erected in the late 1780s – early 1790s. The tenets of Methodist teaching and church order were formulated in the Bahamas before the death of the founder of Methodism, Rev. Fr. John Wesley in 1803.

The socio-economic-political climate had changed from the eighteenth century to the twentieth century in the Bahamas and was still evolving. The Methodist Church in the Bahamas was a district in the West Indies in the 1950s of the Methodist Overseas Division of the Wesleyan Methodist Church in Great Britain. The Methodist Church in the Bahamas had many local preachers and auxiliary preachers both black and white who were the lifeline in keeping Methodism alive throughout the Bahamian islands as a connextion. The Bahamian Methodist as an itinerant Methodist Minister was rare.

Historically, the first Bahamian candidate for the Methodist Ministry was Mr. Alexander Thompson in the 1870s. Mr. Thompson was sent to Jamaica as the first student for the newly established theological college for the training of Methodist ministers in the West Indies, York Castle Theological College.

The Desegregation of the Methodist Church

The Methodist Church in the Bahamas gained a strong influence in the country; however, the church had a race problem. In churches where there were mixed races, the white people sat on one side and the black people sat on the other side. In some cases, church organizations were separated by race and met on different days. When Rev. Mr. Alexander Thompson returned to the Bahamas after his studies, he was sent to Green Turtle Cay to help ease the racial tension due to the seating arrangement. The race problem was not settled in the church or the country in the 1870s and still persisted in the 1950s. Another race problem was in the area of Education. Queen's College, a Methodist educational institution only accepted white students. The Methodist Church in Great Britain, sensitive to the situation, sent ministers with the specific focus of ending racial tension and division in the Bahamas in the beginning and in the middle of the twentieth century.

The sparse number of candidates stretched over the years in the Bahamas. However, in the 1950s there was a change on the horizon which was a reflection of the ecceslesiatical, cultural and societal change. Previously, the Methodist clergy were white Europeans, but now indigenous black Caribbean clergy were coming to the Bahamas.

Local blacks were now candidating and being accepted as ministers in training for the ministry of Word and Sacrament. The era had come where the decolonization of the Methodist pulpit was a reality being embraced globally. Rev. Charles Curry was not the first black candidate for the ministry but he was the one who was confident, consistent and faithful to the end.

To candidate, Rev. Curry's process included a mentorship where he had to spend time in the home of a Methodist minister for a period of time. Rev. Curry had this exposure to the ministry under the guardianship of Rev. Armstrong at Hope Town, Abaco. Having completed the prerequisite exams, Rev. Curry went on to formal theological studies and ministerial formation in Jamaica in 1955 at Union Theological Seminary. Rev. Curry found the academic theological training challenging, enlightening and stimulating. He possessed ability, zest and zeal. The educational caliber of the Methodist minister was highly esteemed and respected in the community.

Upon the completion of his studies, Rev. Curry was assigned to the Bahamas, his home country where he was stationed at what was known as the Windward Mission, which included Andros, Cat Island, Acklins and Long Island. As an itinerant ordained Methodist minister, Rev. Curry was transferred to the Jamaica District and then back to the Bahamas.

Rev. Curry's Service and Ministry

Rev. Curry's sermons were said to be exegetical. Profound but simple enough to be understood by both children and adults in the congregation. In one of his eulogies conducted he was remembered for praising the deceased, who in his humble way was faithful to God and stated declared that he desired that as his life goal he desired to be faithful to God.

Rev. Curry served as Secretary to the District Synod and subsequently elected Chairman and General Superintendent of the Bahamas/Turks and Caicos Islands District of the Methodist Church in the Caribbean and the Americas. Rev. Curry was the first Bahamian-born minister to fill this high office of Methodism in the Bahamas in 1978.

Rev. Curry sought to fulfill his office with spiritual discernment, compassion, truth, justice and a heart of love. He was a gentleman but not one to be taken for granted. A tribute to him echoed the sentiments of his colleagues at seminary 'This is the first time we are meeting a gentle policeman'. He was deliberate and held his convictions even if he had to walk out of a meeting. As the voice and symbol of Methodism in the Bahamas and Bahamian Methodism to the world, Rev. Curry was concerned about the continuous thrust of the education of youth, work among youth, the mission of the church and the integrity of the church as being holy, catholic, apostolic and united.

Rev. Charles Curry took ill suddenly while conducting an induction service on the island of Eleuthera, he was airlifted to the capital, Nassau, where he died a few days later. His funeral was held at Ebenezer Methodist Church and buried at Ebenezer graveyard alongside other Methodist ministers including Rev. William Turton. A favorite hymn of Rev. Curry 'Thou God of truth and love' gives a perspective into his sense of intimate spirituality, family life, pastoral life, and mission and congregation life.

Rev. Charles Curry was, indeed a "Bahamian Who Made a Difference" in every aspect of the phrase!

E. Clement Bethel

(February 11, 1938 – August 24, 1987)

Bahamian Cultural Icon

INTRODUCTION - "THE E. CLEMENT BETHEL AWARDS"

During "exam time," usually towards the end of the academic year, thousands of eager students, from throughout the length and breadth of the Commonwealth of the Bahamas, participate in the examinations for the E. Clement Bethel Awards. These students, after years of diligent preparation compete for awards in varied subjects including music, vocal as well as instrumental renditions, poetry, drama, dance and other cultural disciplines. Those who excel are afforded the rare, distinguished and delightful opportunity to attend the impressive E. Clement Bethel Awards Ceremony at Government House.

Always, "with pride and joy," the nervous young recipients feel highly honoured to be presented with their awards by the Governor General!

Now, while diligently preparing for these awards, very few of the thousands of students who participate in the highly competitive examinations for these prestigious awards know much about the great Bahamian in whose name and recognition they are held.

Our purpose, here then is to learn about this great Bahamian cultural icon - Edward Clement Bethel.

Early Life and Education

Edward Clement Bethel (or Clement Bethel) was born on February 11th, 1938 into a well-respected old Bahamian family, who resided on East Bay Street, "up east" as many Bahamians referred to that section of the island of New Providence. Youngest of the six children born to Edward and Lillias, Clement, by name and nature, demonstrated that he was a very gifted person early in his life. His father passed while Clement was still a small child and his saintly mother, Lillias, made sure that he attended Sunday school at the nearby Central Gospel Chapel bringing him up "in the nurture and admonition of the Lord. Thus, at an early age, he made a commitment of his life to Christ. A brilliant student, "young Clement Bethel" excelled in the very highly competitive entrance examinations for the then prestigious Government High School, winning a scholarship to that then very prestigious institution of secondary education.

It was at the Government High School that the narrator/chronicler first met Clement Bethel that he demonstrated his academic ability in the entrance examination, he was expected to maintain this high standard throughout the four years he spent there. For, he worked under the watchful eye of one of the great Bahamian educators, Mr. Cecil Valentine Bethel, a strict disciplinarian of the old school, Mr. Bethel served as Senior Master and Teacher of Spanish, (*Profesor de Español*).[xcvii]   One of the few Bahamians on the staff comprised mainly of white expatriates, he gained the patriotic respect of all students, next only in authority to the highly respected Headmaster, A. Deans Dr. Peggs. All students knew that they were expected to do their best in the classes of "CV." Young Clement Bethel was no exception, referring to the Revered Senior Master in private conversation with his school pals as "Uncle Cecil" while, respectfully addressing him in class as "Mr. Bethel"/"Sr. (Señor) Bethel!"

Clement Bethel, or "Bethel VI" did very well in all his studies. He excelled in the Cambridge Senior Examinations, gaining "Distinctions" in several subjects, notably English Language and English Literature!

Besides excelling in academia, the multi-talented young Clement Bethel proved to be an excellent musician; a pianist demonstrating deft mastery of the keyboard. With obvious delight and a deep sense of appreciation, he always spontaneously admitted that the person who helped him most in developing this particular talent was none other than Mrs. Meta Davis Cumberbatch.[xcviii] For, she, like "Uncle Cecil" was a strict disciplinarian "from the old school." Thus, she insisted that Clement should engage in diligent music practice for at least two hours every day.

A native of Trinidad, this remarkable lady came to the Bahamas with her husband, the highly respected dentist affectionately known as "Dr. Cumberbatch."

A talented and very competent musician in her own right, she truly identified with the people of her adopted homeland, performing at many concerts and imparting skills to many of its young people.[xcix]

Evidently, this observant, fine, dignified lady "saw something" in the budding Bahamian artist and sought to enable him to develop it to the fullest. (We must always bear in mind that our English word "education" is derived from two Latin expressions being "e" meaning "out of" and *"ducere"* meaning "to lead or draw out." Thus, education is not so much imparting knowledge to another as seeking to develop his/her natural or God-endowed abilities and talents.)

Now, during spring-time every year, coaches and other officials "in the world of sport" come to the Bahamas. The objective of these "talent scouts" is to observe the performance of our young people, mainly in basketball, baseball, softball and athletics. Those who demonstrate great potential are afforded the opportunity to study and participate in highly competitive athletic activities in American universities. In a way most profound, Mrs. Meta Davis Cumberbatch was the "talent scout" who discovered the talented Clement Bethel, the tutor who diligently instructed him in developing his musical talent, and the mentor, who affectionately encouraged him to aspire to "become the best that he could be!!!

Rapid Ascendency to Recognition as Bahamian Cultural Icon

After graduation from the Government High School in 1953, the industrious, ambitious and enthusiastic Clement Bethel assiduously pursued his education at tertiary level while concentrating on music. However, this multi-talented "young Bahamian" did not neglect his prowess in other cultural disciplines: playwriting, choreography, painting Bahamian scenery, Bahamian folklore, Junkanoo, etc.

In pursuit of the specialized academic qualifications required for competence and recognition in the field of cultural education, Mr. Bethel studied at institutions of tertiary education abroad, notably the prestigious Royal School of Music, London, United Kingdom and at the University of California, the United States of America.

As a result of these studies, the brilliant Bahamian scholar earned impressive academic credentials attaining recognition as:

Graduate of the Royal School of Music (GRSM)

Licentiate of the Royal School of Music (LRAM)

Associate of the Royal College of Music (ARCM)

A patriot, Clement Bethel was always interested in "things Bahamian," especially Bahamian folk lore vividly described as "Tellin' ole stories" in the Bahamian community.[c] Both in Nassau and the Out Islands (subsequently known as the "Family Islands") there were members of the older generation who imparted these stories (Ber Bookie and Ber Rabbie) to the delight of "the younger generation," being passed down from generation to generation by means of oral tradition.

Now Clement Bethel as a patriotic young Bahamian applied his talents and training to Bahamian folklore (and as we shall see Junkanoo). Thus he was instrumental in bringing to the people of the Bahamas "The Cat Island Legend of "Sammie Swain." Indeed, this story eventually spread beyond the borders of the Bahamas, gaining international acclaim.

Clement Bethel continued to serve the Bahamas in ways "many and varied" in keeping with his ability as a multi-talented individual. While devoting much of his time and energy to teaching, he also was very active in playing at concerts, establishing the Renaissance Singers and promoting the development of Bahamian Culture. Interestingly

356

enough, much of this work was done in collaboration with another Bahamian cultural icon - Timothy Gibson, author of the Bahamian National Anthem.

In recognition of his competence and deep concern for the cultural development of the people of the Bahamas, Clement Bethel was appointed the first Director of Culture of the Ministry of Education, Science & Technology (then the Ministry of Education and Culture). It was, indeed, the crowning achievement of his career and he served with great dedication and enthusiasm.

Indeed, Edward Clement Bethel proved to be an excellent Director of Culture of the Ministry of Education setting a very high standard for anyone who was appointed to serve in the top post in the challenging field of Cultural Education!

Happy Home & Family Life

While a student at "The Old Government High," Clement Bethel often spoke, with admiration about one Keva Eldon. According to Clement she was one of the most brilliant students at Queen's College. He would go on to tell how well she did in the Cambridge Senior Examinations. Yet, there was something about the way in which he spoke about this female student at Queen's College which betrayed an interest in her which was "more than academic!'

Thus, it was not surprising when he married "the love of his life" Keva, a beautiful young lady destined to make a major contribution in the field of education. This happy union of two outstanding educators produced two children - Edward (named after his father) and lovely little Nicolette, (Dr. Nicolette Bethel-Burrows). These two young people continue to serve the Bahamian community, literally "following in the footsteps of their famous parents." Concisely, there is Edward following in the footsteps of his mother by serving in the field of education, and Nicolette, following in the footsteps of her father, by demonstrating keen interest and competence in the cultural aspect of the development of the people of the Bahamas

The E. Clement Bethel Awards

There can be no doubt that Edward Clement Bethel (or E. Clement Bethel as he preferred to be known) was a very remarkable man! Multi-talented, he was nevertheless humble, blessed with the saving grace of humour, was always very observant, a keen judge of human character, meticulous, and thorough in everything he attempted. He had no tolerance for mediocrity or half-heartedness.

While no nationalist or social activist, Clement Bethel, was at heart a patriot who deeply loved his homeland- its people and its products. Developing his own God-endowed talents to the fullest, he was also deeply interested in encouraging all his fellow Bahamians to do the same.

His great pride in being Bahamian was dramatically demonstrated early in his eventful life. Thus while in his late teens, he proudly represented the Bahamas at an International Youth Conference.

There, literally hundreds of young people drawn from all the nations and colonies of the Commonwealth, were all smartly attired in the native dress of their homeland. But Clement Bethel "stole the show," appearing in a brightly coloured, tropical outfit topped by a two foot tall Bahamian straw work hat!

Yes, that was Clement Bethel "at his finest hour" – representing his beloved Bahamaland abroad! Always proudly promoting "things Bahamian," very proud to represent his homeland wherever he went! It was indeed this sense of patriotism which was the key to his major contribution in life.

This is why he was instrumental in the promotion of "The Legend of Sammy Swain." By the same token, Clement Bethel took a keen interest in the promotion of what has become the premier, internationally recognized epitome of Bahamian culture– Junkanoo.

Clement in his studies at home and abroad, devoted much of his time in tracing the History of Junkanoo from its roots in Africa and its gradual evolution in the Bahamas. Indeed, he must be ranked with cultural giants such as Winston "Gus" Cooper, "Chippie" Chipman, Jackson Burnside, Arlene Nash-Ferguson, Percy Vola Francis and a host of others including his daughter Nicolette who dedicated their energy and talents to making Junkanoo the powerful cultural celebration that it is today.

Clement Bethel, then, was passionate about the development of Bahamian culture during his life time; he worked tirelessly along with others in tracing the cultural development of the Bahamas. The narrator vividly recalls Clement Bethel and Timothy Gibson visiting and talking with his legendary Aunt Lily[ci] about the historical development of the culture of our nation. For, when Clement Bethel began to take a lively interest in Bahamian culture, he soon found that it was no easy undertaking. There were, indeed, those who opined that "we have no culture" or denied that there, was such a thing as Bahamian culture. It was this general feeling of apathy about Bahamian culture which resulted in many Bahamians resorting to the culture of other nations. Thus, budding Bahamian singers would imitate the distinctive style of foreign artists. Thus, in the popular concerts held in "Over the Hill" communities, contestants would begin by saying that "I sing like Nat "King" Cole" or "I sing like Louis 'Satchmo' Armstrong" or some other, often black American, singer. This imitation of foreign singers, musicians and even Rappers, has continued until the present. Hence the popularity of the reggae singers from Jamaica, beginning with the famous visit of Bob Marley, and the rise of many, young Bahamian Reggae singers and Rappers. Concisely, there have been and continue to exist many Bahamians who lack pride in the culture of their homeland. This is manifested by the fact that often foreign artists attract large crowds of Bahamian youth, while some Bahamian entertainers complain that their performances are poorly attended."

Yet over the years there have been those Bahamians who have sought to develop the culture of the Bahamas and have done what they could to encourage their fellow Bahamians to do the same. It has often proved to be an "uphill struggle" and, at times, discouraging.[cii] Clement Bethel was certainly amongst those Bahamians who dedicated their lives to the development of the culture of our young nation.

Their efforts have not been in vain! For, today, young Bahamians can take pride in the culture of their homeland, indeed, there can be no doubt that it is now well recognized that we as a people do have a culture, peculiar to these islands, which merits to be developed to the fullest by ourselves and shared with others. This is why the Clement Bethel awards are so crucial to the cultural development of our young nation. For at its heart is the encouragement of young Bahamians to dedicate their God-given talents to the growth and recognition of the culture of these islands. They need not be ashamed of "Things Bahamian" but can, with great pride, develop the culture of our nation - whether in song, drama or painting or dance - and share the fruit of their endeavors with people "in every corner of the globe."

Retrospectively, there can be no doubt that this wonderful achievement has come about, largely through the determination of Edward Clement Bethel, who passed at the comparatively young age of forty-nine, to promote the all-around development of the unique culture of the people of the-Commonwealth of the Bahamas!

This attitude of 'dogged determination', of trying again and again to achieve one's goal, of persevering against all odds, what some Bahamians describe as "stickability" which motivated Clement Bethel , throughout his eventful life, is well encapsulated in the immortal words of his major musical contribution:

When the road is rough,

When you've had enough -

>Don't cry, don't sigh ...wonder why,

>Just keep on tryin'

>Keep on tryin'
>Tomorrow's another day[ciii]

This song certainly "lifts the spirits" of all who sing it! The chronicler vividly recalls that it was a favorite musical item during his tenure at the Boys Industrial School (now the Simpson S. Penn Centre for Boys).

The young residents of this correctional institution sang this Bahamian national musical rendition with such sincere and great emotion that it pierced the heart of all who listened to them. For, they themselves had first hand experiences of "having enough" of the rough road of suffering abuse, of trying to do their best only to be involved in anti-social behaviour, leading, in some cases, to criminal activity. Yet, evidently, they were struggling to do their best...or to make amends for their bad behaviour in the past, seeking to be lifted from their state of moral degradation to one of being law-abiding citizens of our beloved Bahamaland. Yes, it brought a message that they really needed in their endeavor to do, yea, to be better.[civ]

But the message of this lyric which, profoundly epitomizes the legacy of E. Clement Bethel is relevant, not only to young people under discipline but to people "in all walks of life in the world today!" for, there are times when each and every one of us must face experiences which are most challenging and demanding. There are times when we all feel that "we've had enough". Times when we feel "so stressed out" by the trials and tribulations of life that we feel like giving up. Times when, indeed, the road on which we travel is rough and we feel like "throwing in the towel."

For its encouraging and edifying theme is that we should not, in such moments of depression, "give up" in despair, regret or grief, or wallow in self-pity! Rather, we must get up, "pick up the pieces," and just:

"Keep on tryin' . . . Keep on tryin'

Then, there is the revitalizing assurance that if we do not succeed today, there is tomorrow when we can continue "To keep on tryin' until we attain the place when, having triumphed, by the grace of God, we may be able to look back, declaring

"Stony the road we've trod."[cv]

For, in the final analysis, persistence is the secret of success in all fields of human endeavour ...physical, mental, moral and spiritual[cvi]

Edward Clement Bethel

Pianist

Poet

Prophetic visionary

Perfectionist "par excellence"

Patriot

Promoter of Bahamian Culture

Bahamian Cultural Icon

Truly, "A Bahamian Who Made a Difference!"

Questions for Group Discussion & Exercises

1. How did E. Clement Bethel contribute to the cultural development of the Bahamas?

2. There, is a difference between a "nationalist" and "patriotism." Discuss with special reference to the life and contributions of E. Clement Bethel.

3. Write short notes on two of the following

"Sammie Swain,"

Carnival/Junkanoo

"Cultural Icon "

"Tellin' Old Stories"

4. E. Clement Bethel was a multi-talented person, who excelled in many cultural disciplines. What do you consider are your God-given talents and abilities? Are you using them to the best of your ability? If not, what do you intend to do about it?

6. E. Clement contributed greatly to the cultural development of the Bahamas. Give the names of three others who have served in this way. (300 words each)

7. Bahamians have no real culture of their own. That is why they so often copy the culture of other nations." Discuss.

Patricia Cozzi, Attorney-At-Law

First Bahamian Female Lawyer

(ca 1926 – April 8, 2006)

"Actions speak louder than words!"

Traditional Proverb

There is something unique and absolutely fascinating about being or "coming first!' Thus, the person who manages to be "The First" to accomplish something in any field of human endeavor is always very highly respected. After all, there can be only one "first!' It is precisely for this reason why those who aspire to positions of leadership, who desire "to make a difference" strive to be first or at least "to be the best that they can be!'

And although this propensity to strive for primacy is discerned in every field of human endeavor, nowhere is it more prominent than "in the world of sports". Thus, thousands of persons from every corner of the globe drawn "from all walks of life" may compete in the marathons which have become popular in large cities today. Yet, in

THE REV. DR. JOSEPH EMMETTE AUGUSTUS WEIR, OM JP

these days of "photofinishing" accuracy, with events measured in fractions of seconds, only one can "come first!'

This competitive spirit is so strong that if we are not able to "come first," we identify with and admire greatly those who can. This is why outstanding Jamaican sprinter Usain Bolt is so very popular "in the world today".

It is said that when it comes to "The Olympics," the Chinese seek "to come first" because they claim that while the one who comes first is well-respected and long remembered, no one remembers the person who comes second, third, fourth, or indeed, any other position after the race. Concisely, as far as the Chinese coaches are concerned, only one position really matters—first!

This passion to attain superiority is also evident in many and varied professions, posts and jobs where most people "make a living". Yes, when a person becomes a pioneer in any profession, he/she inevitably attains immediate fame and (sometimes) fortune.

Accordingly, history was made on July 10, 1953 when a beautiful young Bahamian lady was called to the Bar Council of the Bahamas and although she was not the only person called to the Bar that rainy morning (there was also a young man) the focus of national attention was upon her. It was "big news" (fully covered in the media) because she was the first Bahamian woman to enter the legal profession, which literally for hundreds of years, had been dominated by men!

Her name. Patricia Cozzi—being married to an Italian—must have sounded strange and foreign to most Bahamians. As a matter of fact, however, she was a proud descendant of a distinguished, well established, ancient Bahamian family—the Coles of Nassau.

Now, three outstanding features were demonstrated by this particular young lady as she stood before the Bar Council of the then Colony of the Bahamas on that historic occasion.

A COURAGEOUS YOUNG LADY!

First and foremost, she demonstrated courage...great courage!

It is germane to bear in mind here, that throughout the long history of humankind, those who have been called to or attained positions of leadership have come from backgrounds and conditions "many and varied". They have emerged from very varied radical, social, political, national, and religious backgrounds, being very different in physical appearance, character, temperament and competence.

If there is one virtue, however, which has proved to be common to them all, it is...courage! Call it bravery, sheer determination, grit, guts or what you will, it is that indefatigable passion to excel, that daring to be different, essential for leadership in every field of human endeavor!

Thus, it took courage for Father Abraham, in response to the Divine Call to leave the "comfort zone" of his home as a millionaire in Mesopotamia to go to a strange country to which he was directed. It took courage for Christopher Columbus to defy those naysayers who believed the earth to be flat, and set out on a voyage of discovery culminating in landing at San Salvador here in the Bahamas on October 12, 1492, one of the greatest events of the history of humankind. It took courage for The Rev. Dr. Martin Luther King, Jr., to stand before a huge crowd in Washington, DC and declare "I have a dream that one day people, all people will be judged, not by the color of their skin but by the content of their character!" And it took courage for a young white Bahamian girl, namely Patricia Cole back in the forties to buck long established tradition by deciding to become a lawyer!

The courage of Miss Cole in moving in this direction becomes abundantly clear when it is realized that for over two hundred and thirty years (since the Bahamas was established as a Colony of Great Britain) the Bahamian legal profession had been dominated by males. Indeed, when she did so, the idea of becoming a lawyer did not "cross the mind" of the vast majority of Bahamian women or girls.

Indeed, the Narrator recalls certain of the female students of primary and secondary education he attended, bitterly complaining how limited were their options upon graduation. Whereas, the boys had many choices open to them, the girls complained that their prospects for occupation (other than domestic chores) were limited to four:

1. A teacher

2. A nurse

3. A secretary

4. A housewife

There was one other option for them—to become an "old maid"; for most young ladies expected to be married by the time they reached their early twenties. None of them desired for this to happen to them. Such, then, were the limited opportunities available to women in the Bahamas...before Patricia Cole came along!

A WELL QUALIFIED LAWYER!

There are, indeed, a few countries on the planet in which lawyers are held in high esteem than the Commonwealth of the Bahamas. Over the many years since democracy was established in 1729, members of the legal profession have been dominant in all branches of government. There is no wonder, then, that people in all walks of life do have a great admiration for lawyers, who still are attired in attractive garb, including black gowns and wigs, dating back to colonial times.

Thus, in addition to the well qualified lawyers, who had been trained in the chambers of leading legal luminaries, or had been to London before being called to the Bar, there have always been a cadre of young men who have become self-taught "lawyers". Thus, they imitate the professionals, adopting such terms as "M'lord," "My learned friend," "I am putting it to you," etc. And even a Latin expression or two! Some, indeed, excel and there have been those who defending themselves have proven competent in the Courts being acquitted.

Patricia Cozzi, however, the first Bahamian female to enter the legal profession, was indeed, very well qualified.

She was the child of Mr. & Mrs. Cole. Like many children of the Cole family, she received her education at both primary and secondary levels, at Queen's College. A Methodist Foundation, it was one of the two secondary institutions of education in the Colony at the time. From all reports, she was a diligent student, who maintained a high academic record while at QC. The Principal (or Headmaster) of that leading institution of education was the Rev. Richard Dyer, who served in that capacity for many years.

LEGAL LUMINARY...BAHAMIAN BEAUTY!

Sometimes, women when entering into a field of human endeavor, traditionally dominated by men, try to prove themselves as equal, or even superior to their male counterparts. Thus, they may become "Tomboyish," harsh and highly competitive in any given responsibility or project.

But not Patricia Cozzi! Always neatly, attired, this petite, polite young Bahamian lady was indeed the epitome of female professionalism at a time when many thought that "A woman's place is in the home!' Indeed, with her ponytail hair nearly covered by the traditional judicial wig, her dark colored coat suit, her "tower high" high heel shoes, she could aptly be described as "the prettiest lawyer Bahamians had ever seen...until other female lawyers came on the scene! She certainly set the pattern of being smartly attired for which Bahamian women in the legal profession have been admired ever since! Yes, it could be conclusively declared that Patricia Cozzi knew how "to dress to impress!' She really did!

Perhaps the reason why she proved so impressive was simply she did not give the impression of trying to impress! In this regard, it is of interest to bear in mind that there are those, who have attained "a first" continually boast about their achievement. They seize upon every opportunity to remind others of what they have done to the point sometimes of becoming boring or overbearing!

They seem to take as their motto the dictum "Blow your own trumpet; for no one else will blow it for you!"

But not Patricia Cozzi! She may have done so in private or family settings, but nowhere is it recorded that she boasted about being the first Bahamian woman to become a lawyer! Rather, she assumed her position and carried out her responsibilities with a "cool" confidence and delightful dignity which earned her the respect and admiration of Bahamians "in all walks of life"...including "The Narrator!' She did not boast about making a difference. Rather, she made a difference by being different!

Thus, that she made a difference there can be "not a shadow of a doubt!' For, she was indeed "a trail blazer". For more than two hundred years, the legal profession in the Bahamas was dominated by men. As indicated, "it never crossed the mind" of the vast majority of Bahamian women in the Bahamas early in the twentieth century to even attempt to enter the male dominated legal profession. Then, the calm, confident, courageous Patricia Cole-Cozzi came along forever changing the Bahamian legal landscape! For, once the door to the legal male club had been opened by this young lady, a host of other females entered it. Amongst these pioneers were Jeanne Thompson, who excelled both as a lawyer and writer, and Eileen Dupuch-Carron who succeeded her father as editor of The Tribune. It was not long before other women, including the Hon. Janet B. Musgrove Bostwick were also called to the Bar. Thus, when the Bahamas celebrated its fortieth anniversary of Independence on July 10, 2013 there were more than women in the legal profession and more female students than males studying at institutions of tertiary education "at home and abroad"—to become lawyers!

In the annals of humankind, there have been those who made a difference by what they said. Such were the prophets, preachers, politicians, priests and philosophers, who have deeply influenced their fellow human beings and the course of human history by their powerful oratory, sermons and fiery speeches!

Then, there were those "who made a difference" by what they did. Such were the kings, conquerors, athletes and innovators of the human family. Others made a difference by what they wrote. Such were the poets, historians, editors and masters of communications who have influenced the thinking and actions of others. Finally, there have been those who made a difference simply by who they were. Such a person was Patricia Cole-Cozzi, first Bahamian female to be called to the Bar Council of the Commonwealth of the Bahamas! For, she made a difference...by being different!

Now, it has been observed that Mrs. Patricia Cole-Cozzi was not the only person who was called to the Bar on that rainy morning July 10, 1953. A young man was also called to the Bahamas Bar Council. Who was he? None other than a brilliant young lawyer who had just graduated from Law School in London...Lynden Oscar Pindling!

The contrast between these two young persons simultaneously called to the Bar could hardly be greater! Physically and socially they could not be more different. She while not tall was of medium height and was as white as snow; he, like the Biblical Zacchias and the famous French General Napoleon was short of stature and black as ebony. She came from the prosperous background of a well-established wealthy white Bahamian family. He, on the other hand was the son of a working class couple who grew up on East Street.

Yet, despite these differences, they did have much in common. First, being amongst the few Bahamians who could qualify to be called to the Bar they must have been ambitious and determined. Indeed, they shared in rich measure that virtue which motivates all who aspire to greatness...courage. They were, indeed, both ambitious and as such were destined to play an important role in the development of the Colony.

Those who assembled at the Bar Council for the swearing in of the two young lawyers certainly realized that Patricia Cozzi was "making history" in becoming the first Bahamian woman to be called to the Bar. But little did they realize that the young man beside her on that august occasion would soon enter the arena of politics and that exactly twenty years later he would make history in becoming the first Prime Minister of the Commonwealth of the Bahamas!

While these two young people were very different, as noted they did have much in common.

Indeed of all the things that united them there was one which was of overarching significance—they were both Bahamians, a proud son and daughter of the Bahamian soil. They both achieved greatness. They were both motivated by a deep love, a strong patriotic bond to the land of their birth.

In a sense most profound, all Bahamians could be justly proud of them. Reflection on their sterling contributions, certainly appeals to the patriotic spirit of all thinking Bahamians. It is that patriotism which is at the heart of that great patriotic hymn, which is the school hymn of Queen's College.

COZZI AND PINDLING

In retrospect, it must be deemed nothing other than providential and prophetic that she, a white Bahamian female was making history by being the first Bahamian of her gender to be called to the Bar at the same time as the black Bahamian male, who would rise to become the first of his race to serve as Premier of their common homeland!

Land of my birth Father in Heaven, who lovest all,

O help thy children when they call

That they may build from age to age

An undefiled heritage.

Teach us to bear the yoke in youth;

With steadfastness and careful truth;

That in our time, thy grace may give

The Truth whereby the nations live.

Teach us to rule ourselves always,

Controlled and cleanly night and day;

That we may bring, if need arise,

No mean or worthless sacrifice.

Teach us to look, in all our ends,

On Thee for judge, and not our friends;

That we with Thee may walk uncowed

By fear or favor of the crowd.

Teach us the strength that cannot seek

By deed or thought, to hurt the weak:

That under Thee, we may possess

Man's strength to succor man's distress.

Teach us delight in simple things,

And mirth that has no other springs;

Forgiveness free of evil done

And love to all men 'neath the sun.

Land of our birth, we pledge to thee

Our love and toil for the years to be

When we are grown, and take our place

As men and women of our race.

Father in Heaven, who lovest all

O help Thy children when they call

That they may build from

An undefiled heritage.

Teach us to rule ourselves always

Controlled and cleanly night and day.

That we may bring, if need arise

No maimed or worthless sacrifice.

Teach us to look in all our ends

On Thee for Judge, and not our friends

That, under Thee, we may perceive

Man's strength to succor man's distress.

Paul Lawrence Adderley, M.A., LL.B.

(August 15, 1928—September 19, 2012)

Brilliant Attorney-at-Law, Versatile Administrator, Great Bahamian Patriot

INTRODUCTION

"DESTINED FOR GREATNESS!"

"Some are born great,

Others achieve greatness

And some have greatness thrust upon them!"[cvii] With this profound observation, William Shakespeare, that great English playwright/philosopher, describes the varied contributions of humankind in terms of greatness.

First there have been those who were born great, these include the kings, queens and princes who have so greatly influenced the course of history, those who were born into royalty and those who inherited wealth. Then there have been those who achieved greatness. These include the great conquerors, the powerful generals and warriors, scientists and inventors and, of course, the rags to riches billionaires of our own time. Finally, there have been and continue to be those who have neither been born into great families, or have done much to achieve greatness, nevertheless, have found themselves in positions of greatness.

While most people fall into one of these categories, here and there (very rare!) have been, and continue to be those who, having been born into circumstances which were fortuitous and conducive to the pursuit of greatness, who have indeed, taken full advantage of all opportunities which have come their way and then have achieved greatness in their own right. Now such a person was Paul Lawrence Adderley!

Son of a well-known and influential Bahamian family. The Adderleys of Nassau, Paul Lawrence was born August 15, 1928. His parents were The Hon. Alfred Francis Adderley, CBE, very prominent Attorney-at-Law and statesman, and Mrs Ethel Adderley, MBE. His grandfather was the very distinguished William Parliament Adderley, who served for many years as a member of the House of Assembly. Paul Lawrence then, was born into a family background which would inspire one to strive for greatness, and this, he certainly did with extraordinary education.

Versatile and most competent, this multi-talented gentleman made major contributions in fields of human endeavour including law and order, education, finance and foreign affairs.

EDUCATION

Paul Lawrence Adderley received his education at primary level at the then well-known private school operated by Mrs Wright, located on Delancey Street, walking[cviii] distance from the Adderley homestead on Meeting Street.

He then continued his education, along with his elder brother Francis, at the Government High School, where he had the opportunity to meet other ambitious young men, Arthur Hanna and Cecil Wallace Whitfield, who certainly contributed to his educational development. It was while at the old GHS that he demonstrated great ability to debate, indicative of a career in the field of law.[cix]

At tertiary level, he studied law at St. Catherine's College, Cambridge University, where he earned the degrees Bachelor of Arts in Law (1950) and Bachelor of Law (1952). He continued his legal studies at Court Law School at Middle Temple, London.

It has to be stated that the young Paul Adderley, like his elder brother Francis, was no book worm, who spent all of his time in the study or library, rather he was quite athletic and played several games, especially cricket.

Returning home, Paul Adderley was called to the Bar in 1953[cx], the same year as other attorneys including Sir Lynden Pindling, and Mrs Patricia Cozzi, First Bahamian female attorney-at-law.

The winds of political change were blowing, like Caribbean tropical storms, with increasing intensity. For it was in that year that the Progressive Liberal Party was established by Mr. Milton Taylor. While other Bahamian attorneys including Lynden Oscar Pindling and Arthur Hanna immediately joined the PLP, Paul Adderley, however, made sure that he had established himself as a leading attorney before venturing into the arena of politics.

His entry into the competitive arena of politics was dramatic and most significant, thus, he was elected to the House of Assembly as a representative of the Western District, representing the Progressive

Liberal Party in 1961. He won by a large majority in the midst of great rejoicing!

In 1965 he left the PLP and led a party known as the Bahamas Democratic Party, which ideally was designed to appeal to all Bahamians, however, in the highly polarized situation of the sixties, there was no place for such a political grouping. Thus he returned to the PLP early in 1972.[cxi]

By then the winds of political change were blowing furiously as the people of the Bahamas were preparing for Independence. Paul Adderley was amongst those who attended the historic conference in London in 1972 when the details of Independence were discussed with the officials of the United Kingdom.

When the Bahamas became independent in 1973, Paul Adderley was appointed to serve as the Attorney General, the first AG in an independent Bahamas. He served in this extremely important capacity until 1989, and as such proved to be most influential in dealing with major legal issues of the Commonwealth of the Bahamas. Many of the laws which have proved of tremendous significance in the development of the Bahamas were piloted through the legislature of the Bahamas by Paul Adderley. His knowledge of the law was encyclopaedic. Gifted with a photographic memory, he was able to quote the laws of the nation with great accuracy in any given context—whether in parliament or in debate with others, in the courts or in lively debates with his peers. All respected him for his great ability as a lawyer, and it is most appropriate that the present headquarters of the Attorney General is named in honour of his major achievements in the field of law.

Paul Adderley was nurtured in a family and environment in which very high priority was placed on education, thus his contribution in the field of education must be placed next only to those in the legal field of human endeavour.

He was appointed Minister of Education in the year 1980 and served in this capacity. During his tenure, major development in education took place. The Bahamas Junior Certificate of Education was established as a major requirement for persons who would become public servants, moreover, the Bahamas Certificate of General Education (BGCSE) was established as the standard for the completion of education at secondary level in the Bahamas. There can be no doubt, then, that Paul Lawrence made an indelible impact upon the development of education in the Commonwealth of the Bahamas.[cxii]

MINISTER OF NATIONAL SECURITY

The Hon. Paul Lawrence Adderley's outstanding ability as an administrator was ably demonstrated when he was appointed Minister of National Security even when being responsible for the administration of the Ministry of Education!

As Minister of National Security, he had to deal, in principal, with two major "burning issues"—the influx of illegal immigrants and the control of the consumption and distribution of illegal 'drugs', including marijuana, cocaine, etc. As a very patriotic, courageous Bahamian, Mr. Adderley tackled booth these challenges "head on" with typical energy and decisiveness.

Accordingly, he was instrumental in the establishment of the OPBAT Operations, whereby the powerful armed forces of the United states of America, 'our great neighbour to the north', were permitted to cooperate with the local law enforcement agencies in the Bahamas, Turks and Caicos archipelago, in combatting the trafficking of illegal drugs.

FOREIGN AFFAIRS

In the complete field of Foreign Affairs, Mr. Adderley was very active in the negotiation of legal assistance treaties with the developed nations of the North Atlantic, including the United States of America, Canada and the United Kingdom. These deliberations were essential for the progress of the banking and financial services business, the second pillar of the Bahamian economy! Concisely, the Hon. Paul Lawrence Adderley made most significant contributions to the political and socio-economic development of the Bahamas at home and abroad![cxiii]

MINISTER OF FINANCE

There can be not a shadow of a doubt that, in any organization-social, political, commercial or religious—that a tremendous amount of authority and responsibility devolved upon the person(s) who "controlled the purse", only those who have earned the trust of their colleagues are allowed to serve in this capacity, accordingly, the amazing, versatile administrative ability of the Hon. Paul Lawrence Adderley was unequivocally demonstrated by his appointment to serve as Minister of Finance for The Commonwealth of the Bahamas on October 1, 1970.

Serving in this most important, and indeed, powerful position, he adopted a conservative approach, exercising what the Hon. Fred Allen liked to describe as "fiscal discipline". This called for the control of spending based on the concept of a balanced budget. He served in this post for two years.

Upon completing his comparatively short tenure as Minister of Finance, Mr. Adderley gradually reduced his participation in the political arena. In the General Election of 1972, he won his seat as a Member of Parliament, representing the St. Michael's Constituency. Very significantly, he was content to serve as a "back bencher" after many years in the Cabinet! Then, in 1997 he retired from 'frontline politics', returning to his 'first love'—the practice of law in his chambers!

What then can we say, summarily, about Paul Lawrence Adderley?

Well, for starters, it can be said that he was certainly "a family man". He was married to the former Lilith Rosena Thompson, whom he greatly loved and cherished. Eventually, they became the proud parents of three lovely daughters, all of whom have excelled in their chosen fields of human endeavour. These are Catherine, a dentist who serves in the Health Services in Grand Bahama; Rosanne, a noted historian, and Paula, who, by becoming a lawyer, is following in the footsteps of her father...and grandfather!

Secondly, there can be no doubt that Paul Adderley was an honest individual in every way. In this regard, the narrator recalls a conversation with a gentleman in Freeport about him. *"'Rev', I can tell ya two tings about Paul. Paul ain' gur lie and Paul ain gur teef; and ya can bribe Paul!"*[cxiv] He declared.

Like the late great Elijah Cummings, courageous African American champion of social justice, it could be truly said of Paul Lawrence

Adderley "He was at once impeccably fair and exceedingly fearless!"[cxv]

It is sometimes said that politics is a dirty game! Well, Paul Adderley managed to play the game of politics for decades without ever becoming dirty!

Then, despite the fact that there were some Bahamians who regarded him as "haughty", Paul Adderley was at heart a humble person. His daughter, Dr. Catherine Adderley, shared with the narrator that her father shunned any form of adulation.[cxvi]

In this regard, he recalls passing by the chambers of Paul Adderley, early one morning, while he was in private practice, there was Paul, with his broom diligently sweeping the floor. Evidently, he exercised the same diligence and thoroughness which characterized his service in the simple task of making sure that his office was clean before any clients came there. His action reminded one of the hymns which indicates that when a person works diligently in any task he/she

"Makes drudgery divine[cxvii]

Who sweeps a room,

As for thy laws,

Makes that and the action fine."

Most of all though, Paul Lawrence Adderley was a patriot! As such, he loved his fellow Bahamians and, indeed, all things Bahamian...with a passion! It was the loyalty to the land of his birth, which was the motivating force behind his many years of faithful service to the Bahamas. Indeed, like his colleagues, the Hon. A. D. Hanna and the

Hon. Loftus Roker, he was a fierce Bahamian nationalist, who despite his many achievements, eschewed the colonial honours, which were coveted by so many others of his generation! Throughout his life, in his many and varied contributions to the political, mental, and moral development of his homeland, he epitomized the service and aspirations of the people of the Bahamas as encapsulated in its motto, as taught by the Rev. Dr. Philip Rahming.[cxviii]

> "I pledge my allegiance to the flag and to The Commonwealth of The Bahamas, for which it stands. One people united in love and service."

Paul Lawrence Adderley, a Bahamian Who Made a Difference in ways more than one!

Questions for Group Discussion

1. What were the factors in the early life of Paul Adderley which contributed to his greatness?

2. "Paul Adderley was more of a statesman than a politician": Discuss.

3. Is there a difference between "a patriot" and "a nationalist"?

4. Why is it so important that a person should work to the best of his/her ability in any given responsibility? Support your answer by reference to the life and contribution of Paul Lawrence Adderley.

5. Write short notes on three of the following:

The Government High School

The Ministry of National Security

OPBAT

Negotiation of legal assistance treaties

The Bahamas Junior Certificate of Education (BJC)

Illegal Immigration in the Bahamas

6. Paul Adderley, despite his many achievements, did not accept honouring awards by the British Government. Do you think he should be honoured posthumously by the Government of the 'Bahamas? Give the reasons for your answers.

About
The Book

From *Pompey to Pindling* is an informative and engaging narrative; it features a compilation of 21 Bahamian patriots of yesteryear, who had passed on before the writing of this work written by my husband the late Reverend Dr. Joseph Emmette Weir. It was his intention to cover those individuals who had passed on before him. He has provided here a useful reference for students and at the same time, a "good read" for those who love and are inspired by history.

Very special thanks and appreciation to Ava Forbes for the skillful typing and working so very diligently; with the preparation of this book.

Ena Weir

---

[i] Rolihlahla Madiba Nelson Dalibunga Manson Mandela (1918-2013) of South Africa spent many years in prison for his strong opposition to its Apartheid (racial segregation) policies. Yet, he emerged from prison without any sign of acrimony or revenge towards his persecutors. He became its President and led it in a campaign for its reconstruction in which all its citizens were

united to move together for the common good. Highly respected internationally, Mandela must be ranked with the Prophet Amos, Mahatma Gandhi and Dr. Martin Luther King, Jr. as amongst the great champions of social justice of humankind.

[ii] See Wendell Jones "The 100 Greatest Bahamians of the Twentieth Century."

[iii] There was great concern in the Bahamian Black community that the film "No Way Out" featuring Bahamian American Sydney Poitier was shown at "The Savoy Theatre" from which they were banned. McPherson Williams was active in a group which was formed to protest against this act of racism. Indeed it was ironic that Black Bahamians were barred from the theatre where this film featuring a Black Bahamian

[iv] In preparing this nostalgia on East Street in the early post-World War II era, the writer was greatly assisted by telephone conversations with Mrs. Gertrude Burnside, who resided there in those days, and childhood memories of visits to the home of his cousin, the Late Leo Roberts, son of "Bulla Roberts" His wife Sylvia Roberts née Weir, who resided at the Roberts homestead on East Street. The site (now vacant) is opposite the Lily of The Valley Church of God.

[v] The Late Shirley Wright, who served for many years at the Audit Department, remarked when the UBP was formed in 1956 that its political executive had been acting together "as a party" for many years.

[vi] Source

[vii] See "Front Porch by Simon, 'The Freeport News' Friday, October 23, 2013, AD.

[ix] For detailed discussion of the role of the Church in nation building in the years leading up to Independence see J. Emmette Weir, Let us Build a Christian Nation, Freeport, Bahamas, 2014.

[x] Ibid, p. 263.

[xi] See Let Us Build a Christian Nation.

[xii] Majority Rule Day, January 10, was observed as a Public Holiday for the first time in 2014.

[xiii] See COB Magazine.

[xiv] William Temple, Christianity and The World Order.

[xv] See "Growing up on East Street," pp. 4–15.

[xvi] See J. Emmette Weir, Let Us Build a Christian Nation. Freeport, 2004, AD.

[xvii] With regard to Liberation Theology see the writer's "Exodus and Sinai in the Theology of Liberation. An Inquiry into the Relationship Between Biblical and Marxist Concepts in Latin America Liberation Theology with Special Reference to the Works of Jose Porfirio Miranda and Gustavo Gutierrez: Dissertation in fulfilment of the requirements for the award of the Degree Doctor of Philosophy, the University of Aberdeen Scotland, U.K., 1985.

[xviii] See the magazine published in Celebration of the 25th Anniversary of the Establishment of the Royal Bahamas Defence Force.

[xix] Young patriot Bahamian artist Kishan Munroe has vividly described the events of "The Flamingo Incident" in a series of historic paintings "Swan Song of The Flamingo."

[xx] See "On Their Shoulders" The Life and Times of Lynden Oscar Pindling, public lecture delivered by the Hon. Obediah Wilchcombe, Minister of Tourism of the Commonwealth of the Bahamas, at First Baptist Church, Freeport, Grand Bahama, on June 26, 2013.

xxi   Don   Maples,   <u>The   Making   of   the   Bahamas</u>,   (Essex   England: Pearson/Longman and Kingston, Jamaica: Carlong Publishers Caribbean, Ld. 2004). Historian who has lectured in Bahamian History at Queen's College and the College of The Bahamas.

xxii Michael Craton, <u>Pindling the Life and Times of The First Prime Minister</u>, Oxford, Macmillan Education, and Nassau, The Pindling Family Estate, 2002), p. 240.

xxiii <u>Ibid</u>. p. 419.

xxiv <u>Ibid</u>. p. 65.

xxv The demise of Sir Lynden Pindling brought to the attention of many, especially Bahamian males, the health challenges caused by cancer of the prostate gland. In a public lecture, Dr. Devaughn Curling, Oncologist, warned that this disease is especially prevalent amongst mature adult black males, urging them to exercise regularly, to avoid red meat and get an annual check-up. The lecture was delivered at Freeport, Grand Bahama on Tuesday, September 9, 2014 under the auspices of "You too, A Body Dedicated to Preventing Prostrate Cancer."

xxvi Cited from verse of the Sacred Song.

xxvii See Public Lecture by The Hon. Obediah Wilchcombe cited above, Note 20.

xxviii See Tony Sewell, <u>Garvey's Children, The Legacy of Marcus Garvey</u>, Oxford: MacMillan Education, 1990, p. 22

xxix Most significantly, Bishop Gilbert Thompson in his scholarly, <u>A Goodly Heritage, A Concise History of The Diocese of The Bahamas and The Turks and Caicos Islands</u>, Nassau: 12 Avenue Graphics, 2011 A.D. See p. 201 includes Dr. Love amongst "Bahamian Priests Abroad."

xxx Thompson, idem.

xxxi The writer has discussed the contribution of the Latin American Liberationist theologians in detail in his "Exodus and Sinai in the Theology of Liberation: A Discussion of the Relationship between Biblical and Marxist Concepts in Liberation Theology with Special Reference to the Works of Jose Porfirio Miranda and Gustavo Gutierrez", Thesis submitted in Fulfilment of the Requirements for the Degree Doctor of Philosophy, The University of Aberdeen, 1984 A.D.

xxxii Sewell, idem.

xxxiii Ibid, p. 23.

xxxiv Ibid., "Foreword"

Questions for Group Discussion

1. "A prophet is not without honour, save in his own country." Discuss with special reference to the life and contributions of Dr. Robert Love.

2. Although comparatively well-known in Jamaica and Haiti, comparatively little is known about him in the Bahamas. What can, and should be done, so that many more Bahamians may get to know more about this great Bahamian?

3. Dr. Love, "born and bred" in the Bahamas, attained wide recognition and fame abroad. Give the names of two other Bahamians who also achieved much abroad.

4. Tell what you know about two of the following (300-500 words):

    a. "Grant's Town in 1839"

    b. Cynthia Love

c. Marcus Mosiah Garvey

5. On the basis of your knowledge of the life and contributions of Dr. Love, what answer would you offer to a person who claims, "Politics and religion should not be mixed"!

For Further Reading and Research

Resources for the study of The Life of Dr. Robert Love are varied but not many! Persons who desire more basic knowledge about this great Bahamian priest/politician, may read:

1. Bishop Gilbert Thompson, <u>A Goodly Heritage: A Concise History of The Diocese of The Bahamas, Turks and Caicos Islands</u>, (Nassau: 12 Avenue Graphics, 2011 A.D.)

2. Hartley Saunders, <u>The Other Bahamas</u>, (Bodab Publishers, January 1, 1991)

3. Tony Sewell, <u>Garvey's Children: The Legacy of Marcus Garvey</u>, (Oxford: MacMillan Education, 1990 A.D.)

Persons, however, requiring detailed information about this most interesting Bahamian priest/politician must be prepared to engage in diligent research!

In this regard, there can be no doubt that the most scholarly, detailed, and authoritative work is the doctoral dissertation of Dr. Goveia, renowned Caribbean historian, who lectured, for many years, at the University of the West Indies.

Accordingly, it is to be found in the Library of The University of the West Indies, Mona, Kingston 7, Jamaica.

The other major source is the large collection of works on Dr. Love in the Library of Mr. Kenneth Love, Photographer, Nassau, Bahamas.

[xxxv]See Randol Fawkes, *The Faith that Moved the Mountain Memorial Edition* edited by Rosalie Fawkes, Nassau, Bahamas, 2003, p. 29. Dr. Walker was a mentor to Sir Randol Fawkes, as he was to many other outstanding Bahamians of his generation!

[xxxvi]"The People" in the time of Dr. Walker, early to mid-twentieth century was used in a socio-economic manner, to refer specifically to predominantly Black Bahamian Community, many of whom were suffering from the effects of poverty and racial discrimination. See also the chapter on Sir Lynden Pindling and the works of Dr. Cleveland Eneas.

[xxxvii]On the old Colonial constitution of the Bahamas, see Randol F. Fawkes, *Know Your Government*, 1950, Nassau, Bahamas.

[xxxviii]See Sturrup, *The Bay Street Boys,* Nassau, Bahamas

[xxxix]See Luke 19:1-10; 1 Samuel 17.

[xl]On the Burma Road Riot and the eventful rule of the Duke of Windsor, who after abdicating the British Throne was appointed Governor of the Bahamas see Orville Turnquest: *The Duke of Windsor.*

[xli]The expression "the wretched of the earth" was coined by a well-known sociologist philosopher who hailed from the French Caribbean island of Martinique to describe the depraved socio-economic condition of many of its people. Dr. Walker, who was very well read, no doubt knew it and applied it, most aptly, to the plight of the poor hard working people of the Bahamas!

[xlii]The wages of the workers were increased, more significantly "in the long run" The Burma Road Riot stabilized the rights of workers that they were not

to be exploited, and indeed, set in motion the events which culminated in the attainment of independence for the Bahamas on July 10, 1973.

[xliii]The motto of "The Voice" in Latin *Vex Populi Vox Dei* reflected the great linguistic ability of Dr. Walker. It originated in ancient Rome to assert the rights of the working classes in their struggle for power against the nobles and aristocrats of the Roman Empire. Thus, although pagan in origin, it was adapted by Christians and may be liberally rendered "The voice of the people is the voice of God." Interestingly enough, it was quoted by the Hon. Bradley Roberts in commenting on the results of the General Election of 2017 AD.

[xliv]These include The Herald and The Bahamian Times, edited by Sir Arthur Foulkes.

[xlv]The first institution of tertiary education of the colony was the Bahamas Teacher's College, established in 1948, long after Dr. Walker returned home with several degrees from leading American Institutions of tertiary education.

[xlvi]The English term "education" is directly derived from two Latin words and it means literally "to draw out". Education then, fundamentally speaking is not so much the imparting of knowledge as enabling persons to develop to the fullest their God endowed talents and abilities. In this sense, Dr. Walker, with his commitment to bringing out the best in others was, indeed, a great educator!

[xlvii]These include the C. R. Walker Technical School and the Mabel Walker Primary School.

[xlviii]Dr. Walker met the dynamic American lady who became his wife in a German class. According to "The Dilly Tree Sip", much of their courtship was conducted in German. Interestingly enough, their eldest had a German

name, Rinehart, which also was the name of the hotel erected by the ambitious builder Dr. Walker!

[xlix]Dr. Walker, evidently took great pride in his knowledge of the Bahamian dialect!

GLOSSARY

"Da Dilly Tree Sip". There were times when the people of the African Bahamian communities, including Grants Town, Bain Town, Fox Hill, Adelaide, Gambier gathered to discuss the local and national matters known as "the latest". The Sapodilla Tree, with its thick foliage evergreen foliage and delicious fruit, was an ideal meeting place for such community gatherings. The writer recalls that there was a large dilly tree in the yard of Wesley Methodist Church, Grants Town and also in the backyard of the home of his 'Aunt Lilly' at the corner of Meeting Street and Blue Hill Road.

[l]See Judges 5:30. For more detailed accounts, see voluminous works of historian Arnold Toynbee.

[li]On the suitability of the central and southern islands for the growing of cotton, therefore proving attractive to the Loyalists, see Don Maples, The Making of the Bahamas. Kingston, Jamaica: Carlong Publishers, 2004, A.D., p. 59.

[lii]W. Claypole and J. Robottam, in Caribbean Story. 2003 A.D. describe vividly the development of the sugar cane industry in the central and southern islands of the Caribbean. Cuba, nearest Caribbean Island to the Bahamas, has, for many years been the largest producer of sugar in the world.

[liii] Gail Saunders, Slavery in The Bahamas, Nassau: The Nassau Guardian, 1985), p. 61.

[liv] Don Maples, Ibid. p. 62.

---

iv See Gail Saunders, Ibid. p. 160 and Gilbert Thompson, <u>A Goodly Heritage,</u> <u>A Concise History of the Diocese of The Bahamas and the Turks and Caicos</u> <u>Islands,</u> Nassau: The Diocese of the Bahamas and the Turks and Caicos Islands, 2011 A.D.) p. 43.

Questions for Group Discussion and Exercises

1. Although the story of Kate was well known in the Bahamas and abroad in the Nineteenth Century, very little is known about her in the Bahamas today. What can be done so that many more Bahamians get to know about the life of this courageous young Bahamian who impacted that of many in those days?

2. Do you think that Kate should be named a Bahamian National Hero?

3. "No one is above the law!" Discuss.

4. Write short notes on two of the following:

    When "Cotton was King" in the Bahamas

    The United Empire Loyalists

    The Abolition of the Slave Trade

For additional reading:

1. Don Maples, <u>The Making of The Bahamas</u>, (Kingston, Jamaica: Carlong Publishers Caribbean Ltd., 2004 AD)

2. Allan G. Murray, <u>Bahamian History Highlights</u>, Nassau, Bahamas: Media Publishing, 1999). Chapters 11–13.

3. Saunders, Gail Saunders, <u>Slavery in the Bahamas 1648-1838</u>, Nassau: The Nassau Guardian, 2000 AD. <u>Bahamian Loyalists and Their Slaves</u>, (London: Macmillan Education Ltd. 1983).

[lvi] The colourful events leading up to the establishment of democracy in the Bahamas in ,due to the efforts of first Governor Woodes Rodgers, are vividly described by Don Maples, *"The Making Of The Bahamas"* (Essex, England: Pearson & Kingston, Jamaica: Carlong pp.49 – 53.

[lvii] M. Patricia Patterson, Jamaican Literary Authority, has contributed the official biography of Sir Milo Butler, Milo Broughton Butler, *Bahamian A Call To Service* (Nassau, Bahamas: Sir Milo Butler & Sons) 2011 AD henceforth identified by the abbreviation, MBB.

[lviii] MBB, p.2.

[lix] On conditions during slavery in the Bahamas, see Gail Saunders *Slavery in the Bahamas* (Nassau, Bahamas: The Nassau Guardian, 1985.

[lx] According to Bahamian patriot, the Rev. Dr. Philip Rahming, author of the Bahamian National Pledge "Rahming" is amongst the few African surnames which has survived, as it dates back to Africa before slavery and emancipation.

[lxi] The contemporary quest of people of African descent in the USA and the Caribbean was initiated by eminent African/American Alex

Haley, who in his monumental book--*Roots*, traced his ancestry back to Africa.

[lxii] The powerful economic and political clout of The Bay Street Boys is described by the writer in dealing with the life of Sir Lynden Pindling.

[lxiii] Murray, *Bahamian History Highlights* (Nassau: Media Press), p. notes that during this period there were "demonstrations for secret ballot in elections led by Milo Butler."

[lxiv] MBB, p. 26.

[lxv] MBB, p. 154

[lxvi] MBB, p. 160.

[lxvii] It is extremely important to bear in mind that in the Biblical account of The Creation of the world, it was by means of the spoken word that God acted. In the text, for instance: "Then GOD said 'Let there be light and there was light.'" (Gen. 1: 3, NRSV.) See also Gen. 1: 6, 11, 20, 24, etc.). Every act of Creation, then, is prefaced by the expression "God said" Concisely, according to Genesis, the spoken word of The Almighty is the act of creation. Charles Wesley, the great hymn writer of Methodism, echoes this concept in one of his hymns praising God, "who spake the world" into being.

[lxviii] Exodus 5:1; 6:10

[lxix] 1 Kings 17:1; 18–19.

[lxx] It is extremely important to bear in mind that in the Biblical account of The Creation of the world, it was by means of the spoken word that God acted. In the text, for instance: "Then GOD said 'Let there be light and there was

light."' (Gen. 1: 3, NRSV.) See also Gen. 1: 6, 11, 20, 24, etc.). Every act of Creation, then, is prefaced by the expression "God said" Concisely, according to Genesis, the spoken word of The Almighty is the act of creation. Charles Wesley, the great hymn writer of Methodism, echoes this concept in one of his hymns praising God," who spake the world" into being.

lxxi This statement of its mission, often described as "The Motto of Methodism", was issued at The Conference of Methodism held in Bristol, England in 1788. Presiding was John Wesley, The Founder of Methodism under GOD.

lxxii The writer has dealt with the important and essential role of the Clergy in the stride of the Bahamas towards Independence *In Let us Build a Christian Nation,*

Freeport, Grand Bahama, Bahamas, 2004ad.

lxxiii In this, perhaps his most profound statement, Dr. Cooper asserted confidently that if life is worth living, it should be lived at its best. Providing much food for thought, it reflects the teaching of St. Paul "For me to live is Christ." (Philippians 1:21) It also informed the contribution of the famous Cardinal Sheen, who in the mid-twentieth century produced the Religious Televised Broadcast "Life is Worth Living". The concept was a major principle of the teaching of Bahamian internationally known preacher, teacher, motivator and author Dr. Myles Munroe.

lxxiv Mrs. Cheryl Strachan spent the formative years of her life as an active member of Mission Baptist Church, and therefore had the opportunity to hear Dr. Cooper preach on many occasions. Author of the book she and her husband, Mr. Orthland Strachan are the proprietors of Compusec in Freeport and "Beyond all Flags" in Nassau.

lxxv The late Mr. Gordon Cooper, taxi man, a relative of Dr. Cooper, informed the narrator that he had lively discussions with him on the "pros and cons" of tourism as the engine of the Bahamian economy!

lxxvi There is always a need, in a country such as the Bahamas, which is dedicated to Christian nation building, for a journal in which all matters are discussed from a Christian perspective. Thus Evangelist Dr. Rex Major used to contribute articles of such a nature, which were published in "The Nassau Guardian" in the seventies. Then "Christian Commentary", written by Ministers of the Gospel under the auspices of the Bahamas Christian Council used to be published in "". No such contribution, however, is to be found today when the need is great.

lxxvii The Brown family were traditionally involved in maritime industries, serving as navigators, boat captains and marine pilots. Lester Brown's father was a boat captain, as was his brother, Geoffrey before he too became a realtor!

lxxviii Bear in mind that Squadron Leader Lester Brown was born just over six years; after the Wright Brothers made that historic first flight of an aircraft!

lxxix Hinsey, Shananda M. "Women Suffrage: Suffrage Women". LibGuides (Libraries' Research Guides). Nassau: University of the Bahamas. Retrieved November 9, 2017

lxxx The Rt. Rev. Gilbert Thompson, Assistant Bishop of The Diocese of The Bahamas, Turks & Caicos Islands, A Goodly Heritage, A Concise History of The Diocese of The Bahamas, Turks & Caicos Islands, Nassau: Avenue Graphics, 2011, P. 292.

lxxxi Ibid., p. 292

lxxxii Ibid., 294,

[lxxxiii]On the matter under discussion here, see Walther Bulmann, <u>The Coming of The Third Church</u>, ET (Brit. Ed.), London: SCM Press, 1978, Amer. ED. Maryknoll, New York, 1977. Buhlmann, a German Catholic Missionary, in this contribution, discusses the rapid numerical growth and growing influence of Christianity in the nations of the Third World.

[lxxxiv] Archdeacon Bain was interviewed by the narrator in the vestry of Christ the King on April, 2015.

[lxxxv]Bishop Laish Boyd's evaluation of Bishop Michael Eldon's legacy recorded on the front page of "The Tribune" under the headline "Bishop Eldon: Pastor, Carer, and Listener", vol. 107 No. 64 Tuesday, February 8, 2011.

[lxxxvi] The narrator, also a Minister of the Gospel, growing up on West Street, "Easy walking distance from The Eldon homestead on Delancey Street was, indeed, during the formative years of his life, deeply influenced and impressed by the young Anglican Priest who had been educated for ministry abroad and had returned to serve in his homeland!

[lxxxvii] Bishop Eldon's very long tenure as Chairman of the Council of the Board of The College served as a stabilizing force in the development of that institution. At least five persons served as President during the years he served as Chairman of its Council.

[lxxxviii] On the winds of political change during the service of Bishop Eldon see chapters on Sir Lynden Oscar Pindling and Cecil Wallace-Whitfield.

[lxxxix] On the very significant contribution of the Church to developing and inculcating the concept of Christian nation building into the minds and hearts of the Bahamian people during the period leading up to the granting of Independence on July 10th, 1973, see the writer's "Let us Build a Christian Nation", Freeport, Grand Bahama, on the life and times of The Rev. Reuben Cooper, Sr.

xc In the captioned conversation with Dr. Keva Bethel when she was serving as President of The College of The Bahamas, our attention was on Bahamian theologians, and the narrator had inadvertently omitted the name of Bishop Michael Eldon, and was corrected by his sister. And rightly so! For, Michael Eldon was recognized as a brilliant theologian throughout the region.

xci See Luke 12:48 "But he that knew not and did commit things worthy of stripes shall be beaten with few stripes. For unto whomsoever much is given of him shall be much expected, and to whom men have committed much, of him they will ask the more."

xcii Charles Spurgeon, Morning & Evening, (Peabody, Mass., Hendrickson Publishers, Inc., 1975), p. 289.

xciiiIt is suggested, in accord with the text Luke 12:8, that Bishop Michael Eldon, as a gifted privileged person, in serving so faithfully his LORD, so devoutly in His Church and so diligently in education, always going "beyond the call of duty", indeed, gave back more than was expected of him. Few, indeed are those of whom such a good report may be justly made!

xciv See Doris Johnson, The Quiet Revolution.

xcvSee "Bahamians Who Made a Difference-- Sir Milo Butler ".

xcvi Excerpt quoted from souvenir booklet published in celebration of the 53rd. Annual Founders' Day of Mission Baptist Church and on the occasion of the Ninth Annual Presentation and Investiture of The R.E. Cooper, Sr., National Meritorious Service Award to Mrs. Sylvia Ethlyn Johnson, on Sunday, December 26,

AD, 1993, 3:30 pm.

xcvii Mr. Cecil Valentine Bethel served as a teacher on the staff of Government High School for many years. As *Profesor de español*, he introduced Spanish into the syllabus of that noble institution, where Latin had been taught from its establishment in 1925 (Ms. Marjorie Davis, taught Latin at that time. She later became Director of Education.) He became the first Bahamian Headmaster of GHS. As such he must be ranked amongst the great Bahamian educators such as T. A. Thompson, H. O. Nash, Donald Davis, Thelma Gibson, T. G. Glover, Keva Bethel, and Timothy Gibson. Appropriately a leading Ministry of Education institution of primary education is named in recognition of his major contribution to education.

[xcviii] Mrs. Meta Davis-Cumberbatch, proved to be instrumental in the development of the culture of the Bahamas because she came from Trinidad and Tobago, which has a long heritage of cultural growth. She and her husband Dr. Cumberbatch were the proud parents of two daughters, and amongst their progeny are Mrs. Allyson Maynard Gibson, Attorney General of the Bahamas and her brother Peter Maynard.

[xcix] "Bahamian folklore" or "Tellin' old stories" is the custom of telling stories which have come down to the present generation by oral tradition. Like Alex Haley's world famous "Roots," folklore can be traced back to Africa. "In the old days" before the invention and wide use of radio and television (not to mention the internet), Bahamians were entertained as they got together and repeated these "old stories" often members of the older generation repeated these stories to the delight of the children, who in turn repeated the same to their children when they became adults. On this aspect of Bahamian culture see inter alia Cleveland Eneas' Bain Town and Let the Church Roll On and Peter Maynard, Attorney at Law who has taken a keen interest in Bahamian folklore.

[c] Sir Etienne Dupuch, then Editor of "The Tribune" also took great interest in "The Legend of Sammie Swain" and assisted Clement Bethel greatly in getting this thrilling Bahamian story to the world by publishing it in detail in his largely circulated "daily."

[ci] The narrator has described, in detail the contributions of if Aunt Lily" in the book, Obama in Prophecy, Colorado: Outskirts Press,

[cii] An experienced Bahamian entertainer, lamented the fact that there were no opportunities for Bahamian entertainers to develop their skills because there were no shows in the hotels featuring Bahamian Culture, declared in an interview broadcast on ZNS on Tuesday, May 2, 2017.

[ciii] Clement wrote the words and composed the music of this song, which, over the years has proved to be of tremendous significance. Along with "God Bless Our Sunny Clime" composed by the Rev. Dr. Philip Rahming, it must be ranked next to the Bahamian National Anthem as a musical contribution greatly appreciated by Bahamians "in all walks of life."

[civ] The narrator served as Superintendent of the Boys Industrial School (now The Simpson Penn Centre for Boys) from 1992 - 1996 "When the Road is Rough" was certainly one of the favorite musical renditions of the residents, which they often sang at special services and ceremonies.

[cv] Based on the sentiments expressed in that great song, written by Bahamian-American James Weldon Johnson, "Lift Every Voice and Sing," appropriately described as "The Negro National Anthem."

[cvi] The narrator has examined in detail the place of persistence in prayer in an unpublished work, "Praying Through . . . The Power of Persistence in Prayer."

[cvii] William Shakespeare,

[cviii] "Miss Wright's School" was an institution of primary education operated by the well-respected wife of a prominent Jamaican born dentist Dr. Wright. Many outstanding Bahamian citizens "got their start" in education at this fine education institute of yester year.

[cix] The Government High School was established in 1925 with the purpose of educating young Bahamians to serve in the Civil Service of the then Colony of the British Empire.

[cx] See chapters on Sir Lynden Pindling and Mrs. Patricia Cozzi.

[cxi] On racial discrimination in the Bahamas in the mid twentieth century see chapter on Sir Etienne Dupuch.

[cxii] According to prominent Bahamian educator Gurth Archer, it was largely through the influence of Paul Lawrence Adderley that the Bahamas did not adopt the General Examinations (CXC) of the other English speaking Caribbean nations. Instead the nation established its own national examination—The Bahamas Junior Certificate of Education (BJCs) and The Bahamas General Certificate of Secondary Education (BGCSE).

[cxiii] On the development of banking and financial services as the second pillar of the Bahamian economy see chapter on Sir Stafford Sands.

[cxiv] This statement in Bahamian dialect was given by a taxi operator to the narrator in a conversation with the narrator soon after he came to reside in Freeport in 2000. In Standard English he declared, "Reverend, there are two things I can tell you about Paul Adderley—Paul will not lie and he will not steal. And you can't bribe Paul!"

[cxv] This evaluation is based on the eulogies delivered by former United States of America Presidents William "Bill" Clinton and Barack Obama at the memorial Home Going Service for the famous Civil Rights Advocate on Thursday, October 24, 2019 at Baltimore, Maryland, USA.

[cxvi] It has been the pleasant opportunity on several occasions of the narrator to speak to Dr. Catherine Adderley about the many and varied achievements of her father.

[cxvii] This profound expression is taken from the delightful hymn, "Teach me my God and King," written by George Herbert (1593-1639), The Methodist Hymn Book (London, The Epworth Press, 1933, Hymn No. 597 verse 4.

cxviii The Rev. Dr. Philip Rahming, a Baptist minister, is a Bahamian patriot who has contributed richly to the moral and spiritual development of his homeland. Accordingly, he has authored the National Motto and composed the National Hymn, "God Bless Our Sunny Clime." The Order of Merit was conferred upon him during the presentation of National Honours in October 2019.

Made in the USA
Middletown, DE
14 October 2023